Evangelicals and
Catholics Together
at Twenty

D0067807

Evangelicals and Catholics Together

at Twenty

—

VITAL STATEMENTS ON CONTESTED TOPICS

EDITED BY Timothy George AND
Thomas G. Guarino

BrazosPress

a division of Baker Publishing Group
Grand Rapids, Michigan

© 2015 by Timothy George and Thomas G. Guarino

Published by Brazos Press
a division of Baker Publishing Group
P.O. Box 6287, Grand Rapids, MI 49516-6287
www.brazospress.com

Printed in the United States of America

Library of Congress Cataloging-in-Publication Data is on file at the Library of Congress, Washington, DC.

ISBN 978-1-58743-368-9

Unless noted otherwise, Scripture translations are from the Revised Standard Version of the Bible, copyright 1952 [2nd edition, 1971] by the Division of Christian Education of the National Council of the Churches of Christ in the United States of America. Used by permission. All rights reserved.

Scripture quotations labeled ASV are from the American Standard Version of the Bible.

Scripture quotations labeled ESV are from The Holy Bible, English Standard Version® (ESV®), copyright © 2001 by Crossway, a publishing ministry of Good News Publishers. Used by permission. All rights reserved. ESV Text Edition: 2011

Scripture quotations labeled KJV are from the King James Version of the Bible.

Scripture quotations labeled NIV are from the Holy Bible, New International Version®. NIV®. Copyright © 1973, 1978, 1984, 2011 by Biblica, Inc.™ Used by permission of Zondervan. All rights reserved worldwide. www.zondervan.com

Scripture quotations labeled NKJV are from the New King James Version. Copyright © 1982 by Thomas Nelson, Inc. Used by permission. All rights reserved.

Scripture quotations labeled NRSV are from the New Revised Standard Version of the Bible, copyright © 1989, by the Division of Christian Education of the National Council of the Churches of Christ in the United States of America. Used by permission. All rights reserved.

Lyrics from Graham Kendrick's "Meekness and Majesty" in chap. 7 are © 2003 Thankyou Music (PRS) (adm. worldwide at Capitol CMGPublishing.com excluding Europe, which is adm. by Integritymusic.com) All rights reserved. Used by permission.

15   16   17   18   19   20   21   7   6   5   4   3   2   1

Contents

Preface

J. I. PACKER

When in 1994 the launching statement *Evangelicals and Catholics Together: The Christian Mission in the Third Millennium* was published, envisioning active consensus and collaboration on the kingdom issues of discipling and community, howls of negativity went up from Evangelical isolationists. These critics were reacting in light of their recall of days when Rome seemed bent on political as well as religious control and seemed to be seeking the death of Protestantism as a heretical excrescence. They saw Evangelicals and Catholics Together (ECT) as a subversive Roman Catholic power play and accused some who endorsed it of forgetting what Rome stood for, or, while knowing, going theologically soft about it, or perhaps signing the launching statement without reading it.

But the era that this thinking represented is past, and Vatican II has slammed the door on it, ensuring that it cannot return. Today, so I urge, partnership between historically affirming Evangelicals and historically affirming Roman Catholics for communicating Christ to unbelievers and upholding Christian order in an increasingly post- and sub-Christian world, up to the limit that individual convictions allow, does indeed need to grow everywhere, as ECT has insisted from the start. The centuries-old question, "Where do we differ?" has not of course gone away, but ECT's role is urgently to explore the new question: "How much agreement—doctrinal, ethical, spiritual, ecclesial, and perspectival—can we muster for cooperation in fulfilling the Great Commission, the kingdom task that Christ has given to us all?" In pressing this question, which has surely come to stay, ECT maintains a ministry that in my view is truly prophetic.

Perhaps I should not have been so surprised as I was by the heat of initial negative Protestant reaction. Years back, it dawned on me that fear is a stronger motivating factor in North America than is ever acknowledged. The sitting-on-a-volcano feeling is very American and is easily exploited. And fear clouds the mind, breeds inertia, generates defensive responses that drive wisdom out of the window, and thus keeps people from taking the long view about matters of principle. Also, church communities that are conservative about the contents of the Christian faith tend to react conservatively to any new policy proposals; and ECT is, from one standpoint, a novel policy proposal. So it was perhaps to be expected that there should have been, and will be still, deep suspicion of ECT's program.

As one who was a committed participant in ECT for its first two decades, until old age ruled out the traveling involved, and who still from the sidelines cheers the project on, I count it a privilege here publicly to welcome this consolidated reprint of ECT's first nine documents. While not infallible (nobody claims that), these statements seem to me to be model resources for the grassroots "cobelligerence" (Francis Schaeffer's word) that Evangelicals and Catholics should henceforth be practicing together, identifying common enemies (unbelief, sin, cultural apostasy) and countering them cooperatively up to the limit that conscience permits. The so-called Lund principle, formulated decades ago in light of Jesus's high-priestly prayer for the active, visible unity of all his disciples, lays it down that ecclesiastically divided Christians should not settle for doing separately anything that they can in good conscience do together, and I see ECT as a noteworthy instance of the Lund principle being put into practice. With thanks to God and prayer for continuance, I hereby commend it as such.

Preface

TIMOTHY CARDINAL DOLAN,
ARCHBISHOP OF NEW YORK

The summer of 2014 featured several key encounters between Pope Francis and Evangelical Protestants. The Holy Father hosted influential pastors for a morning of conversation that extended over lunch, and he traveled to an Evangelical congregation in Caserta, Italy, where he visited the pastor in his home and preached in his church. These novelties reflect something of what it means to have a pope from the new world. If the ecumenical priorities of Europe look toward the Orthodox and toward the ecclesial communities of the Reformation—Anglicans, Lutherans, Calvinists, and so forth—the more frequent ecumenical encounters of a bishop from Buenos Aires are with the various worlds of Evangelical Protestantism.

It is no secret that throughout Latin America there has been tension between Catholics and Evangelical Protestants, as some of the former have become the latter. While in Buenos Aires, Cardinal Jorge Mario Bergoglio was notable for *not* pointing an accusatory finger against supposed sheep rustling, but rather inviting an examination of conscience about what Catholics lacked in missionary zeal for proclaiming the joy of the gospel. Though our division is contrary to the will of Christ, the Holy Father judges it Christ's will that until those divisions are healed, we remain fraternal partners in mission.

That would no doubt please the late Father Richard John Neuhaus and his good friend the late Charles W. Colson, who jointly established Evangelicals and Catholics Together in 1994. The encounter we celebrate earned no little criticism twenty years ago. That what was criticized then is now celebrated is largely due to the prophetic courage of those two friends and fellow disciples. Indeed, the greater courage was on Colson's part, as he earned the disapproval even of some of his close collaborators. No doubt his courage was sustained by the friendship he forged with Father Neuhaus, whom I was pleased to hold up in my installation Mass homily (as archbishop of New York) as one of those great New York priests whose impact is felt far beyond our city.

The friendship that made Evangelicals and Catholics Together possible ought not obscure the substantive work that these friends and their colleagues accomplished. There is a tendency in ecumenical and interreligious encounters to set aside doctrinal questions, often considered divisive, in favor of good fraternal relations, cooperation on the corporal works of mercy, defense of religious liberty, advocacy of justice, advancement of peace, alleviation of poverty, and witness to the sanctity of life and marriage.

There is much good in all of that, but Colson and Neuhaus advanced the more ambitious proposal that Christians who are serious about overcoming our divisions ought to discuss doctrinal matters precisely to overcome those divisions. To the extent that divisions are the result of confusion or historical arguments no longer burdened by the history that shaped them, real breakthroughs are possible. To the extent that divisions over doctrine are irreconcilable, serious theological dialogue about them has the capacity to deepen appreciation for both sides, as it were, of those particular truths of the gospel that their formulations seek to protect.

Two recent books by leading Catholic authors have suggestive titles—*Evangelizing Catholics* by Scott Hahn and *Evangelical Catholicism* by George Weigel. Is it not the case that we Catholics have learned something about the missionary, evangelizing mandate of the church from our Evangelical Protestant brethren? Is it not likely that Pope Francis, who repeats insistently that the church exists to form "missionary disciples," learned something about how Christians can be zealous missionaries and devoted disciples from being close to Evangelical Protestants in Argentina? Surely such Evangelical Protestants have also learned from us Catholics some valuable lessons in this exchange of spiritual gifts, but I would leave it to them to enumerate what they are.

Unafraid of tough questions, ECT has over the course of twenty years addressed serious "church-dividing" questions and thereby helped many Christians to understand that we are not as divided as we may have thought. That is no small service as the challenges facing the entire Christian church are growing more acute, from secularist fundamentalism at home to lethal persecution abroad.

What began twenty years ago in the pages of serious journals may have found a popular counterpart in the words and gestures of Pope Francis and his Evangelical friends. Inspired by the meetings of this past summer, I expect that there will be more encounters between Evangelical Protestants and Catholics. When we meet, what shall we discuss? ECT has provided us with a rich agenda for conversation and, perhaps even more important, a model for how to discuss important things—*first things*, we might say. It is a model, to use the more apt phrase from Ephesians, of how to speak the truth in love (Eph. 4:15).

At the beginning of ECT, the first statement began by noting that the participants did not speak officially for their communities, but quickly added that they did "intend to speak responsibly from our communities and to our communities."

Christians in America can be very proud that in Chuck Colson and Richard John Neuhaus we produced two who were able to speak better than most. What they and their collaborators said is a gift for the universal church. Their conversation, we pray, now continues in heaven. It remains for us to continue conversing here below as fellow pilgrims through history.

Foreword

GEORGE WEIGEL

The project that came to be known as Evangelicals and Catholics Together began in a most unlikely place: a Washington cocktail reception, the purpose of which I've long since forgotten. In any event, I was there, and the distinguished Evangelical author Herbert Schlossberg was there. Herb pulled me aside to suggest that, given what was afoot in America in the early 1990s, a much more serious conversation between Evangelical Protestant leaders and Catholic leaders in the United States was imperative. I told Herb I'd think about it, and, as I often did in such circumstances, I called my close friend and collaborator, Father Richard John Neuhaus, to talk it through with him. Father Neuhaus was intrigued; I suggested that he take the lead, given his unique standing among both Evangelicals and Catholics. Father Neuhaus called Chuck Colson, and those two large-scale figures proceeded to invite others into the collaboration that became Evangelicals and Catholics Together.

It was a collaboration that few could have predicted thirty-some years before. Many Evangelical Protestants, in those days, were not quite sure that Catholics were really Christians. Catholics, for their part, had little contact with Evangelical Protestantism, found its talk of being "born again" strange, and sensed the doubts that Evangelicals had about Catholic faith and Catholic piety.

Things began to change, not from the top down but from the bottom up, as Catholics and Evangelicals found themselves cobelligerents in the American culture war. These two communities, historically wary of (and often ill-informed about) each other, found themselves occupying the same foxholes in battles on behalf of the unborn—a wholly unexpected by-product of the abortion license imperiously imposed on the entire country by the Supreme Court in 1973. An old saw has it that there are "no atheists in foxholes." The drama of the pro-life movement—in its contest with those who occupied the cultural high ground in American public life—demonstrated that foxholes are good places to learn who is, in fact, a brother or sister in Christ. Many misconceptions were cleared away in the process, making an initiative like Evangelicals and Catholics Together possible.

Then there was Pope John Paul II, another factor no one could have anticipated. By the courage and resoluteness with which he preached the gospel around the world, this manifestly evangelical Christian leader inspired Catholics to take Evangelical Protestantism's passion for mission more seriously. That John Paul II had committed the Church to a "New Evangelization" was yet another providential development drawing Evangelicals and Catholics together, with the pope being acknowledged as one of the great Christian witnesses of our time by no less an Evangelical giant than Billy Graham.

At the outset of Evangelicals and Catholics Together, as the first statement suggests, our primary concern was to offer a common witness to our faith in Jesus Christ as Lord, particularly as we approached the Great Jubilee of 2000 and the third millennium of Christian history. Concerned as we were with the moral and cultural foundations of American public life, we were convinced that the most important thing we could do together, amid the confusions of late modernity, was to make a simple profession of faith: Jesus is Lord. And it was in light of his lordship that we wished to read and address the signs of our times. That confession of faith led to a common commitment to mission, for we had come to understand that, while there were grave matters of public policy that Christians had an obligation to address, the long-term health of the American republic was a matter of ongoing conversion. Together, we sensed that the venerable notion of America as a republic of virtue was giving way to the coarser idea that ours must be a republic of the imperial autonomous self. Only a rediscovery and reclamation of the moral truths on which the founders had staked the American experiment in ordered liberty and the American claim to national independence could reverse the deterioration in our public life.

We understood that there were issues dividing us theologically, and we thought it appropriate to identify at least some of them. But this was not a matter of throat-clearing prior to the "real world" business of the politics of virtue. It was important, we believed, to signal to our respective communities that there were things that we could learn from each other: things that could deepen our common faith in Jesus as Lord and our common witness in the public square. And in identifying what divided us theologically, we also wanted to make a statement to the public culture: that (as Father Neuhaus often put it) "tolerance" doesn't mean ignoring differences as if differences made no difference; true tolerance means engaging differences in the bond of civility. And in a Christian context, that civility is the bond of charity, the "more excellent way" (1 Cor. 12:31).

Then, and only then, were we ready to address specific issues in American public life.

What we saw there was challenging, and we tried to identify the deeper roots of the distress that many of us felt about the course of American history. Against the notion that democracy and the free economy are matters of mere mechanics, of getting the institutions right and then letting them run by themselves, we affirmed that it takes a certain kind of people, living certain habits of the heart and mind (or what we called "virtues"), to make free politics and free economics serve the cause of genuine human flourishing. Against the complacency that took freedom for granted, we believed that freedom is never free, and that sacrifice for the common good, not the mere aggrandizement of the self, is essential to maintaining free public institutions. Against the moral relativism that was prepared to concede "your truth" and "my truth" but nothing called "the truth," we wanted to make common cause in proposing that a truly just society rested on a secure foundation of culturally affirmed and culturally transmitted moral truths—truths that could be known by reason but were most easily apprehended through the lens of reason informed by biblical faith.

And then there was religious freedom. It seemed to us then, as it has ever since, that religious freedom is the first of human rights and that Evangelicals and Catholics, together, must be champions of religious freedom for all.

There were many other matters on which we found ourselves, at the outset, shoulder to shoulder in the battles of American public life: in defending the unborn, the radically handicapped, and the elderly; in challenging the coarsening of our culture by the violence, promiscuity, and antireligious bigotry that too often characterized popular "entertainment" and self-styled avant-garde "art"; in contesting for an educational system that inculcated the virtues necessary for democratic self-governance to succeed; in lifting up the family as the basic unit of society—the list was quite extensive.

And the urgency with which we assayed the current state of American culture, in itself and in its impact on political and economic life, has not abated over the past twenty years. It has, in fact, intensified.

Evangelicals and Catholics Together has addressed grave issues of public policy over two decades, but that could have been predicted at the outset of this collaboration. What could *not* have been predicted, and what seems in the retrospect of twenty years to have been another providential development, was ECT's evolution into a forum of serious theological dialogue on contested questions like the meaning of salvation, the role of the Bible in the life of the church, the place of Mary and the saints in Christian life, and the other topics on which we have issued the statements collected in this volume. Here, as at the beginning, we have not sought a false and demeaning least common denominator. Where disagreement continued, it was identified as such. But where agreement, perhaps unexpected agreement, was achieved, we were happy to identify that too and to celebrate common understandings achieved as the result of hard digging through the appropriate sources and frank, fraternal conversation and debate.

I think it's fair to say that the first twenty years of Evangelicals and Catholics Together suggested new patterns for Christian ecumenism in the twenty-first century and beyond. At the moment when the post–Vatican II bilateral ecumenical dialogues that had once seemed to hold such promise—Anglican-Catholic, Lutheran-Catholic, Reformed-Catholic, and so forth—were bogging down as a result of the continued implosion of liberal Protestantism, ECT emerged as a new model of biblically grounded and theologically serious ecumenical encounter that addressed hard issues in a spirit of both scholarship and fraternal charity—and that offered others the witness of genuine ecumenical progress where little seemed possible. We did not claim to speak for the churches, but only to and from our respective communities. In having done so, however, we hope that we have offered something useful for official ecumenical dialogue in the future.

There have been other encounters between Evangelicals and Catholics around the world, and the strength that Christian brethren have found in those meetings, conversations, joint biblical study, and common prayer has been important for the world church in its many manifestations. But I don't think I risk a charge of untoward boasting when I suggest that there has been nothing quite like Evangelicals and Catholics Together for seriousness, for depth of theological encounter, and for genuine results.

My hope and prayer for this book is that it inspires many similar efforts throughout the world. For the cause of Christ can only benefit by deepening the conversation between those Christian communities that take revelation seriously and that are committed to a bold, missionary future in the third millennium.

A Theological Introduction

TIMOTHY GEORGE AND THOMAS G. GUARINO

The ecumenical initiative known as Evangelicals and Catholics Together (ECT) began two decades ago with a stroke of insight by Chuck Colson and Richard John Neuhaus. Their bold intention was to advance unity and fellowship among Christians by establishing a serious theological dialogue between Evangelicals and Catholics, the two largest Christian groups in North America.

Both men were concerned that religion in general and Christianity in particular were being increasingly relegated to the margins of public life in the United States. Religious faith, the most comprehensive and foundational of all realities, was being consigned to the provincial arena of private devotion and sectarian belief. Colson and Neuhaus argued, however, that the Christian faith is indispensable to understanding and addressing the great issues of the day. Evangelicals and Catholics needed to be fully engaged in the complex social, cultural, and political questions that the nation faced—illuminating them with the truth of the gospel. They concluded that if a common and public witness was to thrive and bear lasting fruit, it needed to be founded on a joint commitment to theological and spiritual unity, a unity for which Christ himself prayed (John 17). This fraternal union in Christ was the cornerstone on which ECT was founded.

But there was another element central to the founding of ECT. Tensions between Evangelicals and Catholics had been proliferating in various parts of the world, particularly in South America. Colson and Neuhaus feared that "animosities between evangelicals and Catholics threatened to mar the image of Christ by turning Latin America into a Belfast of religious warfare."[1] They hoped that a sincere and comprehensive collaboration between Evangelicals and Catholics— a collaboration that honestly faced theological differences—could also offer a useful word to the brethren in South America. A sincere ecumenical dialogue would serve to overcome the "stereotypes, prejudices and conventional ideas" that had been entrenched for decades and, indeed, for centuries.[2]

It was with these goals in mind—to work together for Christian unity and to live together with a deep sense of Christian fraternity— that Colson and Neuhaus founded Evangelicals and Catholics Together in 1994.

Theological Roots of Ecumenism

But the primordial roots of ECT extend far deeper into history, down to the beginnings of the ecumenical movement. The initial impetus for ecumenical dialogue is normally traced to the International Missionary Conference that convened at Edinburgh, Scotland, in 1910. On that occasion, several denominations came together to discuss their common witness to Jesus Christ, with the hope of putting an end to useless and counterproductive rivalries.[3]

After this initial meeting, the "ecumenical movement" continued to grow among mainline Protestant churches. Catholicism initially kept its distance from this initiative, fearing that it would lead to

---

1. *Evangelicals and Catholics Together: Toward a Common Mission* (Nashville: Thomas Nelson, 1995), xi.

2. Ibid., ix.

3. For a history of the ecumenical movement and an examination of the achievements of various dialogues, see *Celebrating a Century of Ecumenism*, ed. John A. Radano (Grand Rapids: Eerdmans, 2012).

relativism, with specific doctrines lost in a misguided attempt to achieve baseline beliefs to which all Christians could subscribe. This was the point of Pope Pius XI's encyclical of 1928, *Mortalium Animos*, in which he warned against "pan-Christianity," fearful that this would lead to a vapid faith, absent distinctively Catholic dimensions. Most Evangelicals also held back from ecumenical efforts represented by the World Council of Churches. They feared that a blending of Christian churches would water down the clear and forceful meaning of the Bible.

Even so, interest in ecumenism persisted. In the 1920s, Catholic and Anglican theologians met in Belgium for what were known as the "Malines Conversations" discussing possible unity between Rome and Canterbury. And in 1937, Yves Congar, later one of the principal theologians at the Second Vatican Council (1962–65), wrote a groundbreaking book entitled *Divided Christendom*, in which he argued for the authentic gifts found in Protestantism and insisted that one could affirm the same biblical truth from different perspectives.[4] Authentic Christian unity was possible without uniformity or compromise.

This accent on a healthy diversity within a foundational unity had been gaining theological favor within Catholicism for decades. In the 1930s and 1940s, for example, theologians argued that differing approaches to the mysteries of faith can, in fact, possess a profound harmony, rooted in the gospel itself.[5] It was precisely in service to this notion of legitimate pluralism that led some theologians to champion the axiom *diversi sed non adversi* (different but not opposed), a maxim indicating that there can be diverse approaches to theological issues without thereby sanctioning adversarial paths.[6] Centuries earlier,

4. See Yves Congar, *Divided Christendom* (London: Centenary, 1939).

5. For example, see M.-D. Chenu, *Le Saulchoir: Une école de théologie* (Kain-Lez-Tournai: Le Saulchoir, 1937). A 1985 reprint was issued by Les Éditions du Cerf, Paris. See also Henri Bouillard, *Conversion et grâce chez S. Thomas d'Aquin: Étude historique* (Paris: Aubier, 1944). Of the many recent books on the *nouvelle théologie*, we have found helpful Hans Boersma, *Nouvelle Théologie and Sacramental Ontology: A Return to Mystery* (Oxford: Oxford University Press, 2009).

6. See Henri de Lubac, "A propos de la formule: *diversi, sed non adversi*," *Recherches de science religieuse* 40 (1952): 27–40, and Hubert Silvestre, "*Diversi sed non adversi*," *Recherches de théologie ancienne et médiévale* 31 (1964): 124–32. We are grateful to Marcus Plested for bringing de Lubac's essay to our attention.

this Latin phrase had been invoked to argue that the accounts of the four evangelists, while different, are nonetheless fully coherent. In the Middle Ages, the slogan was adduced in order to acknowledge that one may speak of a consensus among early Christian writers (*consensus patrum*) even if these authors displayed some differences in their interpretations of the Scriptures. The fundamental point, once again, is that variety in expression does not necessarily mean incommensurable or opposing positions.[7]

On the Evangelical side, the founding of ECT in the early 1990s would not have been possible without the prehistory that included the catalytic ministries of Harold J. Ockenga and Billy Graham. These leaders were pioneers in forging a new way in American Protestant life in the post–World War II era. The "new evangelicalism," as it came to be called, found itself engaged in a struggle on two fronts. One was *modernism*, as mainline, liberal Protestantism was called in those days. The other front was known as Romanism, a pejorative term for Catholic Christianity. The post–World War II reformers hoped that a reinvigorated Evangelicalism, shorn of its fundamentalist drag, would both restore true biblical Christianity and rescue American society itself by resisting the forces of modernism/secularism, on the one hand, and Catholicism, on the other. When Colson and Neuhaus proposed the ECT project in the 1990s, both of those fronts looked completely different. Protestant liberalism no longer enjoyed the kind of hegemony it had once claimed in American religion. On the Catholic side, the Second Vatican Council had introduced a renewal of the Catholic Church and made Christian unity a priority. At Vatican II, the Catholic Church entered the ecumenical movement and, by doing so, transformed it.

The council should not be understood simply as an event within the Catholic Church. It should be recognized, rather, as perhaps the greatest ecclesial event of the twentieth century, with profound significance for all Christians. Its *Decree on Ecumenism* (promulgated in November 1964) makes clear that unity with the "separated brethren" is one of the principal and essential goals of the Catholic Church. This

---

7. Congar pursued this point at great length for the sake of ecumenical unity. See, for example, his *Diversity and Communion*, trans. John Bowden (Mystic, CT: Twenty-Third Publications, 1985).

Decree (and Vatican II generally) endorsed several specific theological ideas—ideas warmly received by the many Protestant observers and theologians in attendance at the council—which have allowed the contemporary dialogue between Evangelicals and Catholics to flourish.

Three Themes at the Heart of Ecumenism and of ECT

(1) The Content of the Christian Faith

One central conciliar theme is that a difference exists between the *content* of the Christian faith and the *modes of expression* used to formulate it. Pope John XXIII explicitly sanctioned this point of view in his speech opening the council on October 11, 1962: "The deposit of faith is one thing, and the manner in which it is expressed is another."[8] So significant was this distinction that Yves Congar, the great ecumenist, remarked that these few words encapsulated the essential meaning of the council.[9] And this distinction is entirely traditional. Already in the early fifth century, Vincent of Lérins had exhorted Christians: *dicas nove non dicas nova* (speak in a new way but don't say new things).[10] The Eastern writer John Damascene endorsed a similar position a few centuries later.[11] And the same idea may be found in the great Reformed theologian Karl Barth reflecting on the Augsburg Confession.[12]

8. "Gaudet Mater Ecclesia," *Acta Apostolicae Sedis* 54 (1962): 792.

9. See Congar, *A History of Theology*, trans. Hunter Guthrie (Garden City, NY: Doubleday, 1968), 18–19. Giuseppe Alberigo, a significant historian of Vatican II, called John XXIII's distinction one of the decisive motifs of the council. See "Facteurs de 'Laïcité' au Concile Vatican II," *Revue des sciences religieuses* 74 (2000): 211–25.

10. *Commonitorium*, no. 22. Vincent argues that although the specific words *homoousios* (Jesus is of the same substance as God the Father) and *Theotokos* (Mary is the Mother of God) are not found in the earliest tradition, they perfectly express biblical faith.

11. See John of Damascus, *On the Divine Images*, trans. David Anderson (Crestwood, NY: St. Vladimir's Seminary Press, 1980), 71. Gregory Nazianzen expressed the same thought in the fourth century when he said that there exists "a great deal of diversity inherent in names," for it is a matter of "meanings rather than words." See *Oration* 31.24. In the thirteenth century, Thomas Aquinas argued that new words are sometimes necessary to express the ancient faith. See *Summa Theologiae* I, q. 29, a. 3, ad 1.

12. "The *Augustana* and the other Reformed confessions did not want to be confessions in so far as they had no new faith to confess—but they were confessions

Authentic pluralism allows for complementary concepts and expressions that throw into relief unseen or overlooked aspects of a doctrine's truth. By admitting that traditional Christian teaching could be expressed in new ways, the council sought to make the faith more intelligible to men and women of the day, to expose previously hidden dimensions of the mysteries of faith, and, crucially, to acknowledge that *the formulations of Protestant and Orthodox Christians might differently, but complementarily, mediate the truth of Christian doctrine as found within Roman Catholicism.*

Vatican II's *Decree on Ecumenism* champions this accent on legitimate diversity when it states, "While preserving unity in essentials, let all members of the Church . . . enjoy a proper freedom in the various forms of spiritual life and discipline, in the variety of liturgical rites, and even in the theological elaborations of revealed truth" (no. 4). The decree insists that a proper understanding of pluralism will give "richer expression to the authentic catholicity and apostolicity of the Church." The underlying issue here is always the same: How can the Christian faith speak robustly and vigorously in every age—the new wine of the gospel always in fresh skins?[13] G. C. Berkouwer, a prominent Reformed theologian who was one of the observers at Vatican II, saw the conciliar distinction between the truth of revelation and its historically conditioned formulation as an important ecumenical advance since one formulation alone could never exhaust the mysteries of faith.[14]

It is just this emphasis on authentic diversity within fundamental unity that constitutes one theological pillar undergirding the work of Evangelicals and Catholics Together. As the original 1994 statement launching ECT affirmed, "Not all differences are authentic disagreements." Differences in theological approaches to the Christian faith

---

in so far as they did confess the old faith anew." See *Church Dogmatics* I/2, ed. G. W. Bromiley and T. F. Torrance (Edinburgh: T&T Clark, 1956), 627.

13. The entire debate over the context/content approach to theological pluralism is discussed at length in Thomas G. Guarino, *Foundations of Systematic Theology* (London: T&T Clark, 2005), 141–67.

14. See G. C. Berkouwer, *The Second Vatican Council and the New Catholicism*, trans. Lewis B. Smedes (Grand Rapids: Eerdmans, 1965), 63–64. Berkouwer's ecumenical theology (and his evaluation of Vatican II) is outlined at length by Eduardo Echeverria in *Berkouwer and Catholicism* (Leiden: Brill, 2013).

need not inexorably mean opposed positions. Could one speak, for example, about the biblical teaching about justification by faith in a way that preserved both of our traditions, but without compromising either?

(2) Scripture and Tradition

A second theological pillar at the foundation of ECT is the new emphasis on Sacred Scripture that emerged in Catholicism at Vatican II—along with the new accent on tradition found among contemporary Evangelical writers. The council, while clearly affirming the importance of tradition in the life of the Catholic Church, also allowed for the interpretation that one could speak of Holy Scriptures as "materially sufficient" for the truths of salvation.[15] In other words, even though tradition is an essential interpretative key for understanding the divine Word (indeed, the council teaches that "it is not from Sacred Scripture alone that the Church draws her certainty about everything which has been revealed"; *Dei Verbum* [*Dogmatic Constitution on Divine Revelation*], no. 9), nonetheless, Scripture contains within itself all that is essential for salvation.[16] For most Catholic theologians, then, the Bible contains within itself the entirety of salvific truth, while tradition, the life of the Church under the Holy Spirit, enables the Church to penetrate the meaning and teaching of Scripture more fully and clearly.

Vatican II itself says of Scripture, "Since everything asserted by the inspired authors or sacred writers must be held to be asserted

15. Congar has shown that the notion of the "material sufficiency" of Scripture has a long history in the church, even prior to the Reformation. See *Tradition and Traditions*, trans. Michael Naseby and Thomas Rainborough (New York: MacMillan, 1967), 107–18. For Joseph Ratzinger's comments on *sola scriptura* and the council, see *Commentary on the Documents of Vatican II*, ed. Herbert Vorgrimler (New York: Herder & Herder, 1969), 3:191–92.

16. Congar rightly states that many Catholic theologians "hold that all the truths necessary for salvation are contained, in one way or another, in the canonical Scriptures." See *The Meaning of Tradition*, trans. A. N. Woodrow (1964; San Francisco: Ignatius, 2004), 106. See also on Vatican II, Avery Dulles, *Revelation and the Quest for Unity* (Washington: Corpus, 1968), 65–81. The preeminent medieval theologian, Thomas Aquinas, taught, "Canonical scripture alone is the rule of faith" (*Sola canonica scriptura est regula fidei*). See his *Commentary on the Gospel of John*, chap. 21, *lectio* 6.

by the Holy Spirit, it follows that the books of Scripture must be acknowledged as teaching solidly, faithfully and without error that truth which God wanted put into sacred writings for the sake of salvation" (*Dei Verbum*, no. 11). One of the principal theological architects of Vatican II framed this primacy of Scripture in unequivocal terms: "Scripture has an absolute sovereignty; it is of divine origin, even in its literary form; it governs Tradition and the Church, whereas it is not governed by Tradition or the Church."[17] This biblical sovereignty is also reflected in the teaching of Aquinas, who wrote, "We believe the successors of the apostles and prophets only in so far as they tell us those things which the apostles and prophets have left in their writings" (*De Ver.*, q. 14, a. 10, ad 11).

Catholicism's new accent on Scripture was much welcomed by the distinguished Protestant observers at Vatican II. Karl Barth, for example, appreciated the council's citation of Jerome's well-known comment, "Ignorance of the Scriptures is ignorance of Christ," and noted that of the six chapters of the *Dogmatic Constitution on Revelation (Dei Verbum)*, four of them are dedicated entirely to Scripture.[18] Lukas Vischer, one of the Swiss Reformed observers, remarked about the council's teaching: "It [Scripture] has authoritative validity, and the Church, in its doctrine and life, must refer to it continually." While acknowledging that tradition is still central to Catholicism, Vischer stated that "the important thing is that it [the Bible] receives a new validity in the life of the Church. For . . . the really decisive thing is whether the Scriptures are read at all and are allowed to develop the strength within them."[19] This renewed accent on the primacy of Scripture in the Catholic Church was an important affirmation, one that brought Catholics much closer to their Evangelical brethren.

---

17. Congar, *Tradition and Traditions*, 422. Given this unwavering affirmation of the uniqueness of Scripture, it is unsurprising to read Congar's comment: "Luther, of course, early on was very strongly convinced . . . of the absolute primacy of Scripture over all other authority, and in that he was completely Catholic" (ibid., 140).

18. Karl Barth, *Ad limina apostolorum* (Zurich: EVZ Verlag, 1967), 51. Barth, prevented from attending Vatican II due to illness, later visited Rome and wrote a brief commentary on the conciliar documents.

19. See Lukas Vischer, "After the Fourth Session of the Second Vatican Council," *Ecumenical Review* 18 (1966): 150–89, at 155, 157.

This Catholic emphasis on the sovereignty of the Bible was complemented by the growing Protestant recognition that tradition, broadly understood, need not be accompanied by negative perceptions. Over the past few decades, Protestantism has acknowledged that *sola scriptura* cannot be understood simply as an antitradition principle since the Reformers themselves were fully committed to the early Christian confessions of faith. For just this reason, the Evangelical theologian Kevin Vanhoozer has stated that the traditional Reformation phrase *sola scriptura* cannot be understood in isolation: "If *sola scriptura* means 'the Bible alone apart from the church and tradition,' it has no future. But this is not what *sola scriptura* means. *Sola scriptura* is a protest not against tradition as such but against the presumption that church tradition (interpretation) and Scripture (text) necessarily coincide."[20] This revaluation of the relationship between Scripture and tradition had led some Evangelical theologians to think about *suprema scriptura* as an apposite phrase, one that recognizes the unique value of Scripture while also acknowledging a place for ecclesial tradition. For example, the Baptist theologian James Leo Garrett has stated, "*Suprema Scriptura*, not a quite literal and restricted *sola Scriptura*, provides the most representative and accurate Protestant answer to the question as to the ranking of channels of religious authority. This means that the Bible always ranks and stands above church and tradition, the divine-human encounter, and any other possible channel of religious authority."[21] In 1995, John Paul II offered a new formulation on the relationship between the Bible and tradition, speaking of "Sacred Scripture as the highest authority in matters of faith and Sacred Tradition as indispensable to the interpretation of the Word of God" (*Ut Unum Sint* [*That They May Be One*], no. 79). This statement is a

20. Kevin J. Vanhoozer, "Scripture and Tradition," in *The Cambridge Companion to Postmodern Theology* (New York: Cambridge University Press, 2003), 149–69, at 167. G. C. Berkouwer also argued that *sola scriptura* was not meant to be an antitradition principle. Rather, with this phrase the Reformation wanted "to bind the church with its confessions and its preaching to the apostolic witness," thereby safeguarding the lordship of Christ over the church and tradition. But "the Reformation call to *sola Scriptura* was not a call to biblicism." See Berkouwer, *Second Vatican Council*, 107, 101.

21. James Leo Garrett, *Systematic Theology*, vol. 1, *Biblical, Historical, and Evangelical*, 4th ed. (Eugene, OR: Wipf & Stock, 1990), 207.

forceful testimony to the primacy of Scripture, while recognizing that tradition can never be regarded as inessential. Whether or not one agrees entirely with any of the above formulations, it is nonetheless clear that a new relationship between the Bible and ecclesial tradition has emerged in both Catholic and Protestant thought.

Of course, it must be remembered that new theological thinking about Scripture and tradition is undertaken not for its own sake but for the purpose of faithfully transmitting the self-manifestation of God that has taken place in ancient Israel and, uniquely, in Jesus of Nazareth. Properly handing on to all generations the truth about God as revealed in Christ and enlivened in the church by the Holy Spirit is a second theological pillar on which ECT has been built.

(3) Ecclesia semper reformanda/purificanda

A third pillar of the Evangelical-Catholic dialogue is the call for ecclesial reform that emerged at Vatican II and, specifically, in the aforementioned *Decree on Ecumenism*. Of course, Protestantism has long been associated with the phrase *ecclesia semper reformanda* (the church always in need of reformation on the basis of the Word of God in accordance with the gospel). At Vatican II, the Catholic Church reprised this crucial theme by insisting that the church is "called by Christ to that continual reformation [*ad hanc perennem reformationem*] of which she always has need insofar as she is an institution of men and women on earth" (*Decree on Ecumenism*, no. 6).

Precisely with this reforming spirit in mind, Vatican II summoned the Catholic Church to remedy any deficiencies that exist in conduct, discipline, and even in the formulation of ecclesial teaching (as opposed to the content of Christian doctrine). To cite the council's own words: "If, in various times and circumstances, there have been deficiencies in conduct, in church discipline, or even in the way that church teaching has been formulated—which must be carefully distinguished from the deposit of faith itself—these should be appropriately rectified at the opportune moment."

Similarly, the council spoke of the Church as "at the same time holy and always in need of being purified" and as continually following the path of penance and renewal (*Dogmatic Constitution on the*

Church, no. 8). The theologian Henri de Lubac noted that the phrase describing the Church as "holy while at the same time always in need of being purified" (*sancta simul et semper purificanda*) appeared to him—and to others, including the Reformed thinker Jean-Jacques von Allmen—as the expression most suitably reflecting the Church's duty of continual reform in Christ.[22]

Whichever phrase is chosen as most apt, it is nonetheless clear that at Vatican II the Catholic Church placed a decided emphasis on the need for self-reformation. While the council did not reverse any of Catholicism's foundational teachings, it issued no anathemas or condemnations. And it certainly spoke with a new accent, expressing the Christian faith in more scripturally oriented formulations. One may discern in the conciliar documents a change of tone and genre, with the Church's message cast in more biblical and evangelical, rather than juridical or scholastic, terms.[23] This change in emphasis reflected the desire of John XXIII, the pope who convoked Vatican II, that the event mark the beginning of a new Pentecost, with the Holy Spirit poured out on the church anew, renewing its life, preaching, and mission. It is no surprise, then, that Benedict XVI, in an important speech, insisted that while the council certainly did not intend a "rupture" with the past, it clearly did engage in a "hermeneutics of reform."[24]

These axial conciliar themes—legitimate diversity within unity, a renewed relationship between the Bible and tradition, and the call for ecclesial reform—received virtually unanimous support from the many Protestant observers and theologians at Vatican II, thereby launching the Catholic Church into the midst of the ecumenical movement. Taken together, these three themes form the theological background to the subsequent advances made by Evangelicals and Catholics Together.[25]

22. Henri de Lubac, *The Motherhood of the Church*, trans. Sr. Sergia Englund (San Francisco: Ignatius, 1982), 33–34.

23. Vatican II's change in the style or rhetorical genre of the Catholic Church is a prominent theme in John W. O'Malley, *What Happened at Vatican II* (Cambridge, MA: Belknap Press of Harvard University Press, 2008).

24. See Benedict XVI, "Christmas Address" (Dec. 22, 2005), *Acta Apostolicae Sedis* 98 (2006): 40–53.

25. While we think that these three themes have been particularly important for the mission of ECT, we recognize that other theological elements emerging from the

Besides some of the theological points noted above, we should also mention a more personal one. Evangelicals and Catholics have now met face-to-face in theological dialogue for over twenty years. We do not form our views apart from each other's perspectives. We do not formulate our opinions on the basis of old stereotypes of our dialogue partners. We know each other well, as both colleagues and friends, and appreciate each other's deep and lively commitment to the Christian faith and each other's continuing desire to live out that discipleship in a profound way. This appreciative Christian friendship has had enormous implications for our deliberations.

It should also be noted that, from the beginning, ECT has made clear that there would be no false irenicism in our discussions, as if there existed no significant differences between us. As the very first ECT statement affirmed, "We reject any appearance of harmony that is purchased at the price of truth." We do have major differences on issues such as the nature and number of sacraments and the structure of the church and its ministry. Ours has been not an easygoing ecumenism that papers over these differences but a serious theological seeking of unity in truth. While we are not in perfect doctrinal communion, we nonetheless share a significant number of the essential and foundational teachings of the Christian faith: belief in the one Triune God, Father, Son, and Holy Spirit; in Jesus Christ, the Eternal Word made flesh, the Lord and Redeemer of all humanity; in the Holy Scriptures as the unique, divinely inspired Word of God that, by the power of the Spirit, is able to make one "wise unto salvation" (2 Tim. 3:15 KJV); and in the need for all to be redeemed, a salvation accomplished only by the grace of God. It is on the basis of these common doctrinal affirmations that Evangelicals and Catholics Together has proceeded with confidence over these past twenty years.

Commenting on ecumenism and on the continuing Christian mission, Pope Francis has recently stated:

> The immense numbers of people who have not received the Gospel of Jesus Christ cannot leave us indifferent. Consequently, commitment

---

council have significance as well, e.g., the "hierarchy of truths" (*Decree on Ecumenism*, no. 11), which teaches that not every element of divine revelation has the same centrality or importance.

to a unity which helps them to accept Jesus Christ can no longer be a matter of mere diplomacy or forced compliance, but rather an indispensable path to evangelization. . . . How many important things unite us [Catholics and Protestants]! If we really believe in the abundantly free working of the Holy Spirit, we can learn so much from one another! It is not just about being better informed about others, but rather about reaping what the Spirit has sown in them, which is also meant to be a gift for us. (*Evangelii Gaudium* [*The Joy of the Gospel*], no. 246)

The Joint Statements of Evangelicals and Catholics Together

This volume presents the nine statements that ECT has issued between 1994 and 2015. Reading through the documents, one will observe that ECT has moved along two lines of thought: a specifically theological track and a theologically informed cultural track. Examples of the former include the statements on justification (*The Gift of Salvation*) and on Mary, the Mother of God (*Do Whatever He Tells You*), and examples of the latter include the documents on the culture of life (*That They May Have Life*) and on religious liberty (*In Defense of Religious Freedom*).

While there will be more extensive introductions to each of the documents, our intention here is to highlight a few major points with regard to the nine agreed statements.

The first, groundbreaking statement is entitled *Evangelicals and Catholics Together: The Christian Mission in the Third Millennium* (1994). This was the innovative document that called forth much reaction, both positive and negative, and that set the tone for the entire project of Evangelicals and Catholics Together. In this statement, ECT insisted on several points: our common witness to, and fraternity in, Jesus Christ; our mandate to seek unity for the sake of the gospel (based on Jesus's prayer in John 17); and the pressing need for Christian cooperation on various societal issues such as the abortion regime.

In reading this initial statement, one is struck by its prophetic power. There is already a strong accent on the importance of religious freedom as the primary and fundamental freedom, reflecting the

dignity of the human person. There is the insistence that the separation of church and state, while legitimate in itself, is not intended to
mean, and indeed can never mean, the separation of religion from
public life. One is also struck by the rhetorical power of the document in phrases such as this: "To propose that securing civil virtue
is the purpose of religion is blasphemous. To deny that securing civil
virtue is a benefit of religion is blindness." In this original statement
of 1994, we have the solid foundation on which ECT was built in
the ensuing years.

Our second statement, entitled *The Gift of Salvation* (1997), deals
with the central Christian theme of justification by faith. We remember well Richard John Neuhaus leaning back in his chair and
lighting a cigarette at the very beginning of our discussion in 1996.
He opened the conversation by saying that, as a former Lutheran
pastor, he had no problem with justification by faith alone. And then
Neuhaus related a story: When considering becoming a Catholic, he
asked Father Avery Dulles about Catholicism's position on the biblical
doctrine of justification by faith alone. Dulles responded, "Justification by faith alone? Justification by faith alone? The only thing the
Bible says about that is to condemn it!" (Dulles was referring to the
Letter of James.) Ostensibly, we were off to a rocky start.

But we made significant headway. Chuck Colson always felt that
the statement on justification was the most important document
issued by ECT, precisely because of the importance of this theme
at the time of the Reformation and still today. Colson subsequently
told one interviewer that Avery Dulles and Richard Neuhaus died in
back-to-back months (December 2008 and January 2009), but not
before God had providentially allowed them to collaborate on our
crucial statement about justification. Colson noted with particular
pleasure that Pope Benedict XVI taught that, if properly understood,
Luther was right. In a routine Wednesday audience on November 19,
2008, Benedict stated:

> Luther's phrase: "faith alone" is true, if it is not opposed to faith in
> charity, in love. Faith is looking at Christ, entrusting oneself to Christ,
> being united to Christ, conformed to Christ, to his life. And the form,
> the life of Christ, is love; hence to believe is to conform to Christ and to

enter into his love. So it is that in the Letter to the Galatians in which he primarily developed his teaching on justification St. Paul speaks of faith that works through love (cf. Gal. 5:14).[26]

Catholics and Lutherans in the United States had already achieved a significant measure of agreement in their 1985 statement *Justification by Faith*.[27] The ECT statement of 1997, *The Gift of Salvation*, was another significant milestone on the road to the groundbreaking 1999 accord between the Catholic Church and the Lutheran World Federation entitled *Joint Declaration on Justification* (an accord subsequently endorsed by several other Protestant churches as well).

Our third statement, *Your Word Is Truth* (2002), deals with the relationship between Sacred Scripture and the church's tradition, long a thorny and controversial theological issue. Over the past fifty years Catholicism has placed an increasingly significant accent on the uniqueness and priority of the Bible, and Protestants have adopted a more complex understanding of the phrase *sola scriptura*, one that does not rule out the importance of tradition (even while subordinating it to Scripture) in the formulation of church doctrine.

We agreed that the Holy Spirit is the true teacher of the church—and that the Bible is, as the traditional axiom has it, the *norma normans non normata* (the rule of faith that is not itself judged by anything else). Of course, even with that said, Catholics and Evangelicals differ on precisely how the Bible is properly interpreted. But this, too, was a significant breakthrough.

Our fourth and fifth statements treat *The Communion of Saints* (2003) and *The Call to Holiness* (2005). In these documents, we affirm that all Christians are called in their personal lives to draw closer to the living Christ and, in so doing, to draw closer to one another—and to the Christians who have gone before us—in both witness and mission.

In 2006, ECT published its sixth statement, *That They May Have Life*, jointly affirming that as followers of Christ, Christians are called

26. See http://w2.vatican.va/content/benedict-xvi/en/audiences/2008/documents/hf_ben-xvi_aud_20081119.html.

27. *Justification by Faith: Lutherans and Catholics in Dialogue VII*, ed. H. George Anderson, T. Austin Murphy, and Joseph A. Burgess (Minneapolis: Augsburg, 1985).

to care for and protect the most marginalized and vulnerable members of our society, including the unborn, the disabled, the dependent elderly, the dying, and the poor. Every human being from conception to natural death is eternally intended by God. Every person then, including those children waiting to be born, should be welcomed in life and protected in law. While written primarily for Christian believers, this statement was also meant to offer guidance to all those in the public square.

Our seventh statement returned to a specifically theological question, the role of Mary in the life of the church. Entitled *Do Whatever He Tells You: The Blessed Virgin Mary in Christian Faith and Life* (2009), the document was described by one wag as "Evangelicals and Catholics Apart." That's a humorous comment, but an exaggeration. We do, indeed, have important differences on the role of Mary in salvation history and in the lives of contemporary Christians. Over the centuries, the Blessed Mother has played an intense role in Catholic life, theology, and devotion, whereas the Evangelical community places virtually its entire emphasis on Christ the Savior, seeing in Mary primarily a sinful human being in need of redemption.

In fact, both Evangelicals and Catholics wish to understand the Blessed Mother in light of her son, Jesus Christ, and his unique salvific role. We agreed that Mary is described in Scripture as the blessed, virgin mother of the Redeemer. As such, it is proper to call her *Theotokos* (God-bearer) or "the one who gave birth to the one who is God." Appropriating the language of the early Christian church (the Council of Ephesus, AD 431) marks an important affirmation by ECT. The Blessed Mother Mary serves as an example of courageous faith, love, and discipleship for all Christians.

The distinguished Reformed theologian Karl Barth once remarked, half humorously, that he had no objection to a Catholic statue of Mary, as long as her statue was placed in the congregation, signifying her eagerness to listen to the Word of God.[28] Insofar as Barth's remark emphasizes Mary as a disciple of Jesus Christ—a unique one,

---

28. Karl Barth, *Karl Barth's Letters 1961–1968*, ed. J. Fangmeier and H. Stoevesandt, trans. Geoffrey W. Bromiley (Grand Rapids: Eerdmans, 1981), 135.

to be sure—then this is a point on which Evangelicals and Catholics are entirely agreed.

In our eighth statement, *In Defense of Religious Freedom* (2012), we outline the bases for religious freedom in the history of Christian thought. Throughout the centuries, a consistent affirmation of Christians (even if not always strictly observed) is that men and women cannot be asked to violate their consciences in religious matters. Indeed, religious liberty goes to the heart of Christian anthropology: all men and women are created in the image and likeness of God; as such, there can be no coercion in matters of faith.

This statement also intends to overcome the manner in which religious freedom is understood by some today: as the right of men and women to worship privately and to cling personally to their beliefs, but without allowing these beliefs to guide all aspects of life in the public square. This profoundly diminished notion of religious freedom is rejected by Evangelicals and Catholics Together, just as it was rejected by the founders of ECT and, indeed, by the founders of the United States. As we said in our statement *That They May Have Life*: "Whatever is meant by 'the separation of church and state,' it cannot mean the separation of public life and public policy from the deepest convictions, including moral convictions, of the great majority of a nation's citizens."

Both Richard Neuhaus and Chuck Colson dedicated their lives to defending the proposition that religious faith—the most comprehensive of realities—could not be reduced to a private or insular dimension of life. Religious belief affects every aspect of existence; its free exercise must be allowed in every forum, public and private. To affirm this is certainly not to endorse religious imperialism. As Neuhaus frequently said, Christians seek neither a sacred public square nor a naked public square but a civil public square open to a wide range of convictions, where religious speech is fully protected as integral to society. People of all religions have a right to conduct their lives and work in accordance with their most deeply held convictions, without government reprisals or interference.

The most recent statement of ECT is entitled *The Two Shall Become One Flesh: Reclaiming Marriage* (2015) and is concerned with the nature of marriage as both a created and a revealed reality.

Marriage as the permanent bond between a man and a woman has been acknowledged for millennia across highly diverse cultures. Over the past several decades, however, the institution of marriage has been weakened by divorce, premarital sex, cohabitation, and a contraceptive mentality. We together agree that the biblical teaching on human sexuality, marriage, and family life is clear but often overlooked, even by those claiming to be disciples of Jesus Christ. And we insist that marriage, as both a created and revealed reality, is based on male-female complementarity. Indeed, as Paul the apostle says, marriage is a profound mystery, signifying the intimate relationship that exists between Christ and his church.

We further agree that same-sex "marriage" is not marriage at all but a dangerous parody of the marital union. Instead of a unique and permanent bond uniting a man and a woman, marriage is now understood as an instrument created by the state to give official status to the relationship between any two human beings. As Evangelicals and Catholics, we hold—no matter the claims and directives of the state—that marriage is the union of a man and woman, each of whom undertakes a permanent relationship that is open to procreation and to the complementary natural roles of father and mother. We urge Christians to stand firm in this belief despite the accusations of intolerance and bigotry to which they will certainly be subjected.

Conclusion

This review of the origins and theological foundations of Evangelicals and Catholics Together would not be complete if we did not mention two well-known theologians who were at the heart of this enterprise from the beginning, Avery Dulles and J. I. Packer. Their status as internationally respected thinkers added immensely to the stature of ECT, particularly since a few had suggested that the dialogue was more a convenient political alliance rather than a mature theological encounter. The work of ECT over the years has given ample evidence that the dialogue is a witness to the gospel in all of its dimensions.

At the conclusion of their introduction to the volume announcing ECT's mission, Colson and Neuhaus wrote that Evangelicals and Catholics Together exists in service to the claim that God was reconciling the world to himself in Christ (2 Cor. 5:19). They added that "the final test of ECT will be whether it strengthens the church's witness to [this] gospel of reconciliation."[29] It is our firm hope that Evangelicals and Catholics Together is meeting that challenge. Both editors of this volume joined ECT in 1995, when Colson and Neuhaus were assembling a core group charged with continuing the theological dialogue. In the ensuing two decades, we have seen this ecumenical initiative grow in maturity and refinement, with both Evangelicals and Catholics deeply grateful for our common witness to all that God has done in the history of ancient Israel, and, uniquely, in the Redeemer of the world, Jesus Christ.

Over the past two decades, Evangelicals and Catholics have learned much from one another and our joint commitment to biblical and doctrinal truth. We live in an age when the very idea of truth is often called into question. And yet we believe that the Bible teaches God's truth, a truth that is able to be known and understood, appropriated and lived, under the agency of the Holy Spirit. It is the task of ECT to formulate that truth in a way that assists contemporary men and women to live as committed disciples of Jesus of Nazareth.

Not long before his death in 2009, Richard Neuhaus made clear that he wished to see the important work undertaken by ECT continue. Chuck Colson, too, just months before his own passage to God in 2012, was insistent that ECT was one of the most powerful initiatives in the United States for communicating the truth of the gospel. No matter the obstacles, he said, Evangelicals and Catholics must stand side by side in their public witness to biblical truth. The intention of ECT is to continue the prophetic mission of its founders.

Evangelicals and Catholics do not know how Christian unity will come about but look forward to that day when we are fully united in the common witness for which Jesus Christ himself prayed. It is the editors' hope that readers will find theological and spiritual nourishment in the statements collected in this volume. Our prayer is that God may continue to bless the work of Evangelicals and Catholics Together.

29. *Evangelicals and Catholics Together: Toward a Common Mission*, x.

Postscript

The list of signatories to each of the statements is found in an appendix at the end of this volume. In some statements, the institutional affiliation of the signatories was indicated at the time of publication; in other statements, such affiliation was omitted. We have reprinted the signatory lists as they originally appeared.

Further, several of our agreed statements have prefaces that recap earlier agreements and discuss ECT's ongoing theological progress. While these prologues are not constitutive parts of the statements themselves, we have reprinted them here, placing them in italics. They help to establish the context in which the various statements came to fruition.

Finally, we have not asked the contributors for uniformity in biblical citations. Various biblical translations have been utilized; occasionally we have standardized translations, conforming them to the RSV.

We have also made slight orthographical changes in the statements for the sake of consistency.

1

Unity

Introduction

TIMOTHY GEORGE

In 1534, Abbot Paul Bachmann published a virulent anti-Protestant booklet entitled "A Punch in the Mouth for the Lutheran Lying Wide-Gaping Throats." Not to be outdone, the Protestant court chaplain, Jerome Rauscher, responded with a treatise of his own titled "One Hundred Select, Great, Shameless, Fat, Well-Swilled, Stinking, Papistical Lies." Such was the tenor of theological discourse among many of the formative shapers of classical Protestantism and resurgent Roman Catholicism in the sixteenth century. Such rhetoric was brought from the Old World to the New. Fueled by local prejudice and nativist traditions, it continued to deepen the divide between the heirs of the Reformation debates.

Imagine, then, the surprise—in some circles, the shock—when on March 29, 1994, the statement *Evangelicals and Catholics Together: The Christian Mission in the Third Millennium* was released in New

York. Here the old hostility between Catholics and Evangelicals was replaced by a new awareness of their common Christian identity—a shared life in Jesus Christ. The core affirmation of the first ECT statement, and of the entire project, was this declaration: "All who accept Christ as Lord and Savior are brothers and sisters in Christ. Evangelicals and Catholics are brothers and sisters in Christ. We have not chosen one another, just as we have not chosen Christ. He has chosen us, and He has chosen us to be his together."

On the following day, the story of the new Evangelical and Catholic initiative was carried on the front page of the *New York Times*, the *Chicago Tribune*, and other newspapers across the country. The reaction was immediate and explosive. While some saw this new effort as a hopeful sign, others, especially some conservative Evangelicals on the right, were disturbed and distraught. Best-selling author Dave Hunt wrote of the ECT statement: "I believe the document represents the most devastating blow against the gospel in at least 1,000 years."[1] For their part, many left-leaning progressives, both Catholics and Protestants, dismissed the statement as a publicity stunt tied to conservative politics.

It seemed to me that both of these narratives had badly misjudged the situation. When I was asked to write a lead editorial on ECT for *Christianity Today*, I described the new project in this way:

> Here is an ecumenism of the trenches born out of a common moral struggle to proclaim and embody the Gospel of Jesus Christ in a culture of disarray. This is not merely a case of politics making strange bedfellows. It is more like Abraham bargaining with God for the minimal number of righteous witnesses required to spare the sinful city of Sodom. For too long, ecumenism has been left to Left-leaning Catholics and mainline Protestants. For that reason alone, evangelicals should applaud this effort and rejoice in the progress it represents.[2]

Of course, ECT did not come out of the blue. Ever since his 1957 crusade in New York City, Billy Graham had warmly welcomed

1. Dave Hunt, "The Gospel Betrayed," *The Berean Call*, May 1, 1994, www.the bereancall.org/content/gospel-betrayed.

2. Timothy George, "Catholics and Evangelicals in the Trenches," *Christianity Today*, May 1994, 16.

Catholic participants in his evangelistic efforts. John Stott, an Anglican pastor with worldwide influence, had long engaged with Catholics in serious theological discussions on issues of mission and world evangelization. Further, an "ecumenism of the trenches" was already at work among many Evangelicals and Catholics in local communities who found themselves standing side by side in opposing abortion on demand and advocating for the traditional values of chastity, family, and community—all derived from deeply held religious convictions.

The 1994 ECT statement, however, did represent something different. First, it was not an official, church-endorsed ecumenical dialogue but rather an ad hoc group of Catholic and Evangelical theologians brought together by Richard John Neuhaus and Charles W. Colson Jr. The ECT participants were clear that they spoke *from* and *to* but not *for* their respective churches and denominations. While ECT might have raised some ecumenical eyebrows, its independent status made it more flexible and more responsive than traditional patterns of discourse. From the beginning, the Vatican was aware and encouraging of the project. On one occasion, Cardinal Edward Idris Cassidy, then the president of the Pontifical Council for Promoting Christian Unity, addressed the ECT group. At the same time, some Evangelical members of ECT continued to participate in official bilateral dialogues between the Catholic Church and Baptists, Pentecostals, and the World Evangelical Alliance.

Second, ECT represented a move beyond cobelligerency. While sharing many common moral concerns in what were then called the "culture wars," the framers of ECT determined to address these issues precisely as believers in Jesus Christ. They took seriously the prayer of Jesus in John 17:21—"that they may all be one; even as thou, Father, art in me, and I in thee, that they also may be in us, so that the world may believe that thou hast sent me."

Third, the framers of ECT were well aware that Jesus's desire for his disciples to be one also encompassed his prayer for them to be "sanctified in the truth." As Jesus said, "And for their sake I consecrate myself, that they also may be sanctified in truth" (John 17:19 ESV). Both Catholic and Evangelical participants recognized that the only unity worth having was unity in the truth. They determined to practice an ecumenism of conviction, not an ecumenism of accommodation.

In this regard, they were encouraged by the words of Joseph Ratzinger, now Pope Emeritus Benedict XVI: "Our quarreling ancestors
were in reality much closer to each other when in all their disputes
they still knew that they could only be servants of one truth which
must be acknowledged as being as great and as pure as it has been
intended for us by God."[3] Thus, from the beginning, ECT addressed
theological matters still dividing Catholics and Evangelicals as well
as issues of public policy and the common good.

These concerns were each represented in the five major sections of
the first ECT statement. "We Affirm Together" includes a common
embrace of the Apostles' Creed and the christological and trinitarian consensus of the early church. "We Hope Together" quotes
the Great Commission of Jesus in Matthew 28 and connects the
quest for Christian unity with the Lord's missionary mandate. "We
Search Together" commits ECT to "disciplined and sustained conversation" through a prayerful reading of the Scriptures and honest
examination of important doctrinal differences between Catholics
and Evangelicals. "We Contend Together" speaks of a togetherness
in witness on matters related to religious freedom, the sanctity of
life, family values, and moral standards in society. And finally, "We
Witness Together" encourages Catholics and Evangelicals to share
the gospel of Jesus Christ among all peoples of the world and to do
so in a spirit of love and humility, avoiding patterns of coercion or
bearing false witness.

Avery (later Cardinal) Dulles and J. I. Packer were the two senior
theologians in the ECT group. Their wisdom and expertise would
guide the ECT process as it moved forward to take up such controverted issues as justification by faith, Scripture and tradition, the
communion of saints, and the role of Mary in the life of the church,
among others. Dulles's renowned work on ecclesiology informed the
ECT dialogue and stressed the importance of seeking full visible unity
within the body of Christ while emphasizing spiritual ecumenism
and intermediate steps that Catholics and Evangelicals could—and
should—take together in the meantime.

---

3. Joseph Ratzinger, *Church, Ecumenism, and Politics: New Endeavors in Ecclesiology* (San Francisco: Ignatius, 2008), 98.

Packer was a major target of the initial Evangelical protests against ECT. In an essay published in 1994, titled "Why I Signed It," he defended the statement and his continuing involvement in the project. "I am a Protestant who thanks God for the wisdom, backbone, maturity of mind and conscience, and above all, love for my Lord Jesus Christ that I often see among Catholics, and who sometimes has the joy of hearing Catholics say they see comparable fruits in Protestants."[4]

Packer recognized that the deep division that had separated Protestants and Catholics since the time of the Reformation had changed in a significant way. The most important fault line today, he argued, was between "conservationists," who honor the Christ of the Bible and of the historic creeds and confessions, on the one hand, and the theological liberals and radicals who do not, on the other. In this new situation, Packer argued that ECT has a vital role to play: "ECT . . . must be viewed as fuel for a fire that is already alight. The grassroots coalition at which the document aims is already growing. It can be argued that, so far from running ahead of God, as some fear, ECT is playing catch-up to the Holy Spirit."[5]

4. J. I. Packer, "Why I Signed It," *Christianity Today*, December 1994, 35.
5. Ibid., 36.

Evangelicals and Catholics Together: The Christian Mission in the Third Millennium

(1994)

We are Evangelical Protestants and Roman Catholics who have been led through prayer, study, and discussion to common convictions about Christian faith and mission. This statement cannot speak officially for our communities. It does intend to speak responsibly from our communities and to our communities. In this statement we address what we have discovered both about our unity and about our differences. We are aware that our experience reflects the distinctive circumstances and opportunities of Evangelicals and Catholics in North America. At the same time, we believe that what we have discovered and resolved is pertinent to the relationship between Evangelicals and Catholics in other parts of the world. We therefore commend this statement to their prayerful consideration.

As the second millennium draws to a close, the Christian mission in world history faces a moment of daunting opportunity and responsibility. If in the merciful and mysterious ways of God the Second Coming is delayed, we enter upon a third millennium that could be, in the words of John Paul II, a "springtime" of world missions (*Redemptoris Missio*).

As Christ is one, so the Christian mission is one. That one mission can be and should be advanced in diverse ways. Legitimate diversity, however, should not be confused with existing divisions between Christians that obscure the one Christ and hinder the one mission. There is a necessary connection between the visible unity of Christians and the mission of the one Christ. We together pray for the fulfillment of the prayer of Our Lord: ". . . that they may all be one; even as thou, Father, art in me, and I in thee, that they also may be in us, so that the world may believe that thou hast sent me" (John 17:21).

6

We together, Evangelicals and Catholics, confess our sins against the unity that Christ intends for all his disciples.

The one Christ and one mission include many other Christians, notably the Eastern Orthodox and those Protestants not commonly identified as Evangelical. All Christians are encompassed in the prayer, "May they all be one." Our present statement attends to the specific problems and opportunities in the relationship between Roman Catholics and Evangelical Protestants.

As we near the third millennium, there are approximately 1.7 billion Christians in the world. About a billion of these are Catholics and more than 300 million are Evangelical Protestants. The century now drawing to a close has been the greatest century of missionary expansion in Christian history. We pray and we believe that this expansion has prepared the way for yet greater missionary endeavor in the first century of the third millennium.

The two communities in world Christianity that are most evangelistically assertive and most rapidly growing are Evangelicals and Catholics. In many parts of the world, the relationship between these communities is marked more by conflict than by cooperation, more by animosity than by love, more by suspicion than by trust, more by propaganda and ignorance than by respect for the truth. This is alarmingly the case in Latin America, increasingly the case in Eastern Europe, and too often the case in our own country.

Without ignoring conflicts between and within other Christian communities, we address ourselves to the relationship between Evangelicals and Catholics, who constitute the growing edge of missionary expansion at present and, most likely, in the century ahead. In doing so, we hope that what we have discovered and resolved may be of help in other situations of conflict, such as that among Orthodox, Evangelicals, and Catholics in Eastern Europe. While we are gratefully aware of ongoing efforts to address tensions among these communities, the shameful reality is that, in many places around the world, the scandal of conflict between Christians obscures the scandal of the cross, thus crippling the one mission of the one Christ.

As in times past, so also today and in the future, the Christian mission, which is directed to the entire human community, must be advanced against formidable opposition. In some cultures, that mission encounters resurgent spiritualities and religions that are explicitly hostile to the claims of Christ. Islam, which in many instances denies the freedom to witness to the gospel, must be of increasing concern to those who care about religious freedom and the Christian mission. Mutually respectful conversation between Muslims and Christians should be encouraged in the hope that more of the world will, in the oft-repeated words of John Paul II, "open the door to Christ." At the same time, in our so-called developed societies, a widespread secularization increasingly descends into a moral, intellectual, and spiritual nihilism that denies not only the One who is the Truth but the very idea of truth itself.

We enter the twenty-first century without illusions. With Paul and the Christians of the first century, we know that "we are not contending against flesh and blood, but against the principalities, against the powers, against the world rulers of this present darkness, against the spiritual hosts of wickedness in the heavenly places" (Eph. 6:12). As Evangelicals and Catholics, we dare not by needless and loveless conflict between ourselves give aid and comfort to the enemies of the cause of Christ.

The love of Christ compels us, and we are therefore resolved to avoid such conflict between our communities and, where such conflict exists, to do what we can to reduce and eliminate it. Beyond that, we are called and we are therefore resolved to explore patterns of working and witnessing together in order to advance the one mission of Christ. Our common resolve is not based merely on a desire for harmony. We reject any appearance of harmony that is purchased at the price of truth. Our common resolve is made imperative by obedience to the truth of God revealed in the Word of God, the Holy Scriptures, and by trust in the promise of the Holy Spirit's guidance until Our Lord returns in glory to judge the living and the dead.

The mission that we embrace together is the necessary consequence of the faith that we affirm together.

We Affirm Together

Jesus Christ is Lord. That is the first and final affirmation that Christians make about all of reality. He is the One sent by God to be Lord and Savior of all: "And there is salvation in no one else, for there is no other name under heaven given among men by which we must be saved" (Acts 4:12). Christians are people ahead of time, those who proclaim now what will one day be acknowledged by all, that Jesus Christ is Lord (Phil. 2:9–11).

We affirm together that we are justified by grace through faith because of Christ. Living faith is active in love that is nothing less than the love of Christ, for we together say with Paul: "I have been crucified with Christ; it is no longer I who live, but Christ who lives in me; and the life I now live in the flesh I live by faith in the Son of God, who loved me and gave himself for me" (Gal. 2:20).

All who accept Christ as Lord and Savior are brothers and sisters in Christ. Evangelicals and Catholics are brothers and sisters in Christ. We have not chosen one another, just as we have not chosen Christ. He has chosen us, and he has chosen us to be his together (John 15:16). However imperfect our communion with one another, however deep our disagreements with one another, we recognize that there is but one church of Christ. There is one church because there is one Christ and the church is his body. However difficult the way, we recognize that we are called by God to a fuller realization of our unity in the body of Christ. The only unity to which we would give expression is unity in the truth, and the truth is this: "There is one body and one Spirit, just as you were called to the one hope that belongs to your call, one Lord, one faith, one baptism, one God and Father of us all, who is above all and through all and in all" (Eph. 4:4–6).

We affirm together that Christians are to teach and live in obedience to the divinely inspired Scriptures, which are the infallible Word of God. We further affirm together that Christ has promised to his church the gift of the Holy Spirit who will lead us into all truth in discerning and declaring the teaching of Scripture (John 16:13). We recognize together that the Holy Spirit has so guided his church in the past. In, for instance, the formation of the canon of the Scriptures, and in the orthodox response to the great christological and trinitarian controversies of the early centuries, we confidently acknowledge the guidance of the Holy Spirit. In faithful response to the Spirit's leading, the church formulated the Apostles' Creed, which we can and hereby do affirm together as an accurate statement of scriptural truth:

I believe in God, the Father almighty, creator of heaven and earth.

I believe in Jesus Christ, his only Son, our Lord. He was conceived
by the power of the Holy Spirit and born of the Virgin Mary.
He suffered under Pontius Pilate, was crucified, died, and was
buried. He descended into hell. On the third day he rose again.
He ascended into heaven, and is seated at the right hand of the
Father. He will come again to judge the living and the dead.

I believe in the Holy Spirit, the holy catholic church, the communion of saints, the forgiveness of sins, the resurrection of the
body, and the life everlasting. Amen.

We Hope Together

We hope together that all people will come to faith in Jesus Christ as
Lord and Savior. This hope makes necessary the church's missionary
zeal. "But how are men to call upon him in whom they have not believed? And how are they to believe in him of whom they have never
heard? And how are they to hear without a preacher? And how can
men preach unless they are sent?" (Rom. 10:14–15). The church is
by nature, in all places and at all times, in mission. Our missionary
hope is inspired by the revealed desire of God that "all . . . be saved
and . . . come to the knowledge of the truth" (1 Tim. 2:4).

The church lives by and for the Great Commission: "Go therefore
and make disciples of all nations, baptizing them in the name of the
Father and of the Son and of the Holy Spirit, teaching them to observe
all that I have commanded you; and lo, I am with you always, to the
close of the age" (Matt. 28:19–20).

Unity and love among Christians is an integral part of our missionary witness to the Lord whom we serve. "A new commandment
I give to you, that you love one another; even as I have loved you, that
you also love one another. By this all men will know that you are my
disciples, if you have love for one another" (John 13:34–35). If we
do not love one another, we disobey his command and contradict
the gospel we declare.

As Evangelicals and Catholics, we pray that our unity in the love
of Christ will become ever more evident as a sign to the world of

God's reconciling power. Our communal and ecclesial separations are deep and long standing. We acknowledge that we do not know the schedule nor do we know the way to the greater visible unity for which we hope. We do know that existing patterns of distrustful polemic and conflict are not the way. We do know that God who has brought us into communion with himself through Christ intends that we also be in communion with one another. We do know that Christ is the way, the truth, and the life (John 14:6), and as we are drawn closer to him—walking in that way, obeying that truth, living that life—we are drawn closer to one another.

Whatever may be the future form of the relationship between our communities, we can, we must, and we will begin now the work required to remedy what we know to be wrong in that relationship. Such work requires trust and understanding, and trust and understanding require an assiduous attention to truth. We do not deny but clearly assert that there are disagreements between us. Misunderstandings, misrepresentations, and caricatures of one another, however, are not disagreements. These distortions must be cleared away if we are to search through our honest differences in a manner consistent with what we affirm and hope together on the basis of God's Word.

We Search Together

Together we search for a fuller and clearer understanding of God's revelation in Christ and his will for his disciples. Because of the limitations of human reason and language, limitations that are compounded by sin, we cannot understand completely the transcendent reality of God and his ways. Only in the end time will we see face-to-face and know as we are known (1 Cor. 13:12). We now search together in confident reliance upon God's self-revelation in Jesus Christ, the sure testimony of Holy Scripture, and the promise of the Spirit to his church. In this search to understand the truth more fully and clearly, we need one another. We are both informed and limited by the histories of our communities and by our own experiences. Across the divides of communities and experiences, we need to challenge one another, always speaking the truth in love, building up the body (Eph. 4:15–16).

We do not presume to suggest that we can resolve the deep and long-standing differences between Evangelicals and Catholics. Indeed these differences may never be resolved short of the kingdom come. Nonetheless, we are not permitted simply to resign ourselves to differences that divide us from one another. Not all differences are authentic disagreements, nor need all disagreements divide. Differences and disagreements must be tested in disciplined and sustained conversation. In this connection we warmly commend and encourage the formal theological dialogues of recent years between Roman Catholics and Evangelicals.

We note some of the differences and disagreements that must be addressed more fully and candidly in order to strengthen between us a relationship of trust in obedience to truth. Among points of difference in doctrine, worship, practice, and piety that are frequently thought to divide us are these:

- The church as an integral part of the gospel or the church as a communal consequence of the gospel
- The church as visible communion or invisible fellowship of true believers
- The sole authority of Scripture (*sola scriptura*) or Scripture as authoritatively interpreted in the church
- The "soul freedom" of the individual Christian or the Magisterium (teaching authority) of the community
- The church as local congregation or universal communion
- Ministry ordered in apostolic succession or the priesthood of all believers
- Sacraments and ordinances as symbols of grace or means of grace
- The Lord's Supper as eucharistic sacrifice or memorial meal
- Remembrance of Mary and the saints or devotion to Mary and the saints
- Baptism as sacrament of regeneration or testimony to regeneration

This account of differences is by no means complete. Nor is the disparity between positions always so sharp as to warrant the "or" in the above formulations. Moreover, among those recognized as Evangelical Protestants there are significant differences between, for example, Baptists, Pentecostals, and Calvinists on these questions. But the differences mentioned above reflect disputes that are deep and long standing. In at least some instances, they reflect authentic disagreements that have been in the past and are at present barriers to full communion between Christians.

On these questions, and other questions implied by them, Evangelicals hold that the Catholic Church has gone beyond Scripture, adding teachings and practices that detract from or compromise the gospel of God's saving grace in Christ. Catholics, in turn, hold that such teachings and practices are grounded in Scripture and belong to the fullness of God's revelation. Their rejection, Catholics say, results in a truncated and reduced understanding of the Christian reality.

Again, we cannot resolve these disputes here. We can and do affirm together that the entirety of Christian faith, life, and mission finds its source, center, and end in the crucified and risen Lord. We can and do pledge that we will continue to search together—through study, discussion, and prayer—for a better understanding of one another's convictions and a more adequate comprehension of the truth of God in Christ. We can testify now that in our searching together we have discovered what we can affirm together and what we can hope together and, therefore, how we can contend together.

We Contend Together

As we are bound together by Christ and his cause, so we are bound together in contending against all that opposes Christ and his cause. We are emboldened not by illusions of easy triumph but by faith in his certain triumph. Our Lord wept over Jerusalem, and he now weeps over a world that does not know the time of its visitation. The raging of the principalities and powers may increase as the end time nears, but the outcome of the contest is assured.

The cause of Christ is the cause and mission of the church, which is, first of all, to proclaim the good news that "in Christ God was reconciling the world to himself, not counting their trespasses against them, and entrusting to us the message of reconciliation" (2 Cor. 5:19). To proclaim this gospel and to sustain the community of faith, worship, and discipleship that is gathered by this gospel is the first and chief responsibility of the church. All other tasks and responsibilities of the church are derived from and directed toward the mission of the gospel.

Christians individually and the church corporately also have a responsibility for the right ordering of civil society. We embrace this task soberly; knowing the consequences of human sinfulness, we resist the utopian conceit that it is within our powers to build the kingdom of God on earth. We embrace this task hopefully; knowing that God has called us to love our neighbor, we seek to secure for all a greater measure of civil righteousness and justice, confident that he will crown our efforts when he rightly orders all things in the coming of his kingdom.

In the exercise of these public responsibilities there has been in recent years a growing convergence and cooperation between Evangelicals and Catholics. We thank God for the discovery of one another in contending for a common cause. Much more importantly, we thank God for the discovery of one another as brothers and sisters in Christ. Our cooperation as citizens is animated by our convergence as Christians. We promise one another that we will work to deepen, build upon, and expand this pattern of convergence and cooperation.

Together we contend for the truth that politics, law, and culture must be secured by moral truth. With the founders of the American experiment, we declare, "We hold these truths." With them, we hold that this constitutional order is composed not just of rules and procedures but is most essentially a moral experiment. With them, we hold that only a virtuous people can be free and just and that virtue is secured by religion. To propose that securing civil virtue is the purpose of religion is blasphemous. To deny that securing civil virtue is a benefit of religion is blindness.

Americans are drifting away from, are often explicitly defying, the constituting truths of this experiment in ordered liberty. Influential sectors of the culture are laid waste by relativism, anti-intellectualism, and nihilism that deny the very idea of truth. Against such influences in both the elite and popular culture, we appeal to reason and religion in contending for the foundational truths of our constitutional order.

More specifically, we contend together for religious freedom. We do so for the sake of religion, but also because religious freedom is the first freedom, the source and shield of all human freedoms. In their relationship to God, persons have a dignity and responsibility that transcends, and thereby limits, the authority of the state and of every other merely human institution.

Religious freedom is itself grounded in and is a product of religious faith, as is evident in the history of Baptists and others in this country. Today we rejoice together that the Roman Catholic Church—as affirmed by the Second Vatican Council and boldly exemplified in the ministry of John Paul II—is strongly committed to religious freedom and, consequently, to the defense of all human rights. Where Evangelicals and Catholics are in severe and sometimes violent conflict, such as parts of Latin America, we urge Christians to embrace and act upon the imperative of religious freedom. Religious freedom will not be respected by the state if it is not respected by Christians or, even worse, if Christians attempt to recruit the state in repressing religious freedom.

In this country, too, freedom of religion cannot be taken for granted but requires constant attention. We strongly affirm the separation of church and state, and just as strongly protest the distortion of that principle to mean the separation of religion from public life. We are deeply concerned by the courts' narrowing of the protections provided by the "free exercise" provision of the First Amendment and by an obsession with "no establishment" that stifles the necessary role of religion in American life. As a consequence of such distortions, it is increasingly the case that wherever government goes religion must retreat, and government increasingly goes almost everywhere. Religion, which was privileged and foundational in our legal order, has in recent years been penalized and made marginal. We contend together for a renewal of the constituting vision of the place of religion in the American experiment.

Religion and religiously grounded moral conviction is not an alien or threatening force in our public life. For the great majority of Americans, morality is derived, however variously and confusedly, from religion. The argument, increasingly voiced in sectors of our political culture, that religion should be excluded from the public square must be recognized as an assault upon the most elementary principles of democratic governance. That argument needs to be exposed and countered by leaders, religious and other, who care about the integrity of our constitutional order.

The pattern of convergence and cooperation between Evangelicals and Catholics is, in large part, a result of common effort to protect human life, especially the lives of the most vulnerable among us. With the founders, we hold that all human beings are endowed by their Creator with the right to life, liberty, and the pursuit of happiness. The statement that the unborn child is a human life that—barring natural misfortune or lethal intervention—will become what everyone recognizes as a human baby is not a religious assertion. It is a statement of simple biological fact. That the unborn child has a right to protection, including the protection of law, is a moral statement supported by moral reason and biblical truth.

We, therefore, will persist in contending—we will not be discouraged but will multiply every effort—in order to secure the legal protection of the unborn. Our goals are the following: to secure due process of law for the unborn, to enact the most protective laws and public policies that are politically possible, and to reduce dramatically the incidence of abortion. We warmly commend those who have established thousands of crisis pregnancy and postnatal care centers across the country, and urge that such efforts be multiplied. As the unborn must be protected, so also must women be protected from their current rampant exploitation by the abortion industry and by fathers who refuse to accept responsibility for mothers and children. Abortion on demand, which is the current rule in America, must be recognized as a massive attack on the dignity, rights, and needs of women.

Abortion is the leading edge of an encroaching culture of death. The helpless old, the radically handicapped, and others who cannot effectively assert their rights are increasingly treated as though they have no rights. These are the powerless who are exposed to the will and whim of those who have power over them. We will do all in our power to resist proposals for euthanasia, eugenics, and population control that exploit the vulnerable, corrupt the integrity of medicine, deprave our culture, and betray the moral truths of our constitutional order.

In public education, we contend together for schools that transmit to coming generations our cultural heritage, which is inseparable from the formative influence of religion, especially Judaism and Christianity. Education for responsible citizenship and social behavior is inescapably moral education. Every effort must be made to cultivate the morality of honesty, law observance, work, caring, chastity, mutual respect between the sexes, and readiness for marriage, parenthood, and family. We reject the claim that, in any or all of these areas, "tolerance" requires the promotion of moral equivalence between the normative and the deviant. In a democratic society that recognizes that parents have the primary responsibility for the formation of their children, schools are to assist and support, not oppose and undermine, parents in the exercise of their responsibility.

We contend together for a comprehensive policy of parental choice in education. This is a moral question of simple justice. Parents are the primary educators of their children; the state and other institutions should be supportive of their exercise of that responsibility. We affirm policies that enable parents to effectively exercise their right and responsibility to choose the schooling that they consider best for their children.

We contend together against the widespread pornography in our society, along with the celebration of violence, sexual depravity, and antireligious bigotry in the entertainment media. In resisting such cultural and moral debasement, we recognize the legitimacy of boycotts and other consumer actions and urge the enforcement of existing laws against obscenity. We reject the self-serving claim of the peddlers of depravity that this constitutes illegitimate censorship. We reject the assertion of the unimaginative that artistic creativity is to be measured by the capacity to shock or outrage. A people incapable of defending decency invites the rule of viciousness, both public and personal.

We contend for a renewed spirit of acceptance, understanding, and cooperation across lines of religion, race, ethnicity, sex, and class. We are all created in the image of God and are accountable to him. That truth is the basis of individual responsibility and equality before the law. The abandonment of that truth has resulted in a society at war with itself, pitting citizens against one another in bitter conflicts of group grievances and claims to entitlement. Justice and social amity require a redirection of public attitudes and policies so that rights are joined to duties and people are rewarded according to their character and competence.

We contend for a free society, including a vibrant market economy. A free society requires a careful balancing between economics, politics, and culture. Christianity is not an ideology and therefore does not prescribe precisely how that balance is to be achieved in every circumstance. We affirm the importance of a free economy not only because it is more efficient but because it accords with a Christian understanding of human freedom. Economic freedom, while subject to grave abuse, makes possible the patterns of creativity, cooperation, and accountability that contribute to the common good.

We contend together for a renewed appreciation of Western culture. In its history and missionary reach, Christianity engages all cultures while being captive to none. We are keenly aware of, and grateful for, the role of Christianity in shaping and sustaining the Western culture of which we are part. As with all of history, that culture is marred by human sinfulness. Alone among world cultures, however, the West has cultivated an attitude of self-criticism and of eagerness to learn from other cultures. What is called multiculturalism can mean respectful attention to human differences. More commonly today, however, multiculturalism means affirming all cultures but our own. Welcoming the contributions of other cultures and being ever alert to the limitations of our own, we receive Western culture as our legacy and embrace it as our task in order to transmit it as a gift to future generations.

We contend for public policies that demonstrate renewed respect for the irreplaceable role of mediating structures in society—notably the family, churches, and myriad voluntary associations. The state is not the society, and many of the most important functions of society are best addressed in independence from the state. The role of churches in responding to a wide variety of human needs, especially among the poor and marginal, needs to be protected and strengthened. Moreover, society is not the aggregate of isolated individuals bearing rights but is composed of communities that inculcate responsibility, sustain shared memory, provide mutual aid, and nurture the habits that contribute to both personal well-being and the common good. Most basic among such communities is the community of the family. Laws and social policies should be designed with particular care for the stability and flourishing of families. While the crisis of the family in America is by no means limited to the poor or to the underclass, heightened attention must be paid to those who have become, as a result of well-intended but misguided statist policies, virtual wards of the government.

Finally, we contend for a realistic and responsible understanding of America's part in world affairs. Realism and responsibility require that we avoid both the illusions of unlimited power and righteousness, on the one hand, and the timidity and selfishness of isolationism, on the other. American foreign policy should reflect a concern for the defense of democracy and, wherever prudent and possible, the protection and advancement of human rights, including religious freedom.

The above is a partial list of public responsibilities on which we believe there is a pattern of convergence and cooperation between Evangelicals and Catholics. We reject the notion that this constitutes a partisan "religious agenda" in American politics. Rather, this is a set of directions oriented to the common good and discussable on the basis of public reason. While our sense of civic responsibility is informed and motivated by Christian faith, our intention is to elevate the level of political and moral discourse in a manner that excludes no one and invites the participation of all people of goodwill. To that end, Evangelicals and Catholics have made an inestimable contribution in the past and, it is our hope, will contribute even more effectively in the future.

We are profoundly aware that the American experiment has been, all in all, a blessing to the world and a blessing to us as Evangelical and Catholic Christians. We are determined to assume our full share of responsibility for this "one nation under God," believing it to be a nation under the judgment, mercy, and providential care of the Lord of the nations to whom alone we render unqualified allegiance.

We Witness Together

The question of Christian witness unavoidably returns us to points of serious tension between Evangelicals and Catholics. Bearing witness to the saving power of Jesus Christ and his will for our lives is an integral part of Christian discipleship. The achievement of goodwill and cooperation between Evangelicals and Catholics must not be at the price of the urgency and clarity of Christian witness to the gospel. At the same time, and as noted earlier, our Lord has made clear that the evidence of love among his disciples is an integral part of that Christian witness.

Today, in this country and elsewhere, Evangelicals and Catholics attempt to win "converts" from one another's folds. In some ways, this is perfectly understandable and perhaps inevitable. In many instances, however, such efforts at recruitment undermine the Christian mission by which we are bound by God's Word and to which we have recommitted ourselves in this statement. It should be clearly understood between Catholics and Evangelicals that Christian witness is of necessity aimed at conversion. Authentic conversion is—in its beginning, in its end, and all along the way—conversion to God in Christ by the power of the Spirit. In this connection, we embrace as our own the explanation of the Baptist-Roman Catholic International Conversation (1988):

> Conversion is turning away from all that is opposed to God, contrary to Christ's teaching, and turning to God, to Christ, the Son, through the work of the Holy Spirit. It entails a turning from the self-centeredness of sin to faith in Christ as Lord and Savior. Conversion is a passing from one way of life to another new one, marked with the newness of Christ. It is a continuing process so that the whole life of a Christian should be a passage from death to life, from error to truth, from sin to grace. Our life in Christ demands continual growth in God's grace. Conversion is personal but not private. Individuals respond in faith to God's call but faith comes from hearing the proclamation of the word of God and is to be expressed in the life together in Christ that is the Church.

By preaching, teaching, and life example, Christians witness to Christians and non-Christians alike. We seek and pray for the conversion of others, even as we recognize our own continuing need to be fully converted. As we strive to make Christian faith and life—our own and that of others—ever more intentional rather than nominal, ever more committed rather than apathetic, we also recognize the different forms that authentic discipleship can take. As is evident in the two-thousand-year history of the church and in our contemporary experience, there are different ways of being Christian, and some of these ways are distinctively marked by communal patterns of worship, piety, and catechesis. That we are all to be one does not mean that we are all to be identical in our way of following the one Christ. Such distinctive patterns of discipleship, it should be noted, are amply evident within the communion of the Catholic Church as well as within the many worlds of Evangelical Protestantism.

It is understandable that Christians who bear witness to the gospel try to persuade others that their communities and traditions are more fully in accord with the gospel. There is a necessary distinction between evangelizing and what is today commonly called proselytizing or "sheep stealing." We condemn the practice of recruiting people from another community for purposes of denominational or institutional aggrandizement. At the same time, our commitment to full religious freedom compels us to defend the legal freedom to proselytize even as we call upon Christians to refrain from such activity.

Three observations are in order in connection with proselytizing. First, as much as we might believe one community is more fully in accord with the gospel than another, we as Evangelicals and Catholics affirm that opportunity and means for growth in Christian discipleship are available in our several communities. Second, the decision of the committed Christian with respect to his communal allegiance and participation must be assiduously respected. Third, in view of the large number of non-Christians in the world and the enormous challenge of our common evangelistic task, it is neither theologically legitimate nor a prudent use of resources for one Christian community to proselytize among active adherents of another Christian community.

Christian witness must always be made in a spirit of love and humility. It must not deny but must readily accord to everyone the full freedom to discern and decide what is God's will for his life. Witness that is in service to the truth is in service to such freedom. Any form of coercion—physical, psychological, legal, economic—corrupts Christian witness and is to be unqualifiedly rejected. Similarly, bearing false witness against other persons and communities, or casting unjust and uncharitable suspicions upon them, is incompatible with the gospel. Also to be rejected is the practice of comparing the strengths and ideals of one community with the weaknesses and failures of another. In describing the teaching and practices of other Christians, we must strive to do so in a way that they would recognize as fair and accurate.

In considering the many corruptions of Christian witness, we, Evangelicals and Catholics, confess that we have sinned against one another and against God. We most earnestly ask the forgiveness of God and one another and pray for the grace to amend our own lives and that of our communities.

Repentance and amendment of life do not dissolve remaining differences between us. In the context of evangelization and "re-evangelization," we encounter a major difference in our understanding of the relationship between baptism and the new birth in Christ. For Catholics, all who are validly baptized are born again and are truly, however imperfectly, in communion with Christ. That baptismal grace is to be continuingly reawakened and revivified through conversion. For most Evangelicals, but not all, the experience of conversion is to be followed by baptism as a sign of new birth. For Catholics, all the baptized are already members of the church, however dormant their faith and life; for many Evangelicals, the new birth requires baptismal initiation into the community of the born again. These differing beliefs about the relationship between baptism, new birth, and membership in the church should be honestly presented to the Christian who has undergone conversion. But again, his decision regarding communal allegiance and participation must be assiduously respected.

There are, then, differences between us that cannot be resolved here. But on this we are resolved: All authentic witness must be aimed at conversion to God in Christ by the power of the Spirit. Those converted—whether understood as having received the new birth for the first time or as having experienced the reawakening of the new birth originally bestowed in the sacrament of baptism—must be given full freedom and respect as they discern and decide the community in which they will live their new life in Christ. In such discernment and decision, they are ultimately responsible to God, and we dare not interfere with the exercise of that responsibility. Also in our differences and disagreements, we Evangelicals and Catholics commend one another to God "who by the power at work within us is able to do far more abundantly than all that we ask or think" (Eph. 3:20).

In this discussion of witnessing together we have touched on difficult and long-standing problems. The difficulties must not be permitted to overshadow the truths on which we are, by the grace of God, in firm agreement. As we grow in mutual understanding and trust, it is our hope that our efforts to evangelize will not jeopardize but will reinforce our devotion to the common tasks to which we have pledged ourselves in this statement.

Conclusion

Nearly two thousand years after it began, and nearly five hundred years after the divisions of the Reformation era, the Christian mission to the world is vibrantly alive and assertive. We do not know, we cannot know, what the Lord of history has in store for the third millennium. It may be the springtime of world missions and great Christian expansion. It may be the way of the cross marked by persecution and apparent marginalization. In different places and times, it will likely be both. Or it may be that Our Lord will return tomorrow.

We do know that his promise is sure, that we are enlisted for the duration, and that we are in this together. We do know that we must affirm and hope and search and contend and witness together, for we belong not to ourselves but to him who has purchased us by the blood of the cross. We do know that this is a time of opportunity—and if of opportunity, then of responsibility—for Evangelicals and Catholics to be Christians together in a way that helps prepare the world for the coming of him to whom belongs the kingdom, the power, and the glory forever. Amen.

2

Justification

Introduction

THOMAS C. ODEN

The Gift of Salvation came after three long years of contemplation and clarification following the original statement about Evangelicals and Catholics Together published on March 29, 1994. This second ECT document was intended to answer questions raised by the original statement and to take the conversation to deeper levels. The timing of the second document was crucial. During those intervening years, participants were listening carefully to our most active critics and to one another.

The two central issues were *justification by grace alone through faith alone* and *the biblical imperative of global evangelization*. The original ECT statement of 1994 was never intended to answer in detail all the unresolved issues between Evangelicals and Catholics. It was most widely seen as a bold statement of consensus between Evangelicals and Catholics on matters about which they had experienced a history of misunderstandings. Despite a warm reception from most Evangelicals and most Catholics, participants agreed that the first statement had left "perceived ambiguities" that needed to be fully clarified. The participants had written the original statement thoughtfully but with no claim that it was a comprehensive expression of mutual understandings.

Justification by Grace through Faith Active in Love

The most ancient and deepest strains of Catholic teaching never intended to affirm justification *by works* alone, as sometimes perceived by Protestant critics. Nor did the Evangelical traditions intend to affirm justification by grace alone as if it were *without the good works that spring from the life freely justified by the grace of God*. These inaccurate misperceptions require explicit correction whenever they emerge. *The Gift of Salvation* offered thoughtful answers based on three years of deliberation, research, and dialogue.

The ECT dialogues were not the result of any officially sponsored ecclesiastical entity, but rather the searching work of informed and believing individuals who were speaking *from and to, but not for*, our various communities. Our dialogue was different entirely from the type of conversations that were occurring through official bodies, such as the ongoing bilateral dialogues between the Pontifical Council on Christian Unity and official bodies such as the Lutherans, Anglicans, Methodists, Reformed, and Pentecostal traditions. Ours was a dialogue between believing Catholics and believing Evangelicals. Our steady conviction was that, despite differences, we were coming together by God's grace as brothers and sisters in Christ, accountable to the apostolic faith that Jesus Christ is Lord and Savior.

We were keenly aware of Jesus's earnest prayer for his disciples *"that they may all be one. As you, Father, are in me and I am in you, may they also be in us, so that the world may believe that you have sent me"* (John 17:21 NRSV). It is the mighty work of the Spirit to nurture the unity of believers. We sought to manifest that unity, a unity that itself becomes a testimony encouraging the world to believe that the Father sent the Son for the salvation of humanity. If we are one, all who look toward believing Evangelicals and believing Catholics will be more open to faith. Insofar as we are not one, we are not manifesting the unity the Spirit is seeking in us. We viewed our unity in the body of Christ as a gift of grace, not as a goal to be achieved. We were there to celebrate that unity and speak of it with both clarity and charity, grateful for the astonishing convergence we were discovering. At the same time we remained ever mindful of the differences in our historical perceptions.

None of the participants downplayed rigorous doctrinal teaching, since all of them were serious, faithful, and largely traditional theologians. Rather, we understood that the way to unity of belief is to pray for grace that the Holy Spirit will unite us. We regarded our work not as a compromise but as joint thinking in good conscience on how the Spirit is bringing believers together. Pope John Paul II in his encyclical *Ut Unum Sint* (*That They May Be One*, no. 18) confirmed this same conviction: "In matters of faith, compromise is in contradiction with God, who is Truth. In the Body of Christ, 'the way and the truth and the life,' who could consider legitimate a reconciliation brought about at the expense of truth?" This recognition was not a weakening or diluting of faith in order to reach agreement but an agreement in faith that strengthened our conviction. It brought all of us closer to the apostolic testimony and its earliest interpreters who were closest to the salvation event that occurred on the cross and in the resurrection.

The Evangelicals did not seek an accommodation at the expense of Evangelical truth. The Catholics did not seek an accommodation at the expense of Catholic truth. Meanwhile, we were learning that believing Evangelicals and committed Catholics had in common the most important common faith that saves us from sin, the faith that justifies by sheer divine mercy and grace, the faith in God the Father, God the Son, and God the Spirit made known in Jesus.

The Common Faith Expressed in the Earliest Consensual Exegetes

Together we were confirming the truth that the apostles and ancient Christian writers had affirmed concerning God's justifying grace—a truth of historic Christian orthodoxy that had been given doctrinal form centuries before the Reformation and Counter-Reformation controversies that divided us.

Thus it would be entirely mistaken to think of this statement as an act of theological pluralism or the hyper-tolerance that has badly diluted both avant-garde Catholic teaching and much modern mainline Protestant theology. As Evangelicals who hold to classic Reformation teaching, we have joined together with Catholics who are faithful to classic Catholic teaching to seek *no unity other than unity in the truth*. Evangelicals today are finding that they stand much closer to classic consensual Christian teaching than they had once imagined. Catholics are finding that they stand much closer than expected to classic Protestant and Evangelical teaching on justification by faith active in love.

Evangelicals believe that justification by faith alone is at the heart of the gospel. It cannot be diluted without loss of faith itself. Both the Anglican-Methodist traditions and the Lutheran and Reformed traditions are expressed in the statement that "we are accounted righteous before God, only for the merit of our Lord and Savior Jesus Christ by faith, and not for our own works or deservings."[1]

Our first major challenge was to work together to understand our varied language about justification. For the Reformers, of course, justification was the benchmark by which they evaluated all other Christian teaching. *The Gift of Salvation* gives expression to our agreement that ancient Catholic teaching confirms justification by faith alone (*sola fide*). For Evangelicals who might doubt that this is ancient Catholic teaching, we need only quote a few leading voices, Christian teachers who express this conviction from the beginning. Key texts from Clement of Rome, Augustine, and others demonstrate the patristic anticipation of Reformation teaching on justification.

The earliest of Paul's interpreters, Clement of Rome, in his *Letter to the Corinthians* (ca. AD 95) clearly maintained the biblical teaching on justification:

---

1. See Article XI of the Thirty-Nine Articles of the Anglican Church and Article IX of the Articles of Religion, United Methodist Church, echoing earlier Lutheran and Reformed Confessions.

We, therefore, who have been called by His will in Christ Jesus, are not justified by ourselves, neither by our wisdom or understanding or piety, nor by the works we have wrought in holiness of heart, but by faith by which almighty God has justified all those who have faith from the beginning, to whom be glory forever and ever. Amen. What, then, shall we do, beloved? Shall we cease from good works, and shall we put an end to love? May the Master forbid that such should ever happen among us; rather, let us be eager to perform every good work earnestly and willingly. (*Letter to the Corinthians* 32.4–33.1)[2]

Augustine set the pattern that would reappear in Luther. In a letter to Paulinus of Nola, Augustine subtly analyzed the relation of grace and freedom:

Let no one say to himself: "If [justification] is from faith, how is it freely given (cf. Rom. 3.24)? If faith merits it, why is it not rather paid than given?" Let the faithful Christian not say such a thing; for, if he says: "I have faith, therefore I merit justification," he will be answered: "What have you that you did not receive (1 Cor. 4.7)?" If, therefore, faith entreats and receives justification, according as God has apportioned to each in the measure of his faith (Rom. 12.3), nothing of human merit precedes the grace of God, but grace itself enables increase . . . with the will accompanying but not leading, following along but not going in advance. (*Letter to Paulinus of Nola* 186.3.10)[3]

Prosper of Aquitaine stated the teaching on justification in much the same way as Luther and Calvin would later:

And just as there are no crimes so detestable that they can prevent the gift of grace, so too there can be no works so eminent that they are owed justly, having received that which is given freely. Would it not be a debasement of redemption in Christ's blood, and would not God's mercy be made secondary to human works, if justification, which is solely through grace, were owed in view of preceding merits, so that

---

2. W. A. Jurgens, *The Faith of the Early Fathers*, 3 vols. (Collegeville, MN: Liturgical Press, 1970–79), 1:9, sec. 16.
3. Ibid., 3:10, sec. 1446.

it were not the gift of a donor, but the wages of a laborer? (*Call of All Nations* 1.17)[4]

That this faith constantly becomes active in love is evident in early Christian writers such as the African Fulgentius of Ruspe, who taught:

> Without faith it is impossible to please God. For faith is the basis of all good deeds. With faith comes salvation. Without faith no one can attain to the number of the sons of God. Without faith no one will obtain the grace of justification in this life nor possess eternal life in the future. If anyone does not actively walk in faith, he will not arrive at the actuality of faith. Without faith every human labor is empty. (*The Rule of Faith* 1; Heb. 11:6)[5]

Caesarius of Arles adds, "What does it mean to receive the grace of God in vain except to be unwilling to perform good works with the help of his grace?" (*Sermon* 126.5).[6]

Similarly in the Eastern consensual tradition, John Chrysostom taught that faith is not something one does by oneself:

> For "by grace are you saved," Paul says, "through faith." Then, so as to do no injury to free will, he allots a role to us, then takes it away again, saying "and this is not of ourselves. . . ." Even faith, he says, is not from us. For if the Lord had not come, if he had not called us, how should we have been able to believe? "For how," he says, "shall they believe if they have not heard?" (Rom. 10:14). So even the fact of faith is not our own. It is, he says, "the gift of God." (*Commentary on Ephesians* 2.8).[7]

According to these texts, Luther's and Calvin's justification teachings were profoundly anticipated by both Eastern and Western patristic

---

4. Ibid., 3:195, sec. 2044.

5. Ibid., 3:295, sec. 2260.

6. *St. Caesarius of Arles, Sermons, Vol. 2 (81–186)*, trans. Sister Mary Magdeleine Mueller, O.S.F., Fathers of the Church 47 (Washington, DC: Catholic University of America Press, 1964), 219.

7. Mark J. Edwards, ed., *Galatians, Ephesians, Philippians*, Ancient Christian Commentary on Scripture, New Testament 8 (Downers Grove, IL: IVP Academic, 2005), 134.

writers.[8] Luther viewed his work not as his own original discovery but as the *recovery* of classic ecumenical justification exegesis. For his part, Calvin unhesitatingly taught that we are justified by faith alone, but the faith that justifies is not alone, since out of it spring the works of love.

Evangelicals who assume that the ancient Christian writers of the first millennium knew little or nothing about good works as specifically flowing from unmerited grace through faith active in love have not spent time with these classical theologians. This central Reformation teaching was learned by the Reformers from Paul, who taught it to the church fathers, who passed it on without diminution. Jesus said, "No one comes to the Father, but by me" (John 14:6). "He saved us, not because of deeds done by us in righteousness, but in virtue of his own mercy" (Titus 3:5).

Scripture describes the consequences of Christ's redemptive work as justification, reconciliation, restoration of friendship with God, and rebirth from above by which we are adopted as children of God and made heirs of the kingdom. Jesus was "put to death for our trespasses and raised for our justification" (Rom. 4:25). "God, on the basis of Christ's righteousness alone, declares us to be no longer his rebellious enemies but his forgiven friends, and by virtue of his declaration it is so" (*The Gift of Salvation*). It is amazing that in *The Gift of Salvation* faithful Catholics joined faithful Evangelicals in confirming that they were in agreement with what the Reformation traditions have meant by justification by faith alone (*sola fide*). Catholics found in their greatest teachers (Augustine, Pope Leo the Great, and Thomas Aquinas) the warning not to pretend that good works obtain salvation. Jerome wrote: "We are saved by grace rather than works, for we can give God nothing in return for what he has bestowed on us" (*Epistle to the Ephesians* 1.2.1).

The Commission to Tell the Good News to All Humanity

Out of this incomparable gift of God comes the imperative to preach the gospel to all humanity. Since the goodness of this good news is

---

8. See my *Justification Reader* (Grand Rapids: Eerdmans, 2002) for an explicit presentation of patristic exegesis on justification.

intended for all men and women, the believing community is commissioned to tell it to all who have ears to hear. In obedience to this Great Commission of our Lord, we commit ourselves to evangelizing everyone. We must share the fullness of God's saving truth with all, including members of our own communities. We must not allow our witness as Christians to be compromised by halfhearted discipleship or needlessly divisive disputes. Only unity in the truth can be pleasing to the Lord and Savior whom we together serve, for he is "the way, and the truth, and the life" (John 14:6).

The Gift of Salvation left on the agenda many issues to be discussed, which have been dealt with in subsequent ECT documents: the historic uses of the language of justification as it relates to imputed and transformative righteousness; the relation of Scripture and tradition; the invocation of the saints; Marian devotion; the church; Petrine teaching; sacramental grace; and many more.

But in this statement, one may see an extraordinary consensus on a fundamental teaching of the Bible and the Christian tradition. We rejoice that God has allowed us to achieve this measure of unity.

The Gift of Salvation

(1997)

In the spring of 1994, a distinguished group of Roman Catholics and Evangelical Protestants issued a much-discussed statement, Evangelicals and Catholics Together: The Christian Mission in the Third Millennium. *That statement noted a growing "convergence and cooperation" between Evangelicals and Catholics in many public tasks and affirmed agreement in basic articles of Christian faith while also underscoring the continuing existence of important differences. The signers promised to engage those differences in continuing conversations, and this has been done in meetings of noted theologians convened by Mr. Charles Colson and Father Richard John Neuhaus. At a meeting in the fall of 1996, it was determined that further progress depended upon firm agreement on the meaning of salvation and, especially, the doctrine of justification. After much discussion, study, and prayer over the course of a year, the following statement was agreed to at a meeting in New York City, October 6–7, 1997. The conveners and participants express their gratitude to Edward Idris Cardinal Cassidy, President of the Pontifical Council for Promoting Christian Unity, for his very active support throughout this process. In future conversations they intend to address the outstanding questions noted at the end of this statement.*

"For God so loved the world that he gave his only Son, that whoever believes in him should not perish but have eternal life. For God sent the Son into the world, not to condemn the world, but that the world might be saved through him" *(John 3:16–17).*

We give thanks to God that in recent years many Evangelicals and Catholics, ourselves among them, have been able to express a common faith in Christ and so to acknowledge one another as brothers and sisters in Christ. We confess together one God, the Father, the Son, and the Holy Spirit; we confess Jesus Christ the Incarnate Son of God; we affirm the binding authority of Holy Scripture, God's inspired Word; and we acknowledge the Apostles' and Nicene Creeds as faithful witnesses to that Word.

The effectiveness of our witness for Christ depends upon the work of the Holy Spirit, who calls and empowers us to confess together the meaning of the salvation promised and accomplished in Christ Jesus our Lord. Through prayer and study of Holy Scripture, and aided by the church's reflection on the sacred text from earliest times, we have found that, notwithstanding some persistent and serious differences, we can together bear witness to the gift of salvation in Jesus Christ. To this saving gift we now testify, speaking not for, but from and to, our several communities.

God created us to manifest his glory and to give us eternal life in fellowship with himself, but our disobedience intervened and brought us under condemnation. As members of the fallen human race, we come into the world estranged from God and in a state of rebellion. This original sin is compounded by our personal acts of sinfulness. The catastrophic consequences of sin are such that we are powerless to restore the ruptured bonds of union with God. Only in the light of what God has done to restore our fellowship with him do we see the full enormity of our loss. The gravity of our plight and the greatness of God's love are brought home to us by the life, suffering, death, and resurrection of Jesus Christ. "God so loved the world that he gave his only Son, that whoever believes in him should not perish but have eternal life" (John 3:16).

God the Creator is also God the Redeemer, offering salvation to the world. God "desires all men to be saved and to come to the knowledge of the truth" (1 Tim. 2:4). The restoration of communion with God is absolutely dependent upon Jesus Christ, true God and true man, for he is "the one mediator between God and men" (1 Tim. 2:5), and "there is no other name under heaven given among men by which we must be saved" (Acts 4:12). Jesus said, "No one comes to the Father, but by me" (John 14:6). He is the holy and righteous one who was put to death for our sins, "the righteous for the unrighteous, that he might bring us to God" (1 Pet. 3:18).

The New Testament speaks of salvation in various ways. Salvation is ultimate or eschatological rescue from sin and its consequences, the final state of safety and glory to which we are brought in both body and soul. "Since, therefore, we are now justified by his blood, much more shall we be saved by him from the wrath of God." "Salvation is nearer to us now than when we first believed" (Rom. 5:9; 13:11). Salvation is also a present reality. We are told that "he saved us, not because of deeds done by us in righteousness, but in virtue of his own mercy" (Titus 3:5). The present reality of salvation is an anticipation and foretaste of salvation in its promised fullness.

Always it is clear that the work of redemption has been accomplished by Christ's atoning sacrifice on the cross. "Christ redeemed us from the curse of the law by becoming a curse for us" (Gal. 3:13 ESV). Scripture describes the consequences of Christ's redemptive work in several ways, among which are justification, reconciliation, restoration of friendship with God, and rebirth from above by which we are adopted as children of God and made heirs of the kingdom. "When the time had fully come, God sent forth his Son, born of woman, born under the law, to redeem those who were under the law, so that we might receive adoption as sons" (Gal. 4:4–5).

Justification is central to the scriptural account of salvation, and its meaning has been much debated between Protestants and Catholics. We agree that justification is not earned by any good works or merits of our own; it is entirely God's gift, conferred through the Father's sheer graciousness, out of the love that he bears us in his Son, who suffered on our behalf and rose from the dead for our justification. Jesus was "put to death for our trespasses and raised for our justification" (Rom. 4:25). In justification, God, on the basis of Christ's righteousness alone, declares us to be no longer his rebellious enemies but his forgiven friends, and by virtue of his declaration it is so.

The New Testament makes it clear that the gift of justification is received through faith. "By grace you have been saved through faith; and this is not your own doing, it is the gift of God" (Eph. 2:8). By faith, which is also the gift of God, we repent of our sins and freely adhere to the gospel, the good news of God's saving work for us in Christ. By our response of faith to Christ, we enter into the blessings promised by the gospel. Faith is not merely intellectual assent but an act of the whole person, involving the mind, the will, and the affections, issuing in a changed life. We understand that what we here affirm is in agreement with what the Reformation traditions have meant by justification by faith alone (*sola fide*).

In justification we receive the gift of the Holy Spirit, through whom the love of God is poured forth into our hearts (Rom. 5:5). The grace of Christ and the gift of the Spirit received through faith (Gal. 3:14) are experienced and expressed in diverse ways by different Christians and in different Christian traditions, but God's gift is never dependent upon our human experience or our ways of expressing that experience.

While faith is inherently personal, it is not a purely private possession but involves participation in the body of Christ. By baptism we are visibly incorporated into the community of faith and committed to a life of discipleship. "We were buried therefore with him by baptism into death, so that as Christ was raised from the dead by the glory of the Father, we too might walk in newness of life" (Rom. 6:4).

By their faith and baptism, Christians are bound to live according to the law of love in obedience to Jesus Christ the Lord. Scripture calls this the life of holiness, or sanctification. "Since we have these promises, dear friends, let us purify ourselves from everything that contaminates body and spirit, perfecting holiness out of reverence for God" (2 Cor. 7:1 NIV). Sanctification is not fully accomplished at the beginning of our life in Christ, but is progressively furthered as we struggle, with God's grace and help, against adversity and temptation. In this struggle we are assured that Christ's grace will be sufficient for us, enabling us to persevere to the end. When we fail, we can still turn to God in humble repentance and confidently ask for, and receive, his forgiveness.

We may therefore have assured hope for the eternal life promised to us in Christ. As we have shared in his sufferings, we will share in his final glory. "We shall be like him, for we shall see him as he is" (1 John 3:2 NIV). While we dare not presume upon the grace of God, the promise of God in Christ is utterly reliable, and faith in that promise overcomes anxiety about our eternal future. We are bound by faith itself to have firm hope, to encourage one another in that hope, and in such hope we rejoice. For believers "through faith are shielded by God's power until the coming of the salvation that is ready to be revealed in the last time" (1 Pet. 1:5 NIV).

Thus it is that as justified sinners we have been saved, we are being saved, and we will be saved. All this is the gift of God. Faith issues in a confident hope for a new heaven and a new earth in which God's creating and redeeming purposes are gloriously fulfilled. "Therefore God has highly exalted him and bestowed on him the name which is above every name, that at the name of Jesus every knee should bow, in heaven and on earth and under the earth, and every tongue confess that Jesus Christ is Lord, to the glory of God the Father" (Phil. 2:9–11).

As believers we are sent into the world and commissioned to be bearers of the good news, to serve one another in love, to do good to all, and to evangelize everyone everywhere. It is our responsibility and firm resolve to bring to the whole world the tidings of God's love and of the salvation accomplished in our crucified, risen, and returning Lord. Many are in grave peril of being eternally lost because they do not know the way to salvation.

In obedience to the Great Commission of our Lord, we commit ourselves to evangelizing everyone. We must share the fullness of God's saving truth with all, including members of our several communities. Evangelicals must speak the gospel to Catholics and Catholics to Evangelicals, always speaking the truth in love, so that "mak[ing] every effort to keep the unity of the Spirit through the bond of peace . . . the body of Christ may be built up until we all reach unity in the faith and in the knowledge of the Son of God" (Eph. 4:3, 12–13 NIV). Moreover, we defend religious freedom for all. Such freedom is grounded in the dignity of the human person created in the image of God and must be protected also in civil law.

We must not allow our witness as Christians to be compromised by halfhearted discipleship or needlessly divisive disputes. While we rejoice in the unity we have discovered and are confident of the fundamental truths about the gift of salvation we have affirmed, we recognize that there are necessarily interrelated questions that require further and urgent exploration. Among such questions are these: the meaning of baptismal regeneration, the Eucharist, and sacramental grace; the historic uses of the language of justification as it relates to imputed and transformative righteousness; the normative status of justification in relation to all Christian doctrine; the assertion that while justification is by faith alone, the faith that receives salvation is never alone; diverse understandings of merit, reward, purgatory, and indulgences; Marian devotion and the assistance of the saints in the life of salvation; and the possibility of salvation for those who have not been evangelized.

On these and other questions, we recognize that there are also some differences within both the Evangelical and Catholic communities. We are committed to examining these questions further in our continuing conversations. All who truly believe in Jesus Christ are brothers and sisters in the Lord and must not allow their differences, however important, to undermine this great truth, or to deflect them from bearing witness together to God's gift of salvation in Christ. "I appeal to you, brethren, by the name of our Lord Jesus Christ, that all of you agree and that there be no dissensions among you, but that you be united in the same mind and the same judgment" (1 Cor. 1:10).

As Evangelicals who thank God for the heritage of the Reformation and affirm with conviction its classic confessions, as Catholics who are conscientiously faithful to the teaching of the Catholic Church, and as disciples together of the Lord Jesus Christ who recognize our debt to our Christian forebears and our obligations to our contemporaries and those who will come after us, we affirm our unity in the gospel that we have here professed. In our continuing discussions, we seek no unity other than unity in the truth. Only unity in the truth can be pleasing to the Lord and Savior whom we together serve, for he is "the way, and the truth, and the life" (John 14:6).

3

Scripture

Introduction

THOMAS G. GUARINO

When ECT issued its statement on justification, *The Gift of Salvation*, in 1997, it was thought that the most difficult issue separating Catholics and Evangelicals had been successfully tackled. But justification by faith was not the only theological matter that, historically, had divided us. Similarly important was the precise relationship between the Bible and subsequent Christian tradition. Outlining our positions on this question—and seeing if any common ground could be found—was a crucial next step in our ecumenical witness.

Background

For centuries, of course, Protestants have been identified with the phrase *sola scriptura* (Scripture alone), while Catholics have been distinguished by their adherence to both Scripture and tradition.

Indeed, it has become commonplace to argue that, just here, one finds a profound and crucial theological divergence between Evangelicals and Catholics—extending right to the heart of divine revelation. One communion relies solely on the Bible for understanding God's self-communication to humanity, and the other depends on the Bible supplemented by the living tradition of the church.

While these characterizations are not devoid of merit, it is also true that the precise relationship between Scripture and tradition had been changing in both Catholic and Protestant circles, with vigorous debates on just this issue. As noted in the introduction to this volume, in the years prior to Vatican II (1962–65) Catholics had been engaged in robust discussions on the relationship between the Bible and the tradition of the Church. In the very midst of the council, Yves Congar, one of the principal theological architects of Vatican II, wrote, "Scripture and Tradition are not on the same level. Scripture has an absolute sovereignty; it is of divine origin, even in its literary form; it governs Tradition and the Church, whereas it is not governed by Tradition or the Church."[1] Congar did not hesitate to add, "Luther, of course, early on was very strongly convinced . . . of the absolute primacy of Scripture over all other authority, and in that he was completely Catholic."[2]

At Vatican II, Catholicism continued to speak reverently about sacred tradition and insisted that the Roman Catholic Church does not reach certainty about its teachings on the basis of Scripture alone. Nonetheless, the council forcefully expressed its reliance on the Bible and even opened the door for theologians to speak of the "material sufficiency" of Scripture for the truths of salvation. Even if this phrase was understood in a Catholic way (meaning that the Bible only reveals its full meaning within the tradition of the Church), this was nonetheless a significant change of emphasis from the theological manuals that had dominated Catholic thought since the Council of Trent in the sixteenth century. It is no surprise, then, that Vatican II approvingly cites Jerome's well-known comment, "Ignorance of the Scriptures is ignorance of Christ" (*Patrologia Latina* 24.17B).

1. See *Tradition and Traditions*, trans. Michael Naseby and Thomas Rainborough (New York: MacMillan, 1967), 422.
2. Ibid., 140.

Vividly illustrating the issue at hand are the debates that took place at the council regarding the precise relationship between the Bible and the tradition of the Church. In early 1962 (in preparation for the council), the Catholic bishops of the world received a preliminary schema entitled "On the Sources of Revelation" (*De Fontibus Revelationis*). The document, broadly citing the Council of Trent, spoke of Scripture and tradition as two separate sources of revelation. When the conciliar debate on the schema began, many of the bishops—unexpectedly—dismissed it with the words *non placet* (the document is not pleasing as it stands). The criticisms lodged against it were many: the schema was too scholastic; it misinterpreted the Council of Trent (which held that the gospel alone is the *fons*—the one source—of saving truth, and this saving gospel may be found in the written books and unwritten traditions that have been transmitted through the centuries); it failed to take account of recent theological investigations; its tone was insufficiently ecumenical, and so on.[3] Ultimately, Pope John XXIII withdrew the controversial document from the council floor, asking for a new schema composed by members from the Doctrinal Commission and the Secretariat for Christian Unity (a commission devoted to ecumenism). The result was that a very different document on divine revelation (*Dei Verbum*)—one that would place Scripture and tradition in much closer relationship—was approved by Vatican II in 1965.

At the same time that Catholics were reevaluating the Bible, Protestant theologians were taking a second look at the notion of tradition. Even though Scripture is the normative Word of God—and one has no proper access to divine revelation except through the Bible—this did not inexorably imply that the word "tradition" had to be accompanied by negative accents. Already at the Faith and Order Conference in Montreal in 1963, the relationship between Scripture and tradition had been newly evaluated, with tradition—understood as the actualization of the living Word of Scripture—now spoken

3. For the initial discussion, see *Acta Synodalia*, vol. 1, pars 3 (Vatican City, 1971), 27–62. Summaries of the conciliar debates on this schema may be found in many places, most recently in John W. O'Malley, *What Happened at Vatican II* (Cambridge, MA: Belknap Press of Harvard University Press, 2008), 141–52.

of in generally positive tones.[4] As Timothy George has stated, Protestant theology was "searching for a sturdier concept of Tradition than the one bequeathed to it by the legacies of liberalism, pietism and individualism."[5]

Several Evangelical theologians have followed in this train of thought, arguing that the Reformers themselves saw tradition as important as long as it was congruent with biblical teaching. Consequently, *sola scriptura* should never be understood as naked biblicism (*nuda scriptura*), as if the Scriptures could be or should be properly construed apart from the tradition of the church.[6]

The Statement

In the statement *Your Word Is Truth*, ECT outlines the significant common ground that exists between Evangelicals and Catholics on the relationship between Scripture and tradition. That shared faith includes our affirmation (1) that the entire teaching and life of Christ's church is accountable to the authority of Holy Scripture, which is, for both Evangelicals and Catholics alike, the written Word of God; (2) that the New Testament is the authoritative word about God's revelation in Jesus Christ; (3) that the Holy Spirit aids the church in the unfolding of apostolic teaching as this is found in the early Christian creeds and councils (in this sense, then, we together hold that development occurs in the life of the church and that the Spirit has guided the church into the fullness of the Bible's meaning); (4) that Scripture is normative for the life and teaching of the church; (5) that tradition is not a second source of revelation but must itself be informed and corrected by the written Word of God; (6) that Scripture cannot be understood apart from the historical life of the community of faith; and (7) that all Christians are called to an intense and prayerful engagement with the Bible.

4. P. C. Rodger and L. Vischer, eds., *The Fourth World Conference on Faith and Order* (New York: Association Press, 1964).

5. Timothy George, "An Evangelical Reflection on Scripture and Tradition," in *Your Word Is Truth*, ed. Charles Colson and Richard John Neuhaus (Grand Rapids: Eerdmans, 2002), 9–34, at 25.

6. For Evangelical theologians taking this point of view, consult the introduction to this volume, notes 20 and 21.

Even while stating these significant elements of shared belief, ECT nonetheless notes the continuing challenges for each community. Evangelicals acknowledged

> the widespread misunderstanding in our community that *sola scriptura* (Scripture alone) means *nuda scriptura* (literally, Scripture unclothed; i.e., denuded of and abstracted from its churchly context). The phrase *sola scriptura* refers to the primacy and sufficiency of Scripture as the theological norm—the only infallible rule of faith and practice—over all tradition rather than the mere rejection of tradition itself. The isolation of Scripture study from the believing community of faith (*nuda scriptura*) disregards the Holy Spirit's work in guiding the witness of the people of God to scriptural truths and leaves the interpretation of that truth vulnerable to unfettered subjectivism.

Catholics, for their part, recognized that

> we who are Catholics must likewise address the widespread misunderstanding in our community that tradition is an addition to Holy Scripture or a parallel and independent source of authoritative teaching. When Catholics say "Scripture and tradition," they intend to affirm that the lived experience (tradition) of the community of faith through time includes the ministry of faithful interpreters guided by the Holy Spirit in discerning and explicating the revealed truth contained in the written Word of God, namely, Holy Scripture.

In this statement, ECT also makes clear that Evangelicals and Catholics disagree on the proper exercise of teaching authority in the life of Christ's church. To Evangelicals it appears that the Roman Catholic Church stands in judgment over Scripture rather than vice versa. Catholics, in turn, believe that the Church, properly ordered through its apostolic ministry, is guided by the Holy Spirit to explicate the truth of Scripture obediently and accurately.

Future Prospects

The statement *Your Word Is Truth* displays how closely aligned Evangelicals and Catholics are today in their respect for the written Word of God and even in their respect for the tradition that is congruent with it. Some theologians, Evangelical and Catholic alike, have argued that rather than *sola scriptura* or "Scripture and tradition"—phrases popularized in the sixteenth century—one might today speak of *prima scriptura*, or *suprema scriptura*, thereby acknowledging the unparalleled uniqueness and primacy of the Bible while simultaneously recognizing that the tradition of the community of faith can never be separated from the Scriptures. Does *prima scriptura* have a future in expressing the common faith of Evangelicals and Catholics?

One also wonders, given the affirmations in *Your Word Is Truth*, whether ECT can fruitfully address the question of proper development and growth over time. The statement eulogistically speaks of "development of doctrine." Can ECT now more fully elucidate that phrase? Can *sola scriptura*—or *suprema scriptura*—be wedded to a robust notion of doctrinal development, such as the one that clearly occurred in the life of the early church? And would not an apposite notion of ripening and maturation—by drawing out the implications of Holy Scripture—bring Evangelicals and Catholics even closer together in doctrinal unity?

Your Word Is Truth

(2002)

In the spring of 1994, a group of Roman Catholics and Evangelical Protestants issued a much-discussed statement, Evangelicals and Catholics Together: The Christian Mission in the Third Millennium. *That statement noted a growing "convergence and cooperation" between Evangelicals and Catholics in many public tasks and affirmed agreement in basic articles of Christian faith while also underscoring the continuing existence of important differences. The signers promised to engage those differences in continuing conversations, and this has been done in meetings of noted theologians convened by Mr. Charles Colson and Father Richard John Neuhaus. At a meeting in the fall of 1996, it was determined that further progress depended upon firm agreement on the meaning of salvation and, especially, on the doctrine of justification. After much discussion, study, and prayer over the course of a year, the statement* The Gift of Salvation *was agreed to at a meeting in New York City in October 1997 and published later that year. The next question taken up by ECT participants was the relationship between Scripture and tradition. The following statement,* Your Word Is Truth, *is the product of intense and extended deliberation and was first published in a book entitled* Your Word Is Truth, *edited by C. Colson and R. Neuhaus (Eerdmans, 2002). The participants express the hope that those responding with critical evaluations of the statement will consult the scholarly papers prepared for their deliberation and to be found in the book.*

Our Lord and Savior Jesus Christ prayed for his disciples: "Sanctify them in the truth; thy word is truth. . . . I do not pray for these only, but also for those who believe in me through their word, that they may all be one; even as thou, Father, art in me, and I in thee, that they also may be in us, so that the world may believe that thou hast sent me" (John 17:17, 20–21).

We thank God for the years of prayer, study, and conversation in the project known as "Evangelicals and Catholics Together." Among the many blessings resulting from this cooperative effort, we note especially our common affirmation of the most central truths of Christian faith, including justification by faith, in the statement *The Gift of Salvation*. From the beginning of this venture, and at each step along the way, we have insisted that the only unity among Christians that can be pleasing to God is unity in truth. Therefore, we have understood it to be our duty to note, carefully and clearly, matters both of agreement and of disagreement between Evangelicals and Catholics.

Among matters of utmost importance, and involving both agreements and disagreements, is the question traditionally framed as the relationship between Scripture and tradition. As we have together explored this question, we have prayed for the guidance of the Holy Spirit, and we believe that prayer has been answered. We respectfully submit the following considerations and conclusions to the ecclesial communities and transdenominational fellowships of which we are part, with the hope that they will be received and examined as possible contributions to our better understanding of one another and our greater unity in Christ's truth.

From before the foundation of the world, God has desired a people to share forever in his life and love (Eph. 1:4). To that end, God disclosed himself and his loving intention by a sequence of revelatory and redemptive acts that involved the uttering of verbal messages and the producing of written records (Heb. 1:1). He created a world that bears witness to his glory (Ps. 19:1–6), and when humanity sinfully rebelled against his purpose, he chose Israel to be instructed by word and deed in the ways of covenant fidelity in order to become a light to all the nations (Gen. 12:1–3; Deut. 4:1–8). To this people he promised a Savior, who is Jesus the Christ, the very Word of God who was in the beginning with God and who is to be recognized and confessed as the Son of God (John 1:1–14). The God of Israel is the One whom Jesus calls Father and teaches us to call Father (John 17:1–5; Matt. 6:6–13). To Jesus's disciples, and to those who would become disciples through their word, he promised the Spirit to guide them into all truth. Thus the new Israel worshiped, obeyed, and proclaimed the one true God—Father, Son, and Holy Spirit—in faith-filled anticipation of participating in the divine life forever (Heb. 12:18–24; Acts 1:8). Already now, God's promised redemption is fulfilled in the mediatorial ministry of Jesus Christ that is centered in his cross, resurrection, ascension, present reign, and assured return in glory to establish his eternal kingdom (2 Cor. 1:19–20).

God gives his people full and final knowledge of his plan of salvation through Jesus Christ. "In many and various ways God spoke of old to our fathers by the prophets; but in these last days he has spoken to us by a Son, whom he appointed the heir of all things, through whom also he created the world" (Heb. 1:1–2). The Son sent and sends the Holy Spirit who, bestowing the gift of faith, creates the community of faith for whose unity Jesus prayed. Christ himself is the head and cornerstone of his church, which is built on the foundation of the apostles and prophets. In its understanding, believing, celebrating, living, and proclaiming the gospel of Jesus Christ, the church is guided by the Holy Spirit (Eph. 2:19–22).

Both Evangelicals and Catholics affirm the one, holy, catholic, and apostolic church, as set forth in the Nicene-Constantinopolitan Creed, but they define the church and its attributes in distinctive ways. Evangelicals stress the priority of the gospel over the church, whose primary mission is to herald the good news of God's salvation in Christ. For Evangelicals, the church as the one body of Christ extending through space and time includes all the redeemed of all the ages and all on earth in every era who have come to living faith in the body's living Head. Everyone who is personally united to Christ, having been justified by faith alone through his atoning death, belongs to his body and by the Spirit is united with every other true believer in Jesus. Evangelicals maintain that the one church becomes visible on earth in all local congregations that meet to do together the things that, according to Scripture, the church does.

Catholics hold that the church is the body of Christ, a sacramental and mystical communion in which Christ is truly and effectually present and through which his justifying and sanctifying grace is mediated. While Christ is the unique mediator of salvation for all humanity, the church of Jesus Christ "subsists in" and is most fully and rightly ordered in the Catholic Church, meaning the church governed by the bishops in communion with the Bishop of Rome, the successor of Peter. Although there have been variations through history in the exercise of that governance, and may be further variations in order to accommodate a fuller expression of Christian unity, Catholics believe that Christ has endowed the church with a permanent apostolic structure and an infallible teaching office that will remain until the kingdom is fully consummated.

While Catholics and Evangelicals have not been able to reconcile these different views of the church, with both communities finding serious aberrations in the ecclesial understanding of the other, as individual believers we do recognize in one another, when and where God so permits it, the evident reality of God's grace expressed by our trust in Jesus himself as Master and divine Savior. All who truly believe in Jesus Christ as Savior and Lord are brothers and sisters in the Lord even though they are not in full ecclesial fellowship.

In communion with the body of faithful Christians through the ages, we also affirm together that the entire teaching, worship, ministry, life, and mission of Christ's church is to be held accountable to the final authority of Holy Scripture, which, for Evangelicals and Catholics alike, constitutes the Word of God in written form (2 Tim. 3:15–17; 2 Pet. 1:21). We agree that the phrase "Word of God" refers preeminently to Jesus Christ (John 1:1, 14). It is also rightly said that the gospel of Jesus Christ is the Word of God, as is the faithful preaching of the gospel (Acts 6:7; 8:4). Then the canon, the listed set of writings making up the Bible, is recognized by the community of faith as the written Word of God, possessing final authority for faith and life. On the extent of the canon we do not entirely agree, though the sixty-six books of the Protestant canon are not in dispute. In every form—the gospel, the preaching of the gospel, and the Scriptures of the Old and New Testaments—the Word of God is in service to Jesus Christ, the Word of God preeminent.

The divinely inspired writings of the New Testament convey the apostolic teaching, which is the authoritative interpretation of God's revelation in Christ. The early Christian community recognized the authority of the first apostles who planted local churches and urged them to be faithful to the teaching they had received. Still today we possess that apostolic teaching in the New Testament, which, together with the Old Testament of which the New is the authoritative interpretation, is the written Word of God. This entire process of the reception and transmission of God's revelation is the work of the Holy Spirit (John 14:26; 2 Tim. 3:15–17; 2 Pet. 1:20–21).

Evangelicals and Catholics alike recognize the promised guidance of the Spirit in the elucidation and unfolding of apostolic teaching that took place as historic Christian orthodoxy emerged. This continuing work of the Spirit is evident in, for instance, the formulation of the Apostles', Nicene, and Athanasian Creeds and in the conciliar resolution of disputes regarding the two natures of Christ and the triune life of God. Such development of doctrine, typically in response to grave error and deviant traditions built upon such error, is to be understood not as an addition to the apostolic teaching contained in Holy Scripture but as Spirit-guided insight into the fullness of that teaching. In this way, the Lord has enabled faithful believers both to counter error and to make explicit what is implicit in the written Word of God.

In the course of that same history, and in the context of crises posed by philosophical and cultural changes as well as manifest ecclesiastical corruptions, the question of how to determine authentic apostolic teaching came into intense dispute. The mainline Reformers of the sixteenth century posited what is called the "formal principle," which holds that the Scriptures are (in the words of the 2000 Amsterdam Declaration) "the inspired revelation of God . . . totally true and trustworthy, and the only infallible rule of faith and practice." The Reformers vigorously protested what they viewed as deviations from biblical teaching, but they never used Scripture to undermine the trinitarian and christological consensus of the early church embodied in the historic creeds that had come down from patristic times. The Reformers stoutly resisted the charge of innovation: they did not seek to found new churches but sought simply to reform the one, holy, catholic, and apostolic church on the basis of the Word of God.

We who are Evangelicals recognize the need to address the widespread misunderstanding in our community that *sola scriptura* (Scripture alone) means *nuda scriptura* (literally, Scripture unclothed; i.e., denuded of and abstracted from its churchly context). The phrase *sola scriptura* refers to the primacy and sufficiency of Scripture as the theological norm—the only infallible rule of faith and practice—over all tradition rather than the mere rejection of tradition itself. The isolation of Scripture study from the believing community of faith (*nuda scriptura*) disregards the Holy Spirit's work in guiding the witness of the people of God to scriptural truths and leaves the interpretation of that truth vulnerable to unfettered subjectivism. At the same time, we insist that all Christians should have open access to the Bible and should be encouraged to read and study the Scriptures, for in them all that is necessary for salvation is set forth so clearly that the simplest believer, no less than the wisest theologian, may arrive at a sufficient understanding of them.

We who are Catholics must likewise address the widespread misunderstanding in our community that tradition is an addition to Holy Scripture or a parallel and independent source of authoritative teaching. When Catholics say "Scripture and tradition," they intend to affirm that the lived experience (tradition) of the community of faith through time includes the ministry of faithful interpreters guided by the Holy Spirit in discerning and explicating the revealed truth contained in the written Word of God, namely, Holy Scripture.

Together we affirm that Scripture is the divinely inspired and uniquely authoritative written revelation of God; as such it is normative for the teaching and life of the church. We also affirm that tradition, rightly understood as the proper reflection of biblical teaching, is the faithful transmission of the truth of the gospel from generation to generation through the power of the Holy Spirit. As Evangelicals and Catholics fully committed to our respective heritages, we affirm together the coinherence of Scripture and tradition: tradition is not a second source of revelation alongside the Bible but must ever be corrected and informed by it, and Scripture itself is not understood in a vacuum apart from the historical existence and life of the community of faith. Faithful believers in every generation live by the memories and hopes of the *actus tradendi* (the handing on of the tradition) of the Holy Spirit: this is true whenever and wherever the Word of God is faithfully translated, sincerely believed, and truly preached.

We recognize that confessing a high doctrine of the nature and place of Scripture is insufficient without a firm commitment to the intense devotional, disciplined, and prayerful engagement with Scripture. We rejoice to note that in our communities and in joint study involving people from both communities, such engagement is increasingly common. In this engagement with Scripture, Evangelicals and Catholics are learning from one another: Catholics from the Evangelical emphasis on group Bible study and commitment to the majestic and final authority of the written Word of God; and Evangelicals from the Catholic emphasis on Scripture in the liturgical and devotional life, informed by the lived experience of Christ's church through the ages.

There always have been, and likely will be until our Lord returns in glory, disputes and disagreements about how rightly to discern the teaching of the Word of God in Holy Scripture. We affirm that Scripture is to be read in company with the community of faith past and present. Individual ideas of what the Bible means must be brought to the bar of discussion and assessment by the wider fellowship.

"The church of the living God [is] the pillar and bulwark of the truth" (1 Tim. 3:15). Because Christ's church is the pillar and bulwark of truth, in disputes over conflicting interpretations of the Word of God the church must be capable of discerning true teaching and setting it forth with clarity. This is necessary both in order to identify and reject heretical deviations from the truth of the gospel and also to provide sound instruction for passing on the faith intact to the rising generation.

Evangelicals and Catholics alike are concerned with these questions: What does the Bible authoritatively teach? And how does Christ's church apply this teaching authoritatively today? Catholics believe that this teaching authority is invested in the Magisterium, namely, the Bishop of Rome, who is the successor of Peter, and the bishops in communion with him. Some Evangelicals see the communal office of discerning and teaching the truth in the covenanted congregation of baptized believers, while others see it in a wider synodical or episcopal connection. In either case, however, Evangelicals believe that a true understanding of the Bible is achieved only through the illuminating action of the Holy Spirit. For this reason, all attempts at discernment and teaching must rely on prayerful attentiveness to the guidance of the Spirit in the study of Scripture.

While Catholics agree that the entire community of the faithful is engaged in the discernment of the truth (*sensus fidelium*), they also believe that Evangelicals have an inadequate appreciation of certain elements of truth that, from the earliest centuries, Christians have understood Christ to have intended for his church; in particular, the Petrine and other apostolic ministries. While Evangelicals greatly respect the way in which the Catholic Church has defended many historic Christian teachings against relativizing and secularizing trends, and recognize the role of the present pontiff in that important task today, they believe that some aspects of Catholic doctrine are not biblically warranted, and they do not accept any claims of infallibility made for the magisterial teachings of popes or church councils.

With specific reference to the subject of the present statement, we are not agreed on the exercise of teaching authority in the life of Christ's church. To Evangelicals it appears that, in practice if not in theory, the Catholic understanding of Magisterium, including infallibility, results in the Roman Catholic Church standing in judgment over Scripture, instead of vice versa. Catholics, in turn, teach that the Magisterium exercised by the successors of the apostles—which they believe is intended by Christ, is guided by the Holy Spirit, and is in clear continuity with the orthodox tradition—enables the church to explicate the truth of Holy Scripture obediently and accurately. We both recognize that judgments must be made in the life of Christ's church as to what is and what is not scriptural truth. We are not agreed on how such judgments are to be made, nor can either group accept all the decisions that have resulted from what they regard as a flawed way of deciding.

Among the Catholic teachings that Evangelicals believe are not biblically warranted are the eucharistic sacrifice and transubstantiation of the elements, the doctrine of purgatory, the immaculate conception and bodily assumption of the Blessed Virgin Mary, and the claimed authority of the Magisterium, including papal infallibility. Catholics, on the other hand, believe that Evangelicals are deficient in their understanding of, for instance, apostolically ordered ministry, the number and nature of the sacraments, the company and intercession of the saints, the Spirit-guided development of doctrine, and the continuing ministry of the Petrine office in the life of the church. On these and other questions of great importance, we are not agreed. Nor do we agree on how we view our differences. Catholics view

Evangelicalism as an ecclesially deficient community that needs to be strengthened by the full complement of gifts that they believe Christ intends for his church. Evangelicals see Catholicism as centering upon an idea of the church that clouds the New Testament gospel and so needs to be brought into greater conformity with biblical teaching. The contrast here is far-reaching and goes deep.

At the same time, we recognize that, during the past five hundred years, the Holy Spirit, the Supreme Magisterium of God, has been faithfully at work among theologians and exegetes in both Catholic and Evangelical communities, bringing to light and enriching our understanding of important biblical truths in such matters as individual spiritual growth and development, the mission of Christ's church, Christian worldview thinking, and moral and social issues in today's world. We praise God for his faithful work within each community as he has provided instruction and guidance in these and other important areas of Christian faith and life.

As Evangelicals and Catholics we are agreed on what we have said together in the statement *The Gift of Salvation* and on what we have been able to say together in the present statement on Scripture and tradition. The theological disagreements that still separate us are serious and require prayerful reflection and sustained mutual engagement. But in the face of a society marked by unbelieving ideologies and the culture of death, we deem it all the more important to affirm together those foundational truths of historic Christian orthodoxy that we do hold in common.

We are confident that the Lord is watching over his gospel and over those who have been called by the gospel, and we are sure that the forces of hell will not be able to thwart his divine purpose. By God's grace, we will continue to pray for one another, to seek greater mutual understanding in continuing conversations, and, in accordance with our deeply held convictions, to work together to bring the love and light of Christ to all persons everywhere. We earnestly invoke the Holy Spirit's continuing guidance in further establishing and making manifest our unity in the truth of Jesus Christ, so that the world may come to believe (John 17:21). In union with our Lord and Savior Jesus Christ, we together pray, "Sanctify us in the truth; your word is truth" (see John 17:17).

4

Saints

Introduction

ROBERT LOUIS WILKEN

As we move deeper into the twenty-first century and American society becomes more secular, Catholics and Evangelicals have a unique responsibility to bear witness to Christ together. Because of our historic differences, many assume that we have little in common. In several of the statements of Evangelicals and Catholics Together we have attempted to show, even on controversial topics such as justification by grace through faith, that what we share is more binding than how we differ. There is, however, one area where division is most visible to outsiders as well as ourselves, and that is how we understand our oneness in Christ.

There is no more beautiful word in the Christian vocabulary than "communion," a translation of the Greek term *koinōnia* (fellowship). It is familiar from the closing greeting of the apostle Paul in his second letter to the Christian community at Corinth: "The grace of the Lord

Jesus Christ, and the love of God, and the *communion* of the Holy Spirit, be with you all" (2 Cor. 13:14 ASV).

The phrase "communion of saints" is taken from the third article of the Apostles' Creed: "I believe in the Holy Spirit, the holy catholic church, *the communion of saints*, the forgiveness of sins, the resurrection of the body and life everlasting." In the creed it refers to those who have been made "holy" through the working of the Holy Spirit and are in fellowship with one another. Membership in the "communion of saints" is unlike belonging to a civic association, club, or political organization. It is bestowed, not something we choose; it is God's work in us, not our own doing.

The phrase "communion of saints" implies that there is no such thing as a solitary Christian. Christian faith is by its very nature communal. Again and again the New Testament emphasizes that to be in Christ is to be in communion with all those who are joined to Christ in faith. One of the most powerful images for the company of believers is a body, and, like a body, all the parts—the feet, the hands, the ears, the eyes—are necessary and work together. "God has so composed the body," writes Paul, "that there may be no discord in the body, but that the members may have the same care for one another. If one member suffers, all suffer together; if one member is honored, all rejoice together" (1 Cor. 12:24–26).

Yet the fellowship in Christ is a broken communion. We confess belief in one God, one Lord, one baptism, and one church, but in truth the church is deeply divided. Christians go about their lives as though the members of the one body, especially those who practice their faith and worship God differently, are not in "communion" with them. By highlighting the phrase "communion of saints" we wished to proclaim that we are one and to give concrete expression to the unity we share. This is a matter of high importance; in our society there is nothing more vital than for the Evangelicals and Catholics to give a common witness.

Our differences are deep. Even the phrase "communion of saints" is a matter of contention, particularly the word "saint." Of course the New Testament uses the term "saints" to refer to all Christians. At the close of his Epistle to the Romans, Paul greets members of the Christian community in Rome, "Philologus, Julia, Nereus and his sister, and Olympas, and all the *saints* who are with them" (Rom.

16:15). But early in the church's history the term "saint" came to be used also for those Christians who had displayed unusual holiness in their lives, for example, the martyrs. Christians gathered at the tombs of the martyrs, sometimes in the catacombs, to remember their witness. Hence the term "communion of saints" came to designate a fellowship that included not only living Christians but also those who had gone before with a sign of faith. Because of their exemplary lives, the "saints" were asked to intercede before God for the living. This practice continues to this day among Catholics.

Evangelicals, however, do not believe that there is any biblical basis for prayer to the saints. Yet, as we met together, Evangelicals could see that there were spiritual reasons for the ways in which Catholics invoke the saints. At the same time, Catholics came to realize that the Evangelical critique of the abuses in Catholic devotion to the saints was well grounded.

We discussed differences in the way Catholics and Evangelicals worship God. For example, for Catholics the Eucharist, or the Mass, is at the heart of their devotional life. In Catholic churches all over the world the Mass is celebrated every day, and in many places, several times in the course of the day. For Evangelicals the sermon is the principal part of the worship service, and the Lord's Supper is celebrated monthly or several times a year.

Yet by pondering the phrase "communion of saints" we discerned a unity that is expressed in the biblical phrase "people of God." Christians are a "holy nation, God's own people" who have been called "out of darkness into his marvelous light. Once you were no people but now you are God's people; once you had not received mercy but now you have received mercy" (1 Pet. 2:9–10).

Significantly, Evangelicals and Catholics each use "people of God" to signify the church. At Amsterdam 2000, a conference convoked by Billy Graham for evangelists, it was said that the people of God are the "body and bride of Christ, the one Church that is transdenominational" and includes the "redeemed of all the ages, being the one body of Christ extended throughout time as well as space" (Amsterdam Declaration, no. 9).

In like manner the bishops at the Second Vatican Council said that the term "people of God" designates all Christians spread throughout the world. "There is but one People of God, which takes its citizens from every race. . . . All the faithful scattered throughout the world are in communion with each other in the Holy Spirit" (*Dogmatic Constitution on the Church*, no. 13).

From the age of the apostles, words and phrases from the Bible and Christian history have carried and expressed those things Christians hold dear. Think for example of "image of God," "Word became flesh," "true God and true man," "children of God," "contrite heart," "one Lord, one faith, one baptism, one God and Father," "Word of God," and many others. "Communion of saints" is one of those precious phrases that became part of the vocabulary of Christians, was enshrined in the Apostles' Creed, and was handed on to later generations even to our own time. In the early decades of the twenty-first century it remains a treasured inheritance that embodies a deep truth: though Evangelicals and Catholics are in some ways divided in doctrine and practice, we are one in Christ and are bound together as members of the "communion of saints."

The Communion of Saints

(2003)

This statement on the communion of saints (communio sanctorum) *is part of the ongoing project known as Evangelicals and Catholics Together, commonly called ECT. The project began in 1992 with a conference occasioned by growing and often violent conflicts between Catholics and Evangelical Protestants in Latin America. In 1994 we issued a statement,* Evangelicals and Catholics Together: The Christian Mission in the Third Millennium, *in which we explained why it is necessary for us, as "brothers and sisters in Christ," to work with one another, and not against one another, in the great task of evangelization and to support one another in facing up to the ominous moral, cultural, and spiritual threats of our time. The signers of the statement pledged themselves to such Christian solidarity and, while this initiative has not been without its critics, both Evangelical and Catholic, we are greatly heartened by the thousands who have joined in that pledge, both in this country and in other parts of the world. Such solidarity, if it is to be true and enduring, must be grounded in nothing less than the gospel of Jesus Christ. This has been an insistent theme of ECT, reaffirmed every step of the way: the only unity that is pleasing to God, and therefore the only unity we can seek, is unity in the truth. This theme was deepened and exemplified in the 1997 statement* The Gift of Salvation. *In that statement we together affirmed the way in which we understand justification by faith alone as a gift received by God's grace alone because of Christ alone. In that statement, we were able to say together:*

> *We agree that justification is not earned by any good works or merits of our own; it is entirely God's gift, conferred through the Father's*

57

sheer graciousness, out of the love that he bears us in his Son, who
suffered on our behalf and rose from the dead for our justification. . . .
The New Testament makes it clear that the gift of justification is
received through faith. "By grace you have been saved through faith;
and this is not your own doing, it is the gift of God" (Eph. 2:8). By
faith, which is also the gift of God, we repent of our sins and freely
adhere to the gospel, the good news of God's saving work for us in
Christ. By our response of faith to Christ, we enter into the blessings
promised by the gospel. Faith is not merely intellectual assent but
an act of the whole person, involving the mind, the will, and the
affections, issuing in a changed life. We understand that what we
here affirm is in agreement with what the Reformation traditions
have meant by justification by faith alone (sola fide).

At every step along the way, we have also noted carefully the
questions on which, as Evangelicals and Catholics, we continue to
disagree. On the long list of what might be called traditional dis-
agreements between Evangelical Protestants and Roman Catholics
is the relationship between Scripture and tradition. In fact, there are
few disagreements on the list that have been more agitated over the
centuries. The disagreement is often posed in a way that calls for a
stark choice between Scripture alone (sola scriptura), *on the one hand,*
or Scripture and authoritative tradition, on the other. In Your Word
Is Truth, *our statement issued in 2002, we were able to say together:*

> *There always have been, and likely will be until our Lord returns*
> *in glory, disputes and disagreements about how rightly to discern*
> *the teaching of the Word of God in Holy Scripture. We affirm that*
> *Scripture is to be read in company with the community of faith*
> *past and present. Individual ideas of what the Bible means must*
> *be brought to the bar of discussion and assessment by the wider*
> *fellowship. "The church of the living God [is] the pillar and bulwark*
> *of the truth" (1 Tim. 3:15). Because Christ's church is the pillar and*
> *bulwark of truth, in disputes over conflicting interpretations of the*
> *Word of God the church must be capable of discerning true teaching*
> *and setting it forth with clarity.*

Each of the above statements is the result of intensive prayer, study,
and uncompromisingly candid discussion among the Evangelicals

and Catholics involved. In each statement we carefully note that we have not resolved all our differences on the subjects addressed, and it should be evident that we resolutely reject any thought of evading such differences. We believe, however, that these statements go a long way toward creating greater mutual understanding and recasting old disputes in new and promising ways. We understand Evangelicals and Catholics Together as a work in progress. We are convinced that this is a work of the Holy Spirit. This work was under way long before ECT was begun. In recent decades, Evangelicals and Catholics have encountered one another as brothers and sisters in Christ in many forums, and especially as they contend together for a culture of life that will protect the unborn, the aged, the handicapped, and others who are often deemed to be expendable. These encounters and the patterns of cooperation they have produced are aptly described as "the ecumenism of the trenches." ECT can be understood as making explicit what was implicit: that our unity in action is the fruit of our unity in faith. Our unity in action and in faith is by no means perfect. If this is the work of the Holy Spirit, as we firmly believe, it will continue long after the present participants in ECT have departed this life. We do not know how or when, but we do believe that the prayer of our Lord in John 17 will be answered, that his disciples will be one in a way that the world will see and will believe that he was sent by the Father.

Moreover, our historical circumstance makes our common witness increasingly urgent. Our circumstance is one of unremitting conflict between distinct and antithetical worldviews, or understandings of reality. Evangelicals and Catholics together share, and must together contend for, the Christian worldview. Whatever differences there have been between us in the past, and whatever differences persist still today, we stand side by side in contending for the truth of that understanding of reality. Such solidarity in opposition to the forces of unbelief is aptly called cobelligerency, and such cobelligerency is the more solid as it is more firmly grounded in the Bible, the creeds, and our confession and worship of Jesus Christ as Lord. With this statement and related undertakings, we seek to deepen our understanding of the common faith that binds us so that we might more effectively address the common tasks that claim us.

*A century ago, the noted Protestant leader Abraham Kuyper rec-
ognized that the common defense of a Christian worldview made
necessary precisely the kind of effort in which we are today engaged.
Kuyper argued that, when we understand Christianity also as a
worldview, we "might be enabled once more to take our stand by
the side of Romanism in opposition to modern pantheism." In a
similar way, Catholic teaching today, as notably set forth by John
Paul II, strongly encourages the fullest possible cooperation among
Christians in contending for a culture of life and of truth against the
encroaching culture of death and deceit. If, then, anyone asks about
the purpose of this statement and of the ongoing project of which
it is part, the answer is clear: it is to evangelize more effectively, to
bear witness to the world that Jesus is the Lord and Savior sent by
the Father, and to bring that truth to bear on every dimension of
life—just as we are commanded to do. It must be added that ECT
is an unofficial initiative. We speak from and to the communities
of which we are part, but we do not presume to speak for them. We
wholeheartedly support the several official theological dialogues
between Evangelicals and Catholics. ECT is an ancillary initiative,
serving as a kind of advance scouting party to explore possibilities
and, as such, has received much appreciated encouragement from
many sources, both Evangelical and Catholic. We have no illusions
that the centuries-long wounds of our divisions will be quickly or
easily healed. We are convinced that ECT is part of a project that
is God's before it is ours, and is only ours because it is God's. We
offer this statement on the* communio sanctorum *in the spirit of the
concluding words of our first statement in 1994: "This is a time of
opportunity—and if of opportunity, then of responsibility—for
Evangelicals and Catholics to be Christians together in a way that
helps prepare the world for the coming of him to whom belongs the
kingdom, the power, and the glory forever. Amen."*

Introduction

There is, as we have noted, a definite sequence in the continuing
conversation that is Evangelicals and Catholics Together. In the first

round of conversation, we affirmed that, despite serious disagreements, we who recognize one another as brothers and sisters in Christ are called to the missionary task of proclaiming his lordship to the world. Acknowledging that we are together in Christ, we then turned in the second round to address justification as the way in which we come to share in the life of Christ. In the third round, we explored our understanding of the Word of God and found ourselves in agreement that Holy Scripture, faithfully interpreted in the community of believers, is the divinely given rule by which we are to understand our life and mission in obedience to Christ. In the present statement, we examine more closely the nature of our life together. Our life together is communion in the *communio* of the life of God, the Father, the Son, and the Holy Spirit. Evangelicals and Catholics both confess the Apostles' Creed, which speaks of the *communio sanctorum*. In this statement, we address four aspects of that article of faith. First, we look to God as the one who is holy in himself and in whose trinitarian communion we must participate in order to be holy. Second, we examine the relationship of communion among all those to whom God has imparted a share in his holiness. Third, we discuss our participation in sacraments or holy ordinances, which are means of manifesting and fostering the communion that we share. Finally, we reflect on the communion that we now share with those Christians who have gone before us, including those who have exemplified to an exceptional degree the fidelity to which we are all called, whom many Christians honor with the special title of "saint."

I. The Holiness of God

God declared to Israel and declares to us, "I am the Lord who brought you up out of the land of Egypt, to be your God; you shall therefore be holy, for I am holy" (Lev. 11:45). The theme of God's holiness permeates the entire Bible. The holiness of God is the mystery of his ineffable being manifested to us as his glory, which includes his righteous and merciful acts to which we are to conform our own lives. The holiness of God is given classic expression in the *trisagion* of Isaiah 6 where the seraphim cry out, "Holy, holy, holy is the Lord

of hosts; the whole earth is full of his glory" (v. 3). The threefold
holiness of God expressed in this passage is understood by Christians as reflecting the life of the Holy Trinity. All human beings are
called to participate in the holiness of God. The life of Christians
who, by the grace of God, have responded to that call is to be a life
of holiness, which is to say a life of sanctification. Paul writes to his
converts in Thessalonica and to us, "This is the will of God, your
sanctification" (1 Thess. 4:3). Although our communion with God
is impeded by sin, which repeatedly alienates us from him, we are
able to be reconciled through Jesus Christ who prayed to the Father,
"For their sake I consecrate myself, that they also may be consecrated
in truth" (John 17:19). To be holy is to participate in the holiness of
Jesus who is "the way, and the truth, and the life" (John 14:6). The
communion of saints signifies, first of all, communion, through Christ
and in the power of the Spirit, with God the all-holy.

II. Holiness and Communion

Holiness necessarily entails relationships. In the *communio sanctorum*, one cannot be in communion alone. Holiness is, first of all, a
relationship with God in Jesus Christ, the mediator of all holiness.
Such a relationship is necessarily communal, for God's own holiness
is being in communion, namely, the communion of Father, Son, and
Spirit dwelling together in love. To enter into fellowship with God is
to enter into fellowship with all who share in the fellowship of God
(1 John 1:3). To be in Christ is to be one with all who are in Christ.
Our Lord prayed that those who believe in him "may all be one; even
as thou, Father, art in me, and I in thee, . . . so that the world may
believe that thou hast sent me" (John 17:21). Jesus speaks of the
union between himself and the Father as a mutual indwelling that is
to be extended by his and the Father's indwelling in the community
of believers. So intimate is the union and so inseparable is the bond
between Jesus and his disciples that those who persecute them are
persecuting him, as is evident in his words to Saul on the road to
Damascus (Acts 9:4). Similarly, those who are merciful to his disciples
will be rewarded for having shown mercy to Christ himself (Matt.

10:42; 25:34–40). We Evangelicals and Catholics do not now live out together the fullness of the unity for which Christ prayed. Yet we do not lack blessings of unity in the body of Christ, which includes the vast company of believers of all times and places, from Abel the righteous one until our Lord's return in glory (Heb. 11). Our task is not to create unity in Christ, but to give full and faithful expression to the unity that is his present gift. Our union with Christ and with one another is never complete in this life, but it can be intensified and strengthened as we together draw closer to him and to one another. In the body of Christ, we strengthen one another by our strengths, even as we weaken one another by our weaknesses. "If one member suffers, all suffer together; if one member is honored, all rejoice together" (1 Cor. 12:26).

To give expression to and thus to strengthen the fellowship that is already ours, we can and should, despite our different ecclesial allegiances, do many things together. We can gather to listen to the Word of God, responding in prayer, worship, and thanksgiving, together with the whole company of heaven. We can together pray for the many good things that God moves us to desire, and for protection against the evils we rightly fear. Thus do we fulfill the prayer of Paul: "May the God of steadfastness and encouragement grant you to live in such harmony with one another, in accord with Christ Jesus, that together you may with one voice glorify the God and Father of our Lord Jesus Christ" (Rom. 15:5–6). More particularly, together and in our separate gatherings, we should pray for one another. As Paul relied on the prayers of his fellow Christians (2 Cor. 1:10–11), so we benefit from our prayers for one another. Through common study of the Bible we have gained a better understanding of God's Word in the tradition of the great preachers and theologians of earlier centuries, and thus we have learned to read the Bible more faithfully in and with the church. We can together learn to interpret the Scriptures in faithful attentiveness to the Holy Spirit who inspired the Scriptures, the same Spirit who Christ promised would lead the church into all truth (John 16:13). In recent decades, this pneumatological and ecclesial way of reading the Scriptures is being widely recovered, thus protecting the sacred text from individualistic exegesis and those critical methodologies that are indifferent, or even hostile, to God's saving and sanctifying truth. In communal worship, Evangelicals and other Protestants have helped Catholics to value more highly the effective proclamation of the Word of God. At the same time, Evangelicals have learned from Catholics and Orthodox to appreciate more fully the importance of ordered liturgy, including a lectionary based on the seasons of the Christian year. Noteworthy also is the greater use of one another's legacy of hymnody. Patristic and medieval hymns are finding greater currency among some Evangelicals, while Catholics today praise God in the songs of Isaac Watts, Charles Wesley, and others in the Evangelical tradition. In seminaries and programs of ministerial formation, leaders are increasingly being educated in both the unity and diversity of the one Christian movement in world history. Thus do we cultivate an understanding and experience of our belonging to a common Christian tradition.

This understanding is of growing importance in a century in which Christianity is sharply challenged by other world religions, most notably by Islam. Always we are brought back to mission and to exploring how we might be more fully together in mission, for there is no doubt that Jesus speaks to all of us when he commands that we "make disciples of all nations, baptizing them in the name of the Father and of the Son and of the Holy Spirit" (Matt. 28:19). As we are sent by the same Lord, as we go forth in the name of the same Lord, as we proclaim the same Lord, so we ought to evangelize with one another rather than against one another. In the words of the Evangelical leaders gathered at the Amsterdam 2000 conference on evangelization:

> Jesus prayed to the heavenly Father that his disciples would be one so that the world might believe. One of the great hindrances to evangelism worldwide is the lack of unity among Christ's people, a condition made worse when Christians compete and fight with one another rather than seeking together the mind of Christ. . . . In all ways that do not violate our consciences, we should pursue cooperation and partnerships with other believers in the task of evangelism, practicing the well-tested rule of Christian fellowship: "In necessary things unity, in nonessential things liberty, in all things charity." We pledge ourselves to pray and work for unity in truth among all true believers in Jesus and to cooperate as fully as possible in evangelism with other

brothers and sisters in Christ so that the whole Church may take the whole gospel to the whole world. (Amsterdam Declaration, no. 14)

We participants in Evangelicals and Catholics Together join in the pledge of Amsterdam 2000, agreeing also with the words of John Paul II in the 1990 encyclical *Redemptoris Missio* (The Mission of the Redeemer, no. 50):

> The relationship between activity aimed at Christian unity and missionary activity makes it necessary to consider two closely associated factors. . . . We must recognize that the division among Christians damages the holy work of preaching the gospel to every creature and is a barrier for many in their approach to the faith. The fact that the good news of reconciliation is preached by Christians who are divided among themselves weakens their witness. It is thus urgent to work for the unity of Christians, so that missionary activity can be more effective. At the same time, we must not forget that efforts toward unity are themselves a sign of the work of reconciliation which God is bringing about in our midst.

Faithful discipleship requires that we, Evangelicals and Catholics, "do good to all men, and especially to those who are of the household of faith" (Gal. 6:10). We grow in the gift of, and vocation to, holiness as we give ourselves in service to the poor and needy. While individuals may disagree about what constitutes a just social order, we are united in our commitment to certain moral truths and their public recognition. Respecting the sanctity of human life at every stage of development and decline, securing the integrity of marriage and family life, protecting the disabled and vulnerable, caring for the marginalized and imprisoned—these are among the mandates that are bringing, and must increasingly bring, Evangelicals and Catholics together. Heartening also is our common witness and action in defense of religious freedom here and around the world, and an awakened sense of solidarity with persecuted Christians, joined with effective concern for non-Christians denied their rights of conscience. Moreover, Catholics and Evangelicals can assist one another in various circumstances by, for instance, defending one another from unfair public attacks, providing worship space and other facilities in times

of need, and taking up offerings for one another's charitable works.
In all these and in many other ways we can both express and deepen
our communion with one another that is God's present gift.

III. Holiness and Divine Ordinances

Communion among Christians includes the recognition of certain
sacred rites, especially the sacraments or ordinances that come to us
from Christ and the apostles. Although we have different understandings of how Christ orders his church, we agree that communion has
both visible and invisible dimensions. Catholics believe that the full
and right ordering of the church embraces seven sacraments, including the apostolic and sacramentally ordained ministry. Evangelicals,
while differing both with Catholics and among themselves on the
number and importance of sacraments, are agreed in respecting certain practices, such as baptism, the Lord's Supper, marriage, and the
reading of Scripture. Some of these sacred practices and institutions,
though differently understood, are bonds between us that maintain
and deepen our communion. The church itself can be understood as a
sign and instrument of grace, instituted by the one mediator between
God and man, Jesus Christ, and, through the gospel, mediating his
grace to the world. While the ancient formula "Outside the church
no salvation" may lend itself to misunderstanding, we agree that
there is no salvation apart from the church, since to be related to
Christ is necessarily to be related, in however full or tenuous a manner, to the church which is his body. Although Catholics believe that
the church is visible in its universal dimension and not only in local
congregations, we as Catholics and Evangelicals together affirm the
statement of Amsterdam 2000:

> The Church is the people of God, the body and the bride of Christ,
> and the temple of the Holy Spirit. The one, universal Church is a
> transnational, transcultural, transdenominational, and multi-ethnic
> family, the household of faith. In the widest sense, the Church includes
> all the redeemed of all the ages, being the one body of Christ extended
> throughout time as well as space. Here in the world, the Church be-
> comes visible in all local congregations that meet to do together the

things that according to the Scripture the Church does. Christ is the head of the Church. Everyone who is personally united to Christ by faith belongs to his body and by the Spirit is united with every other true believer in Jesus. (Amsterdam Declaration, no. 9)

Similarly, we together affirm the statement of the Second Vatican Council:

All are called to belong to the new People of God. Wherefore this People, while remaining one and unique, is to be spread throughout the whole world and must exist in all ages, so that the purpose of God's will may be fulfilled. . . . It follows that among all the nations of earth there is but one People of God, which takes its citizens from every race, making them citizens of a kingdom which is of a heavenly and not an earthly nature. For all the faithful scattered throughout the world are in communion with each other in the Holy Spirit. (*Lumen Gentium* [*Dogmatic Constitution on the Church*], no. 13)

Because we do not have the same ecclesial structures and do not fully agree on the doctrinal heritage that we share, there are some things that we cannot in conscience do together. Our communion is most manifestly and painfully imperfect in our inability to be one at the table of the Lord in Holy Communion. Evangelicals differ among themselves as to how open or restrictive admission to the Lord's Supper should be. Catholics, for their part, cannot in conscience participate in an observance of the Lord's Supper absent communion with the apostolic ministry that they believe Christ wills for his church. Evangelicals and Catholics together know that our Lord commanded us, "Do this." We know that he intended that we do this together. Our different discernments of what is entailed in doing this obediently prevent us from doing this together. This circumstance is an abiding and heartbreaking sadness. We together pray that our imperfect communion will one day give way to full communion in eucharistic fellowship. At present, we cannot see beyond some disagreements that appear to be intractable. Our visibly fractured fellowship at the Lord's Table can, at the same time, be a salutary reminder of how far we are from the goal of complete unity and a spur to more urgent prayer and work that one day the prayer of Jesus in John 17 will be fully answered. That fulfillment is finally the work of the Holy Spirit, who moves in ways that we cannot always anticipate. In the meantime, however, we recognize that the right ordering of the church and all the means of grace are precisely means. They serve the end of personal union with Christ, and that union is effected, by the grace of God, when believers avail themselves of the means of grace available to them. We Evangelicals and Catholics gratefully acknowledge our unity in being reconciled to God through Christ, and we pray for the day when that unity can be expressed and strengthened by agreement on all the means of grace that Christ intends for his church.

IV. Holiness and the "Great Cloud of Witnesses"

The *communio sanctorum* embraces all Christians, including those whose lives are not notably marked by holiness. In the New Testament, the term "saints" generally refers to all who are baptized and confess Christ as Lord. The Christian tradition, following the New Testament, also lifts up some persons for special respect and veneration. The Letter to the Hebrews, for instance, proposes an honor roll of those in the history of salvation who are exemplars of heroic faith. The lives of such faithful men and women both point to and reflect the holiness of God in Christ.

> Therefore, since we are surrounded by so great a cloud of witnesses, let us also lay aside every weight, and sin which clings so closely, and let us run with perseverance the race that is set before us, looking to Jesus the pioneer and perfecter of our faith, who for the joy that was set before him endured the cross, despising the shame, and is seated at the right hand of the throne of God. (Heb. 12:1–2)

As early as the second century, Christians gathered for worship at the tombs of the martyrs, celebrating the power of God's grace in the lives of these faithful men and women. They prayed to God for spiritual and temporal favors to be granted through the intercession of the martyrs. Indeed, in the early church and through the patristic era, the phrase *communio sanctorum* had primary reference to this enduring bond between the faithful on earth and the faithful who had gone before, especially those whose witness was crowned with martyrdom. While all Christians are properly called saints, the word "saint" soon became a title of honor referring to exemplary lives among the faithful, and most notably the lives of martyrs. Our own time is rightly understood as a time of the martyrs, and it is a most encouraging development that Christians today increasingly recognize and revere those members of the several ecclesial communities who, in the centuries past and still now, offer the ultimate witness to the lordship of Christ. As Christians, we are wayfarers who look forward to joining one day "the assembly of the first-born who are enrolled in heaven" (Heb. 12:23). Scripture indicates that the martyrs beneath the heavenly altar still await their full vindication (Rev. 6:10). They are one with us, and we are one with them, in yearning for the completion of God's plan of salvation in the final establishment of the kingdom of Christ who is "the Alpha and the Omega, the first and the last, the beginning and the end" (Rev. 22:13).

In a world where many believe that this life is all there is, Christians are called to bear bold witness to the solidarity of the *communio sanctorum*, a solidarity secured by our communion with Jesus Christ—crucified, risen, and coming again—and with all, both the living and the dead, who are alive in Christ. Catholics believe that there is a lively interaction, including an exchange of spiritual goods, between ourselves and those who have gone on to glory. This interaction is always in Christ and through Christ. Just as all Christians request the intercession of brothers and sisters on earth, so Catholics rely also on the intercession of the saints in heaven, of whom the Blessed Virgin Mary is foremost, and invoke their aid in prayers, recognizing that prayers to the saints are also prayers with the saints, directed to Christ and to the Father, and that all blessings are received from God. When the saints in heaven act, it is God who acts through them. This understanding is expressed in the *Dogmatic Constitution on the Church* (no. 50):

> It is supremely fitting that we love those friends and fellow heirs of Jesus Christ, who are also our brothers and extraordinary benefactors, that we render due thanks to God for them and "suppliantly invoke them and have recourse to their prayers, their power and help in obtaining

benefits from God through His Son, Jesus Christ, our Lord, who is
our sole Redeemer and Savior." For by its very nature every genuine
testimony of love which we show to those in heaven tends toward and
terminates in Christ, who is the "crown of all saints." Through him it
tends toward and terminates in God, who is wonderful in His saints
and is magnified in them.

Evangelicals do not generally affirm the intercession of the saints
in heaven and do not ask for their intercession, since they do not find
any explicit biblical warrant for such practice. They are sometimes
puzzled, if not repelled, by the intense and various ways in which
Catholics express communion with the saints. They caution, as do
Catholics, against the dangers of abuse and superstition in connection with the cult of saints and of relics. Indeed, the formal Catholic
procedures for beatifying and canonizing saints are intended, inter
alia, to guard against superstition, miracle mongering, and popular
enthusiasms of a possibly heretical nature. While Evangelicals do not
have such formal procedures, they have informal ways in which those
who have lived exemplary lives of faith are recognized as deserving
of particular honor. At the same time, however, some Evangelicals
express concern that the Catholic doctrine of the "merits" of the
saints implies that there is a basis of merit other than Christ the sole
Redeemer, and are not convinced by Catholic assurances to the contrary. These are among the questions in need of further examination
in our continuing conversation.

All Christians of all times have asked how God prepares believers for the beatific vision of the fullness of his glory. Holy Scripture
does not present us with details about what happens to those who
die in Christ—whether, as most Evangelicals believe, they enter im-
mediately into the fullness of God's glory or, as Catholics believe,
ordinarily undergo a period of further preparation. If sanctification
is not complete here on earth, is it somehow completed between
the time of death and the beatific vision? Catholics hold that one
who dies in God's friendship while still suffering from certain sinful
attachments and dispositions will be cleansed by "spiritual fire" in
purgatory. Evangelicals agree that our lives will be reviewed before
the judgment seat of Christ, and all that is unworthy will be burned

away. While Evangelicals find no biblical warrant for the doctrine of purgatory, we together affirm with Paul, "If the work which any man has built on the foundation survives, he will receive a reward. If any man's work is burned up, he will suffer loss, though he himself will be saved, but only as through fire" (1 Cor. 3:14–15).

A detailed exploration of the doctrine of purgatory and related questions is beyond the scope of this round of our conversation. Nor have we examined adequately suffrages for the dead, the question of indulgences, the role of Mary in Christian piety, or the sins of denominationalism against the communion that is God's present gift. Together, however, we do affirm that no true Christian, living or dead, can be outside the *communio sanctorum*, the fellowship of all who live in the crucified, risen, reigning, and returning Lord. Within the body of Christ, we know that we are to pray for one another and to offer up our sufferings for the sake of the church (Col. 1:24). Living as we do in communion with those who have gone before us, we strive to realize in the pilgrim church on earth a life together that more fully anticipates the communion of the church in glory. It is our hope and prayer as Evangelicals and Catholics that by rightly using the means of grace afforded to us in the church here on earth, we will be more fully conformed to Christ and thus be drawn into more perfect communion with one another and with the *communio sanctorum* triumphant, to the glory of the one and immortal God, the Father, the Son, and the Holy Spirit.

5

Holiness

Introduction

CHERYL BRIDGES JOHNS

In 1994, when Evangelicals and Catholics Together launched its efforts to help our respective bodies envision ways of working with each other to further the Christian mission, other similarly motivated initiatives were under way, especially the official bilateral dialogues between Roman Catholics and Evangelical bodies. ECT did not seek to replicate these dialogues. Instead, it created a niche of its own, one characterized by focusing on issues of shared concern, especially those that dominated the landscape of the United States. This niche impacted US Christians in ways the official bilateral dialogues were unable to do. The ECT statements, while theologically robust, were concise and tangible. They offered clear and focused means of making a way through the differences toward unity.

Background

Through the years of working together as Catholics and Evangelicals, it became clear that while there were many issues that divided us, we shared a deep passion for the essential truths of the gospel. We discovered a shared reverence for the beauty and scope of the mystery of salvation found in Jesus Christ. Moreover, we discovered that this gospel is multifaceted, deeper and wider than any of us imagined. Our joint statements express the joy and wonder of these discoveries. Each tradition and each communion has brought to the ECT table a lens for viewing and expressing the great mystery of Christ. Even with the strain of hermeneutical and ecclesial tensions, we began to understand that "together" we could not just see the complexities of our shared faith but also share and rejoice in them.

The Call to Holiness builds upon the previous statement, *The Communion of Saints*. Discussions on that topic were robust as we attempted to tease out the nature of being in communion with one another while in communion with Christ. While there were disagreements on the nature of our communion with Christians who are now in the great cloud of witnesses, we agreed that "our life together is communion in the *communio* of the life of God, the Father, the Son, and the Holy Spirit." We all agreed that holiness characterizes the nature of God's life, and it defines the shape of the communion of saints.

The Statement

In this ECT statement, we sought to clarify the nature of our sharing in the holiness of God's divine life. The work on *The Call to Holiness* began with the common agreement of our previous statement, namely, that all Christians are called to share in the vocation of holiness. This vocation is not for a special group of people but is a universal, corporate calling. It was clear to us that both Evangelicals and Catholics face the scandal of Christians having low levels of commitment to this call to holiness.

There were disagreements between Catholics and Evangelicals as to how the grace found in the gift of salvation worked toward effecting holiness. Furthermore, it would have been easy for discussions on holiness to bog down in intra-Evangelical debates on soteriological concerns. However, as our discussions progressed, we were able to come together as Evangelicals and Catholics and forge agreement on the constitutive nature of the universal call to holiness.

We agreed that the call to holiness begins with divine election. God summoned Israel and later the church to be a "holy nation, God's own people" (1 Pet. 2:9). Our holiness is made possible through Christ's sacrificial death on the cross, and, by the power of the Holy Spirit, we are able to share, as the statement says, in the "holiness that he embodies and accomplishes for us."

The Call to Holiness reflects several main areas of agreement regarding the nature of our holiness in Christ: (1) holiness is participation in the life of God and the life of the church; (2) Christians are called to share in holiness while living out radical "cruciform" love involving a profound gift of self; (3) discipleship is the means toward enabling Christians to live out this cruciform life; and (4) discipleship into a life of holiness involves study of God's Word, participation in the life and worship of the church, and a confession of sin.

The call to holiness places the holiness of the church within the mission of God. For it is through the holiness of the church that nonbelievers are drawn to the beauty of God's holiness. This beauty is best seen in a healed community reflecting God's ultimate mission to heal and restore all creation.

This statement further links the call to holiness with a call to advance a culture of life. The church is called to be a hope-filled culture of vibrant life in contrast to the decaying "culture of death." Christians are also called to contribute to the ordering of society toward this culture of life.

The Call to Holiness ends with an awareness of the sacrifices involved in the pursuit of holiness. When our suffering is joined with Christ's suffering, our union with him is deepened and our holiness is made more perfect. The way of the cross becomes a "royal road to holiness." Hope is born out of this suffering as Christians live out of a reality anchored at "a point beyond this world and its contingencies."

Ten years have passed since the release of *The Call to Holiness*. This statement, perhaps due to the lack of controversial subject matter, received less attention than other statements. However, it may prove to be one of the most important gifts of ECT. Today, both Evangelicals and Catholics face increasing challenges in our common vocation to holiness. We are beginning to realize that our witness to Christ has been greatly compromised as we have failed to live out the beauty of holiness.

In 2012 the Synod of Bishops addressed the task of evangelization. Its final list of statements noted that the "universal call to holiness is constitutive of the New Evangelization that sees the Saints as effective models of the variety and forms in which this vocation can be realized."[1] Among Evangelicals there is a growing awareness that far too often we have fallen prey to a cultural captivity that tarnishes our holiness. In both Roman Catholic and Evangelical circles we find churches with baptized believers who do not understand what is involved in living out the way of salvation. We all are in need of a "new evangelization" that unites baptism with holiness.

The task of catechesis today is more like that of ancient Christians than those living in recent centuries. It is a task of bringing people out of a pagan darkness into the light of Christ. Baptized believers in the twenty-first century will find that the call to live the cruciform life will mark them in ways that cause them to live in stark contrast to the dominant culture. Perhaps *The Call to Holiness* can serve future generations in living out this beautiful and dangerous calling.

1. "The New Evangelization for the Transmission of the Christian Faith," XIII Ordinary General Assembly of the Synod of Bishops final list of Propositions, Proposition 23, October 7–28, 2012.

The Call to Holiness

(2005)

Over more than ten years, this group of Evangelicals and Catholics, speaking as individuals committed to their respective communities but without any official mandate, has explored important areas of agreement and disagreement among us. In our first round of conversations and in the resulting statement of 1994, Evangelicals and Catholics Together: The Christian Mission in the Third Millennium, *we were able to recognize one another as brothers and sisters in Christ and to affirm the positive value of the witness to the gospel rendered by our several communities, notwithstanding differences and disagreements. In 1997, we were able to issue a second statement,* The Gift of Salvation. *In that statement we affirmed that the justification of sinners, which is not earned by any good works or merits of our own, leads us toward the fullness of salvation that is promised in the final kingdom.*

In our third statement, Your Word Is Truth *(2002), we found a notable convergence in our views concerning the transmission of God's saving Word through Holy Scripture and tradition. The following year we took up the interpretation of the phrase* The Communion of Saints *that appears in the Apostles' Creed, and there we affirmed that, by virtue of our communion with Christ, we are in a certain, albeit imperfect, communion with one another in his body, the church. That round of discussions called our attention to the holiness that is proper to God alone but in which human beings are called to participate. Such participation means nothing less than to be drawn into the very life and love of God—Father, Son, and Holy Spirit.*

Holiness is also participation in the life of the church, which is the holy people called into being by God's saving work in Christ.

76

Following up on this theme, we wish now to consider the ways in which our communities and their individual members can and must foster and embody holiness.

As is clear from our earlier statements, we believe that salvation is realized through union with God, who is all-holy (Lev. 11:44–45; 21:6–8; 1 Pet. 1:15–16). The gift of salvation is effected and bestowed only through the one Mediator, Jesus Christ (1 Tim. 2:5–6; Acts 4:11–12). While thanking God for this inestimable gift, we acknowledge our failures and seek to find ways in which we, our communities, and our world can more fully respond to the call to holiness.

We Are Christians

According to the apostolic witness, the call to holiness begins with divine election: God's summons to Israel, and later to the church, to be a holy nation, a people set apart as God's own treasured possession, called to worship, witness, and good works (see Eph. 1:4; 1 Pet. 2:9). All of us are consecrated to the one God—Father, Son, and Holy Spirit—in whose name we are baptized (Eph. 4:4–6). By his sacrificial death on the cross, Jesus Christ enables us, by the power of the Holy Spirit, to share in the holiness that he embodies and accomplishes for us. Our conformity to Christ involves a radical love that is cruciform, requiring a profound gift of self: "If any man would come after me, let him deny himself and take up his cross and follow me" (Matt. 16:24). By incorporating us into Christ, the Holy Spirit also makes us members of his body, the church.

The relationship of the Christian to Christ is expressed in a variety of biblical metaphors. We have already spoken of our being members of his body. We may also speak of our being branches grafted on the vine, who is Christ. The relationship may also be expressed as our inclusion in the covenant of the New Testament—a covenant in which Jesus is the Lord and we are his servants. However expressed, our union with Christ is profoundly transformative.

This transformation manifests itself differently to different people. For some it is experienced as a powerful and specifiable moment, engaging the deepest affections. For others it is experienced as a deepening of faith in Christ and a peaceful sense of being welcomed into the communion of believers. For all it is the knowledge of being called out of darkness into God's marvelous light (1 Pet. 2:9). However differently experienced, the gift of grace is to be preserved and cultivated throughout the life of the Christian.

Our different traditions, notwithstanding their doctrinal differences, agree that faith and baptism, as the sacrament of faith, belong together. Christian faith should always lead to baptism, and baptism, conversely, should always be accompanied by Christian faith. Baptism is mandated, not optional. It is the gateway to the Christian life.

Some of our traditions reckon baptism as a sacrament of constitutive importance for Christian existence. Others see it rather as a sign and expression of a new Christian life already received. But on either view, baptism involves a lifelong engagement to grow in union with Christ and labor in the service of the gospel.

Sadly, the level of commitment is much lower than it ought to be. In all our communities, there are many who are members in name only. Many of us live in a manner that brings disgrace on the name of God. The call to holiness entails a continuing call to repentance and transformation of life. Many, however, have received practically no instruction in Christian doctrine; many fail to measure up to the norms of Christian conduct. Weak and sinful members, we agree, should not be treated with harshness and contempt, but rather with compassion, each of us being painfully aware of our own frailty. We strive to find ways of helping inactive, alienated, and marginal Christians to rise to the dignity that is theirs as children of God.

Becoming Who We Are

Christian existence is by its very nature relational. Christians are related to God as their Father, to Christ as their older brother, and to all their fellow Christians as members of the same family. The Holy Spirit maintains and animates all these relationships. "If we live by the Spirit, let us also walk by the Spirit" (Gal. 5:25).

To be a Christian is always both a gift and a task. We are called to be perfect, as our Father in heaven is perfect (Matt. 5:48). Yet even the most exemplary of Christians must confess with St. Paul, "Not that I have already obtained this or am already perfect; but I press on to make it my own, because Christ Jesus has made me his own. . . . I press on toward the goal for the prize of the upward call of God in Christ Jesus" (Phil. 3:12, 14).

The command, "Be holy, as I am holy," already given under the old law, holds in a special way for Christians (Lev. 11:44–45; cf. 1 Pet. 1:16). Paul exhorts the Philippians to be "children of God without blemish in the midst of a crooked and perverse generation, among whom you shine as lights in the world" (Phil. 2:15). The authenticity of the Christian life is manifested in the fruits of holiness. Jesus taught us that faithful disciples would be known by their fruits (Matt. 7:20).

Holiness entails a transforming encounter with the living Christ. This conversion, which is ongoing in the Christian life, means that one becomes a disciple of Christ, and discipleship necessarily entails discipline. Christians know they are not perfect, but they together constitute a people that is different. In the early church, Christians were able to point to the probity of their lives. They did not steal and murder; they did not practice divorce, adultery, infanticide, or abortion. In the second-century *Letter to Diognetus* the author boasted that Christians "dwell on earth, but are citizens of heaven. . . . What the soul is to the body, Christians are to the world" (chap. 5, sec. 1). Somewhat later, Minucius Felix puts on the lips of the hero of a literary dialogue the words: "While the jails are crammed with your kind, they do not hold a single Christian, unless he be accused on account of his religion, or unless he be an apostate" (*Octavius*, chap. 35). Christians attracted pagans to join them because they excelled in virtue and mutual affection. They were seen to love Christ and his church, even to the point of giving up their lives.

It is a great scandal that so many Christians of our day, while continuing to be identified as members of the church, fail to respond to the call to holiness. Too many, misunderstanding the nature of faith and presuming upon the grace of God, disregard the commandments of God. Such Christians rely on what Dietrich Bonhoeffer called "cheap grace," evading "the cost of discipleship." They have drifted far from the biblical precept: "Confirm your call and election" (2 Pet. 1:10), which is expounded as meaning, "Supplement your faith with virtue, and virtue with knowledge, and knowledge with self-control, and self-control with steadfastness" (2 Pet. 1:5–6). It is time, therefore, for Catholics and Evangelicals, corporately and individually, to recommit ourselves to the life of discipleship that ought to be the distinctive mark of Christians.

Committed as they are to Christ as the source and model of all that is holy, Christians are in no way exempted from obedience to the moral law permanently inscribed by the Creator in human nature (Rom. 2:15). They are bound to the moral precepts of the Decalogue, which are confirmed and brought to surpassing fulfillment in Christ. "If you love me," says the Lord, "you will keep my commandments" (John 14:15). To reject his commandments is to reject him and thus to forfeit our ability to abide in him and to bear fruit (John 15:1–11). While individuals have different vocations, all are called to obey the commandments and especially the commandment of love, the greatest of them all (Matt. 22:37–40).

God has given us ample means to participate in the fullness of his love. We are to hear and study the Word of God, especially as it comes to us in the Holy Scriptures. There is a growing practice among serious Christians—Evangelical, Catholic, and others—to join in Bible study and prayer groups. This is attended by a new appreciation of the *lectio divina*, the devotional and meditative reading of the Bible, notably in the discipline of daily prayer. Encouraged by these developments, we rejoice in a greater measure of common catechesis based on Scripture and the ecumenical creeds that we share.

Corporate worship on the Lord's Day is central to the Christian life. We are agreed that the Sunday gathering should be marked by the proclamation of the Word and the celebration of the Lord's Supper. Catholics are coming to a renewed appreciation of the proclamation of the Word in the eucharistic assembly. Many Evangelicals are recovering historic forms of Christian worship, incorporating the preaching of the Word within the context of communal prayer, worship, and participation in the Lord's Supper (1 Cor. 10:16).

As fellow members of the community of faith, we should also confess our sins and failures to God and one another, especially to those whom we have offended, according to the opportunities and requirements of our respective communions (1 John 1:8–9; James

5:16). In all cases, sinners must be reconciled to God and the church, making a firm resolve to amend their ways. Whether as Catholics or as Evangelicals, we are spiritually responsible for fellow Christians. We should engage in mutual encouragement and correction, performing this duty with love and tact. All of us will be summoned in the end to give an account of our stewardship. Our source of forgiveness is in God's reconciling work in Christ (2 Cor. 5:18), and our accountability is, in this and all else, to Christ the Lord "who is to judge the living and the dead" (2 Tim. 4:1).

Witness and Mission

The church cannot rightly be conceived as a self-created or self-enclosed entity. It is a body of believers gathered by God and sent on mission to the world. In going forth into the world, Christians are not venturing into a foreign territory. By his death on the cross and his glorious exaltation to the Father's right hand, Christ has been made Lord over the whole world, even though his dominion is not universally acknowledged (Phil. 2:9–11). Those who deny his lordship or serve idols and other deities are not beyond the sovereignty of Christ but are, albeit unknowingly, his subjects. The world, insofar as it is captive to sin, is under the power of the evil one and still awaiting the liberation that Christ has won for it (1 John 5:19).

The entire mission of the church may be summarized under the rubric of evangelization. Evangelization in the broadest sense is proclaiming the good news of Jesus Christ to all people and bringing that gospel to bear, by word and deed, on the totality of things. According to the Scriptures, God's Word in Jesus Christ should penetrate into the hearts and minds of believers, governing their ideas and activities and, through their ministry, permeating the cultures and social institutions of the world (2 Cor. 10:5). All of creation, wounded by original sin, is to be healed and redirected in Christ to its true goal, the glory of the Creator (Col. 1:19–20).

The missionary activity of the church should not be understood as the task of a few specialists. The church is missionary in nature. It is the duty and privilege of every Christian to "declare the wonderful deeds of him who called us out of darkness into his marvelous light" (1 Pet. 2:9). The precise form of evangelization to which believers are called depends upon their particular vocations. Some are called to travel to other lands and bring the good news to peoples who have not previously heard or accepted it. All, and especially parents, are called to impart Christian truth within their own families. Those in business and politics are called to bear witness in the marketplace and the public square. Whatever one's work or calling, occasions arise for professing one's allegiance to Christ and for inviting friends and associates, as well as casual acquaintances, to share one's faith.

Lay men and women should not think that the secular character of their vocation consigns them to an inferior rank in the church's mission. On the contrary, the church with its ministerial and sacramental structures is entirely ordered toward the redemption of the secular, meaning this world (the *saeculum*). The Second Vatican Council was not speaking only for Catholics when it declared that the normal vocation of the laity is to "seek the kingdom of God by engaging in temporal affairs and ordering them according to the plan of God" (*Lumen Gentium*, no. 31). The plan of God, in turn, cannot be fully understood apart from Christ and the gospel, which alone disclose the deeper meaning and orientation of all temporal activities. The Amsterdam Declaration affirms, "The salvation Jesus brings and the community of faith he calls forth are signs of his kingdom's presence here and now, though we wait for its complete fulfillment when he comes again in glory. In the meantime, wherever Christ's standards of peace and justice are observed to any degree, to that degree the kingdom is anticipated, and to that extent God's ideal for human society is displayed."

In our first statement, *Evangelicals and Catholics Together*, we pointed out a number of areas in the right ordering of society on which we can and should cooperate. Our response to the call to holiness requires us to exemplify and advance a culture of life. This includes defense of religious freedom and the marriage-based family; resistance to evils such as abortion, euthanasia, eugenics, and coercive population control; and a devotion to justice for all, especially for the poor. We now renew all of these commitments as aspects of our vocation to pursue holiness together. Cooperation among Christians, we believe, vividly expresses the bond that already unites them and sets in clearer relief the features of Christ the Servant (cf. Vatican II, *Unitatis Redintegratio* [*Decree on Ecumenism*], no. 12; Lausanne Covenant, 7).

Suffering and Hope

Christ promised that the pursuit of holiness would be difficult. He said that his disciples would face adversity and persecution (John 16:33). Christians should not be surprised by opposition and setbacks. Paul assures us that God works in all things for the good of those who love him and are called according to his purpose (Rom. 8:28). Stirred by the example of the martyrs who died rather than deny their Lord, Christians today should be prepared to make sacrifices for their faith. Such sacrifices can be a radiant proof of their love of God and a source of inspiration to others.

Contemporary culture tends to look upon suffering and death simply as evils. Christians, however, recognize that in the plan of God suffering, patiently endured, can deepen our union with Christ in his suffering and thus become a royal road to holiness (Phil. 3:10). Although Christ's suffering was sufficient for the redemption of the world, Christians can grow in the life of grace by uniting their own sufferings with his. Paul refers to this great mystery when he speaks of our filling up what was wanting in Christ's afflictions for the sake of his body, the church (Col. 1:24).

We would find it impossible to endure suffering and failure with patience and joy except that Christ has given us by his words, his glorious resurrection, and the gift of the Holy Spirit a sure hope that he will never abandon his disciples. After they have suffered a little while, he will bring them into the fullness of his kingdom (1 Pet. 1:6–7). The world today desperately needs a hope that cannot be disappointed—a hope that is anchored at a point beyond this world and its contingencies.

Our churches, separated though they be, witness to this hope. It is our prayer that, recognizing our solidarity in hope, we may now proclaim it more effectively together. As we preach to others, we attend to ourselves, lest in preaching to them we ourselves become castaways (1 Cor. 9:27). The good example of Christians, indeed, is often the most effective form of witness.

The spiritual renewal of our communities, their missionary activity, their service to society, and their quest for visible unity are, we are confident, indivisible aspects of the Holy Spirit's work in our day. In all these endeavors, holiness and the pursuit of holiness has unquestioned priority. We urge all Christians to devote themselves to these tasks with eyes fixed on Christ, "whom God has made our wisdom, our righteousness and sanctification and redemption" (1 Cor. 1:30).

6

Pro-Life

Introduction

R. R. RENO

It was an irony of history that abortion became *the* social issue for American Christians. In the 1960s, most states prohibited all abortions aside from those necessary to save the life of the mother. Progressives worked to relax those laws. Their goal was to allow abortions in cases where the woman's pregnancy posed a threat to her emotional well-being, or in some cases to allow the abortion of genetically defective children. The feminist movement added urgency, arguing that anti-abortion laws were part of the larger unequal treatment of women that needed to be reversed. Attention was focused on the dangers that illegal ("back alley") abortions posed to women who sought to end their pregnancies.

Christian leaders were not universally opposed to these trends toward liberalized abortion laws. Modern methods of contraception became widely accepted, often affirmed by Christian leaders.

Abortion seemed simply an extension of "family planning" to circumstances when contraception failed. This way of thinking allowed even conservative Protestants to express a degree of support for liberalized abortion laws. In 1971, the Southern Baptist Convention passed a resolution to support abortion in cases where the mother's health was threatened, including her emotional health.

Among mainline Protestants the popular belief that a "population explosion" represented a dire global threat exercised a great deal of influence. In this context the use of contraceptives was transformed into a moral imperative, and abortion became part of a multipronged plan for achieving population control.

Catholic teaching on the evil of abortion was and has remained unequivocal, and Catholics were among the most prominent leaders of opposition to liberalized abortion laws in the 1960s. But the intense controversy over *Humanae Vitae*, the 1968 papal encyclical reaffirming traditional prohibitions against the use of artificial means of birth control, fragmented and to a great degree paralyzed American Catholicism's response. The larger turmoil after the Second Vatican Council also contributed to a sense that everything was up for grabs. Abortion remained a grave sin, to be sure. Some Catholics continued to fight its legalization. But as was the case for many aspects of the sexual revolution and other dramatic cultural changes of that era, Catholicism was disoriented and nearly always on the defensive.

In the early 1970s, then, there was not a united, vigorous Christian witness defending the sanctity of life. An objective observer in those years would have concluded that Evangelical Protestantism, having largely accepted new contraceptive technologies such as the pill, would fall in line on abortion. Mainline Protestants increasingly accepted the goals of the sexual revolution across the board. With progressives on the march in the Catholic Church, it was plausible to imagine that in spite of official doctrine Catholicism would in practice accommodate itself to new sexual mores, including abortion.

Then came the shocking Supreme Court decision in *Roe v. Wade*, announced on January 22, 1973. The *Roe* decision created a constitutional right to abortion, allowing the law to limit only late-term abortions, and even then in a way so qualified that no legal limits could be meaningfully imposed. Even proponents of liberalized abortion laws were surprised by the sweeping scope of the decision. *Roe* was not an incremental change. It was not a measured liberalization of existing abortion laws. Instead, it voided all existing anti-abortion laws.

The extremism of the *Roe* decision had a galvanizing effect. Incremental change can be hard to resist. It's not easy to know when a decisive threshold has been crossed, and coalitions often divide over how to respond to small changes. But the 1973 decision was clear in its consequences, and it forced Christians in America to take sides. Mainline Protestantism stood behind *Roe* and supported the unrestricted abortion license. Evangelicals and Catholics responded with a clarified and increasingly united witness on behalf of the sanctity of life. This clarity and unity was reinforced by an awareness of the horrifying rise in the number of abortions being performed in America after *Roe*. It has been further reinforced by movements promoting euthanasia and doctor-assisted suicide, as well as uses of human embryos in biomedical research.

The extremism of *Roe* had a further effect. By making abortion a constitutional right, the court transformed it into a regime-defining issue. In the aftermath of *Roe*, efforts were made to impose minimal restrictions, but they too have been struck down as unconstitutional. In the early 1990s, some judges expanded the reasoning in *Roe* and other Supreme Court decisions to find a right to doctor-assisted suicide. In this instance, the Supreme Court did not go along and refused to recognize the existence of such a right. Right-to-death advocates have pursued their agenda by legislation and referenda, with success in some instances.

Raising abortion to the level of a constitutional right has contributed to the urgency of the pro-life cause. Though stymied by the logic of *Roe* from progress in restoring legal protections to the unborn, we know that the constitutional regime of *Roe* must be overturned. To do so requires applying overwhelming moral, cultural, and political pressure.

Thus, we must witness to the centrality of life's sanctity in the post-*Roe* political culture of America. The pro-life cause is a matter of life and death, reason enough to make it a priority for any citizen. The Supreme Court's continued insistence that abortion is a constitutional issue means that the defense of life must seek to transform the laws of our society at the most basic level. At the same time, powerful forces continue to work to make death a legitimate "choice" in other areas of life, substituting the nebulous notion of "quality of life" for the gift of life itself. As our society withdraws legal protections for the weak, the vulnerable, and the dependent, the defense of the sanctity of life becomes more urgent.

How, then, should we bear witness to the sanctity of life? There are certainly sound reasons to reject abortion as immoral. That life begins at conception is a scientific fact. That size, maturity, and capabilities ought not to disqualify anyone from the special respect and protection we accord human beings in law and morality would seem self-evident, especially in the American context where we have had to fight against the notion that people's black skin disqualifies them from the full protection of the law. Yet as the 2006 statement by Evangelicals and Catholics Together, *That They May Have Life*, makes clear, these good reasons do not exhaust our Christian witness. The good news of new life in Christ gives a special urgency to our duty to respond to threats to the sanctity of life. The gospel calls us to resist the culture of death and to renew a culture of life.

To speak together as Christians on behalf of the sanctity of life does not mean "imposing" our religious faith on our fellow citizens. Martin Luther King Jr. appealed to the prophets of Israel to rouse the conscience of our nation. In the same manner this statement by Evangelicals and Catholics Together seeks to draw upon the moral wisdom and spiritual power of scriptural truth. For Christian citizenship must not remain satisfied with restraining and limiting the culture of death by overturning *Roe* and protecting the sanctity of life in law. We recognize this is a necessary objective. No sane society can turn God's gift of life into an individual's "choice." But we must seek more. *That They May Have Life* calls us to a higher task: to convert our society to a culture of life, to advance a vision of the common good based on a commitment to welcome, comfort, and succor every vulnerable human being.

That They May Have Life

(2006)

I came that they may have life, and have it abundantly. (John 10:10)

I.

We are grateful that as Christians, Evangelicals and Catholics together, we can speak with one voice on a matter of paramount urgency for our society and the world. We address this statement to all who confess Jesus Christ as Lord and Savior and to all people of goodwill who share our concern for a more just and humane social order.

Recent years have witnessed a new pattern of convergence and cooperation between Evangelicals and Catholics. We are grateful that the project known as "Evangelicals and Catholics Together" (ECT) has played a part in this development—a development that has occasioned both controversy and high hopes within our respective communities. In the public life of our country, the changing relationship between Evangelicals and Catholics has also occasioned curiosity, anxiety, and even alarm.

This convergence has implications for our culture and civil order. In the present statement we intend, however briefly and inadequately, to make the case for what is commonly called "a culture of life" and to do so in a way that invites public deliberation and engages questions of public policy. Our primary purpose, however, is to explain to our communities why we believe that support for a culture of life is an integral part of Christian faith and therefore a morally unavoidable imperative of Christian discipleship.

To those who do not identify with our communities, or with any Christian community, we respectfully suggest that it is in our mutual interest that they try to understand better the reasons and convictions that have recruited so many millions of their fellow citizens to the cause of the culture of life. Greater understanding does not necessarily lead to agreement, but it at least makes possible a more civil engagement of our disagreements.

The present moment in American public life is frequently described in terms of "culture wars," and there is some merit in that description. We need not and must not, however, resign ourselves to unremitting warfare. A culture is composed of many parts, but different cultures are distinguished by different understandings of reality, of the meaning of life and death, of rights and duties, of rights and wrongs.

There is what is called a Judeo-Christian worldview, a worldview that was crucial to the formation of our civilization and is, we believe, clearly reflected in the convictions that inspired the American founding. To speak of American culture today is to speak of a culture marked by different worldviews in conflict. So severe is the conflict, also in the political realm, that many despair of finding any commonalities by which warfare can be replaced, or at least tempered, by civil discourse.

We refuse to join in that despair. We refuse to despair because we share with those who oppose us a common humanity. We also share a common interest in sustaining the American experiment in its aspiration to be a free, just, and virtuous society. In our common humanity, we share a God-given capacity to reason, to argue, to deliberate, to persuade, and to discover moral truths regarding questions related to the right ordering of our life together. As members of the community of Christians, we are obliged to bear an uncompromising witness to our faith. As members of this civil order, we are also obliged to engage respectfully those who do not share our faith. In this statement, we intend to do both.

Between Evangelicals and Catholics there have been long-standing differences on the capacities of human reason. To put it too briefly, Evangelicals (and the Protestant traditions more generally) have accented that human reason has been deeply corrupted by sin. Catholics, on the other hand, while recognizing that human reason has been severely wounded by sin and is in need of healing, have held a higher estimate of reason's capacity to discern truth, including moral truth.

We, as Evangelicals and Catholics together, affirm that the knowledge of God necessary for eternal salvation cannot be attained by human reason alone apart from divine revelation and the Holy Spirit's gift of faith's response to Jesus Christ the only Savior. (These questions are addressed in more detail in our 1997 statement, *The Gift of Salvation*.)

We also affirm together that human reason, despite the consequences of sin, has the capacity for discerning, deliberating, and deciding the questions pertinent to the civil order. Some Evangelicals attribute this capacity of reason to "common grace," as distinct from "saving grace." Catholics typically speak of the "natural law," meaning moral law that is knowable in principle by all human beings, even if it is denied by many (Rom. 1 and 2). Thus do we, as Evangelicals and Catholics together, firmly reject the claim that disagreements over the culture of life represent a conflict between faith and reason. Both faith and reason are the gift of the one God. Since all truth has its source in him, all truth is ultimately one, although our human perception of the fullness of truth is partial and inadequate (1 Cor. 13:12). Thus do we invite those who disagree, including those who do not share the gift of faith in Christ, to join with us in attempting to move beyond "culture wars" to a reasonable deliberation of the right ordering of our life together.

As Christians, we are informed, inspired, and sustained by our faith in a commitment to a culture of life, which includes the protection and care of the unborn, the severely disabled, the dependent elderly, and the dying. The culture of life encompasses also the poor, the marginalized, and those who, for whatever reason, are vulnerable to neglect or exploitation by others. This is not a uniquely Christian commitment. Disagreement on our obligations to those in need should not be viewed as a conflict between Christians and non-Christians.

We are sadly aware that many who identify themselves as Christians do not share our understanding of a culture of life. It is not the case that we wish to "impose" our moral convictions on our fellow citizens or, as some recklessly charge, to establish a "theocracy." Our intention is not to impose but to propose, educate, and persuade, in the hope that, through free deliberation and decision, our society will be turned toward a more consistent respect for the inestimable gift that is human life.

This statement and the questions addressed are emphatically public in nature. Christianity—its Scriptures, doctrine, intellectual tradition, and institutions of communal allegiance and mission—are part of our common history. Christianity claims at least the nominal adherence of the great majority in our society. To be a Christian is a personal but not a private decision. To be a Christian is to be associated with a historical movement bearing public witness to universal moral truths.

Such truths are not accepted by all in our society, nor is there complete agreement about their meaning and implications among all who do accept them. But the assertion of these truths, including their significance for public policy, is part of, and in no way to be excluded from, genuinely public discourse. Whatever is meant by "the separation of church and state," it cannot mean the separation of public life and public policy from the deepest convictions, including moral convictions, of the great majority of a nation's citizens.

As Christian truth claims are public, so also are the questions pertinent to a culture of life. There is no more inescapably public and political question than who belongs to the polis of which we are part. The contention over abortion, for instance, is not about when human life begins. That is a biological and medical question about which there is no reasonable dispute. The moral and political dispute is over which human beings, at whatever state of development or decline, possess rights that we are bound to respect. The question is this: Who belongs to the community for which we accept public responsibility?

In what follows we hope to make the case that the defense of the *humanum* is made imperative by the Christian understanding of reality. Our position with respect to questions such as abortion, euthanasia, assisted suicide, and the creation and destruction of nineteen embryos for research purposes [*in 2005, the government limited federal funding for human embryonic stem cell research to nineteen cell lines*] is integral to that understanding of reality. Every human life is, from conception, created by God and is infinitely precious in his sight. The fulfillment of human life is, by the grace of God, "life and life abundant" through faith in Jesus Christ, who said, "I am the way, and the truth, and the life" (John 14:6).

We believe it is of utmost importance that everyone involved in the public discussion of these questions understand the unbreakable connection between a Christian worldview and the defense of human life. We can no more abandon our contention for a culture of life than we can abandon our allegiance to the lordship of Christ, for our contention is inseparably part of that allegiance.

At the same time, we contend that the public policies pertinent to the defense of the *humanum* are supported by reasons that are accessible to all and should be convincing to all. The term "humanism" is frequently employed in opposition to Christian faith, as in the phrase "secular humanism." We propose a deeper and richer humanism that is firmly grounded in the bedrock of scriptural truth, that is elaborated in the history of Christian thought, that is in accord with clear reason, that honors the best in our civilization's tradition, and that holds the promise of a future more worthy of the dignity of the human person who is the object of God's infinite love and care. This more authentic humanism is in no way alien to Christianity. There is in world history no teaching more radically humanistic than the claim that God became a human being in order that human beings might participate in the life of God, now and forever.

II.

Our contention for a culture of life is made possible and imperative by the gospel of life. The word "gospel" is used in different ways. Gospel (from the Greek *euangelion*) means "good news." The apostle Paul writes: "Now I would remind you, brethren, in what terms I preached to you the gospel, which you received, in which you stand, by which you are saved, if you hold it fast—unless you believed in vain" (1 Cor. 15:1–2). The good news is centered in Jesus Christ—his birth, teaching, healing ministry, holiness of life, redemptive suffering and death, his resurrection victory over sin and death, his present reign, his abiding presence with his disciples, and his promised coming in glory to restore all things to God. "In Christ God was reconciling the world to himself, not counting their trespasses against them, and entrusting to us the message of reconciliation" (2 Cor. 5:19). The good news is that, despite all the evil for which we human beings are responsible, "God so loved the world that he gave his only Son, that whoever believes in him should not perish but have eternal life. For God sent the Son into the world, not to condemn the world, but that the world might be saved through him" (John 3:16–17).

The gospel of life includes the very creation. All that exists is brought into being and sustained in being by love and for love, for "God is love" (1 John 4:8). The whole of creation is a gift and constitutes an order graced by the love of God. In that same love, God bestowed upon humanity a unique dignity. "So God created man in his own image, in the image of God he created him; male and female he created them. And God blessed them, and God said to them, 'Be fruitful and multiply, and fill the earth and subdue it'" (Gen. 1:27–28). Of life in all its created forms we are told, "And God saw everything that he had made, and behold, it was very good" (Gen. 1:31).

God did not recant that judgment even when man turned against God and, as a consequence, against his brother. To Cain, the first murderer, God says, "The voice of your brother's blood is crying to me from the ground" (Gen. 4:10). The cry of innocent blood did not go unheeded but began the long gospel story of restoration, including the covenant with Abraham and the people of Israel that prophetically points toward the culmination of God's self-revelation and redemptive work in Jesus Christ. Thus humanity is called "to Jesus, the mediator of a new covenant, and to the sprinkled blood that speaks more graciously than the blood of Abel" (Heb. 12:24). In Christ the dignity and eternal destiny of humanity is restored. St. Paul declares, "For as by a man came death, by man has come also the resurrection of the dead. For as in Adam all die, so also in Christ shall all be made alive" (1 Cor. 15:21–22).

The radical humanism of Christianity was and is a new thing in history. Irenaeus, the second-century church father, declared, "The glory of God is man fully alive." From the earliest noncanonical Christian writing, the *Didache* (probably written in the latter half of the first century), we learn how Christians confronted the pagan culture of the time:

> There are two ways, a way of life and a way of death; there is a great difference between them. . . . In accordance with the precept of the teaching "You shall not kill," you shall not put a child to death by

abortion or kill it once it is born. . . . The way of death is this: They show no compassion for the poor, they do not suffer with the suffering, they do not acknowledge their Creator, they kill their children and by abortion cause God's creatures to perish; they drive away the needy, oppress the suffering, they are advocates of the rich and unjust judges of the poor; they are filled with every sin. May you be ever guiltless of all these sins! (*Didache* 1.1; 2.2; 5.1–2)

There are many ways in which the dignity of the human person, created in the image and likeness of God, is violated. Both historically and at present there is genocide, unjust war, innocent victims of just wars, economic exploitation, the neglect and abuse of children, the disrespect and mistreatment of women, the abandonment of the aged, racial oppression and discrimination, the persecution of religious believers, and religious and ideological fanaticisms that are the declared enemies of freedom. The depressing list goes on and on. We have no delusions that such evils will be entirely eliminated before Christ returns in glory to set all things right. But, as in the apostolic era, so also in our time, Christian witness and life is to stand in clear contrast and opposition to such evils, for we are called to be "the salt of the earth" and "the light of the world" (Matt. 5:13–14).

While we cannot remedy all the evils in the world, we can—if we are prepared to suffer and even die rather than to do evil—always refuse to willingly participate in, support, or condone the doing of evil. The way of the gospel of life is in the keeping of God's commandments, which are summarized in this: "You shall love the Lord your God with all your heart, and with all your soul, and with all your strength, and with all your mind; and your neighbor as yourself." Jesus said, "Do this and you will live" (Luke 10:27–28).

The love of neighbor takes many forms. In Matthew 25 the righteous are rewarded and the wicked condemned by the measures of whether they fed the hungry, gave drink to the thirsty, welcomed the stranger, clothed the naked, and visited those who are sick or in prison. By these and other measures of love for our neighbor, we all fall short. Love for the neighbor begins, however, with respect for the neighbor's right to be, by honoring the gift of God that is the neighbor's life. Thus the most basic commandment of neighbor-love

is "You shall not kill" (Exod. 20:13; Deut. 5:17). "You shall not kill"
is rightly understood as "You shall not murder."

Recognizing the honorable exception of those who embrace absolute pacifism, Christians believe that there are moral duties to protect
life that may entail the taking of life, as in defense against lethal
aggression. Most Christians, past and present, have also considered
capital punishment to be morally permissible, citing the words of
St. Paul that the ruler "does not bear the sword in vain; he is the
servant of God to execute his wrath on the wrongdoer" (Rom. 13:4).
Some hold that capital punishment is not necessary to protect society
and therefore is not morally permissible, while others hold that it is
both permissible and necessary.

Our differences on capital punishment are not differences between
Evangelicals and Catholics, but are based on different judgments
regarding the need for capital punishment, at least in developed societies, and on the widespread perception that capital punishment
is in tension, if not conflict, with a consistent ethic of life. At the
same time, we are in firm agreement on the critical moral difference
between killing the innocent and punishing those who are guilty of
killing the innocent.

The ominous, and still recent, development in our society and
others is the addition of new justifications for killing. Beyond self-
defense, just war, and capital punishment, the principle is now asserted and supported by appeal to law that we are justified in killing
human beings who are, for whatever reason, unwanted or deemed
to be an excessive burden to others.

There is today no rational disagreement that the child in the womb
is, from conception, a living being that is undeniably a human being.
Barring natural tragedy, as in miscarriage, or lethal intervention, as
in abortion, this being will become what everyone recognizes as a
human baby. It is false and pernicious to claim that the unborn child
is, at early stages of development, only a potential human being. No
life that is not a human being has the potential of becoming a human
being, and no life that has the potential of becoming a human being
is not a human being.

Every human life is intended by God from eternity for eternity.
Human life is sacred because it is the creation of God, the Lord of

life. "For you did form my inward parts, you knit me together in my mother's womb" (Ps. 139:13). Nature shares in the consequences of sin, and innumerable lives are lost before they have an opportunity to develop in the womb, as many die in disasters such as famine, earthquakes, and hurricanes. Mortality is the common denominator of all life on earth. We are morally responsible, however, for the protection and care of life created in the image and likeness of God. The commandment "You shall not kill" is the negatively stated minimum of what we owe to our fellow human beings.

The direct and intentional taking of innocent human life in abortion, euthanasia, assisted suicide, and embryonic research is rightly understood as murder. In the exceedingly rare instance of direct threat to the life of the mother, saving her life may entail the death of the unborn child. Such rare and tragic instances are in sharpest contrast to the unlimited abortion license created by the Supreme Court, resulting in more than forty million deaths since 1973.

The blindness of so many to this moral atrocity has many sources but is finally to be traced to the seductive ways of evil advanced by Satan. Jesus says, "He was a murderer from the beginning, and has nothing to do with the truth, because there is no truth in him. When he lies, he speaks according to his own nature, for he is a liar and the father of lies" (John 8:44).

The direct and intentional taking of innocent human life may be attended by what is believed to be compassion, especially in the case of the dependent and debilitated aged. While we can sympathize with those who view their own life or the life of another as a burden and not a gift, and while, by the grace of God, there can be repentance and forgiveness for those who are guilty of committing great evil, there can be no moral justification for murder. We are determined to employ every legal means available to protect, in law and in life, the innocent and vulnerable members of the human community.

We plead also with our fellow citizens who do not accept the authority of God's commandments or the good news that is the gospel of life to consider the consequences of having created a license to kill. In the present state of our tragically disordered law, citizens are given, in the case of abortion, a private "right" to kill those who are too young, too small, too handicapped, too burdensome, or, for whatever reason, not "wanted." When this "right" and the lethal logic that supports it is established in law, there is no principled reason why it should not be applied to the "unwanted" at any point along life's way, as advocates of eugenics, euthanasia, and assisted suicide logically contend.

The inescapably public question posed is whether we as a political community adhere to the founding proposition articulated in the Declaration of Independence that all people are endowed by their Creator with certain "unalienable rights," beginning with the right to life. The course of progress in our political history has been one of inclusion rather than exclusion. Most notable has been the inclusion of slaves and their descendants and the recognition of the political rights of women. The foundational moral claim on which our polity rests is the claim that all human beings are created equal and are the bearers of rights that we are obliged to respect.

Among the most encouraging developments of recent decades, in our society and the world, is the increased interest in the defense of human rights. This has occurred in large part in reaction to the unspeakable horror of ideologically driven mass murder under the regimes of Nazism and Communism, which denied the equal rights of all. Especially heartening is the growing involvement of Christian communities in the defense of religious, political, and civil rights around the world. Such concern is premised upon the conviction that all human beings are created equal with respect to God-given rights that we are bound to respect. That is the premise attacked by the current abortion regime and related aggressions against the gift of life. Rights are not to be confused with individual desires or felt needs. Rights are joined to duties. Those who cannot assert their rights depend upon others doing their duty. The right to be protected entails our duty to protect.

The inescapable question is this: Why should we care about those who are weak, dependent, burdensome, unproductive, and undeveloped or gravely diminished in their capacity for the interactions we associate with being human? If we are unable to give a morally principled answer to that question, the very concept of human rights is emptied of obliging force and reduced to utilitarian calculation or arbitrary sentiment. The lethal logic invoked in support of the abortion license imperils the lives and well-being of millions who are severely handicapped or who are cared for in the many thousands of facilities for the aged and radically dependent.

Those most in need of defense are those who cannot defend themselves. We are called to speak on behalf of those who cannot speak for themselves. Among the most defenseless are the unborn child, the severely disabled, and the dependent elderly. There are today legal protections of the disabled and elderly, but the unborn are totally dependent and totally vulnerable to the will of others. Once fully born, they are deemed to have rights that are protected in law, even though they are at that point no more human beings and no less dependent than they were hours, weeks, or months before. Yet before birth, and even in the very process of being born, they are now deemed not to have rights that society is obliged to respect. This perverse view of human rights is irrational and incoherent. Its result is the unjust killing of many millions of those who are indisputably human beings and the undoing of the very concept of human rights.

We recognize that, short of Our Lord's return in glory, there will always be great evil in the world. Human history is the drama of conflict between truth and falsehood, light and darkness, life and death. The witness to the gospel of life echoes today the words of Moses to the children of Israel: "I call heaven and earth to witness against you this day, that I have set before you life and death, blessing and curse; therefore choose life, that you and your children may live" (Deut. 30:19). With the apostle Paul, we contend, and call others to contend, against the "principalities" and "powers" of the present darkness (Eph. 6:12).

There will likely always be abortions, as there will be other great evils. In the words of Jesus, "Temptations to sin are sure to come; but woe to him by whom they come" (Luke 17:1). While sin and temptations to sin are constant, the notion that the killing of the innocent is a "right" in law is relatively recent and has thrown our society into legal, political, and moral confusion and conflict. The way to justice and restored civility is a firm commitment to the goal of a society in which every vulnerable human being, including every unborn child, is protected in law and welcomed in life.

The healing professions in our society have been deeply corrupted by the culture of death. Not only in abortion but also in practices such as doctor-assisted suicide, the noble calling of medicine has been grievously debased. In medical education, we witness the ominous abandonment of the Hippocratic Oath and its prohibition of killing.

We earnestly plead with medical practitioners to recover the moral integrity of their profession. With specific reference to the aged, the debilitated, and the dying, it is often the case that restoration to health is not possible. But no life is without value or is unworthy of life. While there is no obligation to prolong the process of imminent death, the intentional hastening of death is morally prohibited. The healing profession is also the caring profession. We cannot always heal, but we can always care. Also in the most difficult of cases, it is a perverse and twisted idea of compassion that seduces medical practitioners into violating the imperative always to care and never to kill. We gratefully acknowledge and prayerfully encourage medical practitioners who strive to restore their profession to the unqualified service of life.

We are keenly aware of the burden of guilt borne, and often painfully experienced, by those who have been complicit in the culture of death. Women beyond numbering mourn for their children whom they denied the living of the life that was theirs. As with King Herod's killing of the innocents, so also now: "A voice was heard in Ramah, wailing and loud lamentation, Rachel weeping for her children; she refused to be consoled, because they were no more" (Matt. 2:18). A striking feature of the movement against abortion is the leadership of women who have experienced the horror and heartbreak of abortion and plead with their sisters to choose life. They and many others work selflessly in helping women with crisis pregnancies and also in assisting with adoptions.

Men beyond numbering are complicit in the culture of death. The legal abortion license has made it easier to exploit women sexually; to abandon them or refuse to support them in the bearing of the new life for which men are equally responsible; and even to coerce them into having the child killed. This is a wickedness of unspeakable proportions and is only compounded by men who self-servingly construe the abortion license as a form of liberation for the women they exploit.

As the sin is great, so is God's mercy greater. "God shows his love for us in that while we were yet sinners Christ died for us. Since, therefore, we are now justified by his blood, much more shall we be saved by him from the wrath of God" (Rom. 5:8–9). As the psalm declares:

> For as the heavens are high above the earth,
>   so great is his steadfast love toward those who fear him;
> as far as the east is from the west,
>   so far does he remove our transgressions from us.
>
> (Ps. 103:11–12)

We thank God for the women and men who, having been complicit in the evil of abortion, have been led to contrition, repentance, and newness of life; for abortionists who have abandoned their trafficking in death; for those who have established thousands of crisis-pregnancy centers to assist women in troubled circumstances to welcome the gift of new life; and for all who have over the years sustained a growing pro-life movement for change toward a culture of life. This is a movement for change that, more than any in American history, claims the allegiance of millions who have no personal stake in the cause other than the protection of the innocent. It is most particularly gratifying that the leadership of this movement is now passing to a younger generation that views with horrified repugnance an abortion regime to which so many of their elders had become morally numbed.

Even as the dark years of the unlimited abortion license may be coming to an end, the culture of death insinuates itself into the sciences and most particularly into the field of biotechnology. The creation and destruction of human life for research, cloning, and related purposes underscore the truth that the pro-life movement is for the duration, meaning until Our Lord returns in glory.

Our churches do not simply support the pro-life movement as a social cause. Because the gospel of life is integral to God's loving purpose for his creation, the church of Jesus Christ, comprehensively understood, is a pro-life movement continuing God's mission until the end of time. In the light of this truth, we plead with Christians who support the legal license to kill the innocent to consider whether they have not set themselves against the will of God and, to that extent, separated themselves from the company of Christian discipleship.

There are no doubt many reasons for our society's perilous drift toward a culture of death. One major cause is the abortion regime established by the Supreme Court by the *Roe v. Wade* decision of January 22, 1973. That decision is rightly described as an act of raw judicial power that eliminated in all fifty states existing legal protections of unborn children. It is an encouraging measure of the moral health of our society that the abortion license decreed by *Roe* has not been accepted by the great majority of Americans. It now seems possible that this question will be returned to the process of democratic deliberation and decision in several states. In that process, we as Evangelicals and Catholics together pledge our relentless efforts to persuade our fellow citizens to secure justice in law for the most vulnerable among us.

While political and legal developments are important, they are not of paramount importance. Deeper and of greater consequence is the moral and cultural impoverishment in our understanding of the gift of life, of our duties to others—especially to those who are most dependent—and of individual freedom that finds its true fulfillment not in license but in love.

Our public culture is debased by distortions of sexuality that are antithetical to the flourishing of marriage, fidelity, and parenthood. The indispensable institution of the family, which is the sanctuary of life, is widely devalued and weakened by divorce. Moreover, while we are not agreed on the moral permissibility of artificial contraception, we recognize the sad effects of a widespread "contraceptive mentality" that divorces sexual love from procreation and views children as a burden to be avoided rather than as a gift to be cherished. We plead with the members of our communities, Evangelical and Catholic, to consider anew the call to be open to new life and the meaning of that call for the relationship between unitive and procreative sexual love within the bond of marriage.

Finally, our society's drift toward a culture of death will not be arrested and reversed without a bolder and more persuasive witness to the gospel of life centered in Jesus Christ who is "the way, and the truth, and the life" (John 14:6). Whatever our cultural circumstance, whatever the ebb and flow of political and legal fortunes, our first duty is evangelization: to share "in season and out of season" (2 Tim.

4:2) the good news of the unsurpassable gift of eternal life, beginning now, in knowing Jesus Christ as Lord and Savior.

To know him is to serve him, and to serve him is to contend for a more just social order that defends the gift of life wherever it is threatened. As did the early Christians to the society of their time, so we propose to our fellow citizens a new humanism. This biblical humanism is deeply grounded in the dignity of the human person at every stage of development, disadvantage, or decline; it is supportive of the founding convictions of our nation; and it holds the promise of keeping at bay the barbaric devaluations of human life to which history is so manifestly prone.

We cannot and would not impose this vision of a culture of life upon others. We do propose to our fellow Christians and to all Americans that they join with us in a process of deliberation and decision that holds the promise of a more just and humane society committed, in life and law, to honoring the inestimable dignity of every human being created in the image and likeness of God. For our part, as Evangelicals and Catholics together, we refuse to despair of the power of public witness and persuasion in the service of every member of the human community, for whom Christ came "that they may have life and have it abundantly."

7

Mary

Introduction

DALE M. COULTER

The statement on Mary was one of the most challenging for Evangelicals and Catholics Together and the only one in which each side composed a kind of "pastoral letter" to the other within the document. Despite the difficulties, both sides agreed upon the necessity of exploring Marian doctrine in order to clarify Catholic teaching, to call Evangelicals to a deeper theological reflection on the role of Mary, and to encourage renewed attention to her status in the history of salvation. The prelude to the statement reflects these underlying concerns when it acknowledges ECT's desire to "turn our attention to the Virgin Mary as an example of God's saving grace, the divinely chosen mother of our Lord, and a model of discipleship." From the outset, soteriology, Christology, and the call to discipleship supplied the framework to affirm the similarities and speak to the differences.

Background

While theological concerns provided the impetus for the document's content, a number of contextual factors contributed to ECT's taking up this subject. The Center for Catholic and Evangelical Theology had recently published a series of essays on Mary in which Timothy George, a long-time ECT member, had made a contribution.[1] Around the same time, Richard John Neuhaus signaled his desire to alert Evangelicals to common misconceptions about Marian dogma, misconceptions confusing veneration and genuine worship. This issue was nowhere more apparent than in the debate between Evangelicals and Catholics in Latin America, particularly over the prominent role of Our Lady of Guadalupe in the devotional life of many Latin Catholics.

Some Evangelicals were also concerned about portrayals of Mary as an example of passive submission—especially as this affected the ongoing role of women in the church. Distortions in Marian teaching could lead to confusions about women and their contemporary vocation. In light of all these issues, addressing the role of Mary took on greater importance as a way for ECT to facilitate a theological and ecclesial renewal that took seriously the Virgin's unique place in the economy of salvation.

The Statement

To read the opening joint statement in isolation from the "pastoral letters" would give the impression that the agreement remains at the basic level of Mary as God-bearer and model for discipleship. While the christological pole of Marian teaching is a crucial feature, clarifying her ongoing subordinate position and thus the nature of her status as model, this serves merely as the starting point of agreement between Catholics and Evangelicals. The "letters" reveal a deeper level of agreement about Mary's unique status in the economy of salvation, even to the point of noting that Calvin, Luther, and Zwingli affirmed

1. Carl E. Braaten and Robert W. Jenson, eds., *Mary, Mother of God* (Grand Rapids: Eerdmans, 2004).

Mary's status as "ever virgin," making the issue one of adiaphora (neither mandated nor forbidden) for Evangelicals.

In their desire to say something theologically constructive about Marian teaching, Evangelicals also affirmed the connection between pneumatology, ecclesiology, and Mariology that one finds within Catholic teaching. Since Mary possesses a unique vocation given by the Spirit, she can be called a type of the church insofar as Mary's motherhood of Christ and the church's motherhood of believers both stem from the one Spirit who breathes life into their wombs. Mary's role in salvation history as the womb of Christ implies that she is more than an analogue to the church as mother. Her motherhood chronologically precedes and gives rise to the church's motherhood. To claim that Mary is "for all Christians" points to her unique role as Mother of the Church for Evangelicals as well as Catholics, although it must be admitted that Evangelicals would not develop this as far as Catholic teaching does. Nevertheless, this important move is part of a call that Evangelical teaching about Mary must be more than an exercise in negative theology.

In an odd way, there is also agreement on the manner in which Marian teaching reinforces the doctrine of grace. It is odd because under the influence of Edward Oakes, the Catholic "word to Evangelicals" affirmed a stronger view of divine election in Marian teaching than the Evangelicals could in light of the divergences between Wesleyan and Reformed wings of the movement. Thus, the Catholic claim that Mary's response of faith was a gift of divine grace flows from the stronger assertion that "Mary was predestined from eternity and uniquely prepared to be the dwelling place of God." Oakes first floated this idea at ECT meetings and then further developed it in the Theotokos Lecture in Theology (delivered at Marquette University) where he argued that the grace given to Mary is the "quintessential example of unmerited grace."[2] Evangelicals affirm *sola gratia* in Mary by pointing toward the manifestation of divine favor in the Spirit's concrete bestowal of grace. Evangelicals utilize the term "election" in a more generic sense, allowing for differences in interpretation.

2. Edward T. Oakes, S.J., *Predestination, Sola Gratia, and Mary's Immaculate Conception: An Ecumenical Reading of a (Still) Church-Dividing Doctrine*, Theotokos Lecture in Theology 4 (Milwaukee: Marquette University Press, 2011).

Despite this rapprochement between Catholics and Evangelicals, the disagreements over Mary still outweigh the basic agreement. Setting aside the obvious differences about whether Scripture teaches Mary's bodily assumption or immaculate conception, Catholics and Evangelicals diverge over what it means to honor or venerate Mary in relation to genuine worship of God. Catholic teaching retains a high Mariology in part because it embeds Marian dogma in a theological framework whereby the saints in heaven actively participate in the life of the church on earth. Marian devotion always points to Christ because Mary stands at the pinnacle of a communion in which all the saints possess a mediatorial role. This is clear in Vatican II's *Lumen Gentium* (chap. 8) and in the Catholic "letter" to Evangelicals found in this statement. All human forms of mediation retain their derivative status in relation to the Incarnate Son. But there is a broader ecclesiological context regarding the church as mediator of grace in relation to the Son that must be taken into consideration.

This broader ecclesiological context indicates that the most significant disagreement is over the authority of the church in relation to Scripture and the development of doctrine. This is not simply a question of the continuity or discontinuity of a particular doctrine, but how to understand doctrinal development as organic growth leading to a dogmatic pronouncement that becomes authoritative and definitive. The Protestant slogan of *semper reformanda* remains grounded in an understanding of the church as not possessing this kind of magisterial teaching authority. It may be that ECT must take up the question of doctrinal development in relation to the nature of the church at some future date.

Future Prospects

The document also hints at areas in which continuing dialogue about Mary may bear fruit. One such sphere is on the doctrine of sin in relation to the doctrine of grace. While Catholic teaching affirms that Mary is preserved from all stain of sin, the Latin term *macula* is cultic, pointing toward the sacrificial system. If the church is without stain in Ephesians 5:27 and yet the church possesses a dual status of members who struggle with the penalty of sin (the *fomes*) while remaining pure before God, one wonders if the same might apply to Mary. The question is whether *macula* points toward sin as guilt or sin as the "punishment for sin," that is, the *fomes* that remain within the forgiven believer. Must Mariology always inform ecclesiology, or can the church as spouse of Christ inform its understanding of Mary? This opens up a host of issues surrounding the doctrine of sin that Evangelicals and Catholics should take up in light of the confusion over disordered desire in relation to guilt that the current cultural debate about human sexuality has brought to the fore.

If the ECT statement on Mary broke new ground, it was primarily as a corrective to excesses or misinterpretations. On the Catholic side, the statement underscored Mary's subordinate status as well as the need to see in her witness the active cooperation with the Spirit that points toward women as active participants in the life of the church. For their part, the Evangelicals called for a renewal of devotion to Mary that honors her as a type of the church whose motherhood of Christ enabled the church to become the mother of believers. One cannot claim that Mary is *Theotokos* without claiming that she is Mother of the Church in terms of the economy of salvation. If Evangelicals simply took that theological insight from this document, it would turn talk about Mary from a negative to a constructive enterprise, placing her back where she belongs as the mother of our Lord.

Do Whatever He Tells You: The Blessed Virgin Mary in Christian Faith and Life

(2009)

In 1994, after intense study, discussion, and prayer, we issued a statement titled Evangelicals and Catholics Together: The Christian Mission in the Third Millennium. *In 1997, we bore common witness to* The Gift of Salvation, *underscoring God's unmerited justification of sinners because of the redeeming work of Jesus Christ, true God and true man and our only hope of salvation. In our third statement,* Your Word Is Truth *(2002), we affirmed a convergence in our understanding of the transmission of God's saving Word through Holy Scripture and tradition, which is the lived experience of the community of faith under the guidance of the Holy Spirit. In 2003, we addressed* The Communion of Saints, *in which we confessed that our communion with Christ means that we are in a certain, albeit imperfect, communion with one another in his body, the church.* The Call to Holiness *in 2005 lifted up our common participation in the life-transforming love of God—Father, Son, and Holy Spirit. The statement* That They May Have Life *(2006) set forth the Christian mandate, based on biblical authority and clear reason, for the protection of innocent human life from conception to natural death.*

In the present statement we turn our attention to the Virgin Mary as an example of God's saving grace, the divinely chosen mother of our Lord, and a model of discipleship. As in previous statements, we wish to emphasize that we speak from and to, not for, our several communities and that we are determined honestly to engage differences between our communities, recognizing that the only unity pleasing to God, and therefore the only unity we may seek, is unity in the truth.

Since the sixteenth century, the subject of the Blessed Virgin Mary has been a primary point of differentiation, and even conflict, between Evangelicals and Catholics. While figures such as Martin Luther, John Calvin, and Ulrich Zwingli retained a special reverence for Mary, this dimension of their teaching and piety was largely lost by their followers in the course of growing animosity between Protestants and Catholics. On the Catholic side, the determination to draw a clear line against Protestantism sometimes led to exaggerations and distortions in Marian devotion.

In our time there is among Evangelicals a renewed interest in Mary, and among Catholics a determination to make clear that the greatness of Mary is in her faithfulness to Jesus Christ, her Lord and ours. In the words of the Second Vatican Council, "No creature could ever be counted as equal to the Incarnate Word and Redeemer. . . . The Church does not hesitate to profess the subordinate role of Mary" (*Lumen Gentium*, no. 62). Whatever is said about Mary is ever and always in the service of what must be said about Christ.

Our purpose in the present statement is not to resolve all the familiar differences on this subject, although we address such differences. Our purpose, rather, is to examine anew, as Evangelicals and Catholics together, the place of Mary in Christian faith and life. In doing so, we acknowledge the primary authority of Holy Scripture. We also recognize the importance of the teaching and practice of the early church, which relied on Jesus's promise to send the Holy Spirit to guide his disciples into all truth.

We recognize that, in discerning such guidance, Catholics have a distinctive view of apostolic authority exercised by bishops with and under the "Petrine ministry" of the Bishop of Rome, a view not shared by Evangelicals. Teaching authority in the Church, or Magisterium, as it is called, may be the subject of a future statement. For our present purpose, we say what we can say together—and what we must say to one another.

At the announcement of the coming birth of the Savior, the angel says to Mary before she conceives that she is "full of grace." Because grace is always a gift, that she is full of grace is God's gift and not her achievement. In her song called the Magnificat, Mary says that "all generations will call me blessed" (Luke 1:48). She is rightly called by us the Blessed Virgin Mary. Mary is the long-awaited daughter of Israel, in fulfillment of biblical prophecy. She stands strikingly between the old covenant and the new, her child being recognized by Simeon in the temple as the long-awaited "consolation of Israel" (Luke 2:25).

In the gospel writings, she is portrayed as the culmination of a prophetic lineage of devout mothers: Sarah, Rachel, and Hannah, along with Tamar, Rahab, and Ruth. Such early Christians as Justin Martyr and Irenaeus acclaimed her as the New Eve in whom was fulfilled the promise to the first Eve that the seed of a woman would reverse the calamitous fall into sin. She is the woman through whom that promise is vindicated in the birth, life, suffering, death, glorious resurrection, and promised coming again of Jesus Christ, her son and her Lord. The typological reading of Mary, and of Christ, in the Old Testament is at the heart of the Christian understanding of the relation of continuity and fulfillment between the old covenant and the new.

Since the days of the apostles, faithful Christians have understood Mary to be the virgin mother of Jesus. In more recent times, the virgin birth became a decisive point of difference between Evangelicals and liberal Protestants. In the apostolic era and among orthodox Christians of all times, it is clearly understood that the doctrine of Jesus's virginal conception is based on the apostolic witness and is intimately connected with the belief that Jesus the Christ, the Son of God and son of Mary, is both true God and true man.

Agreeing on the miracle of the virgin birth, we would also encourage a fuller reflection on the maternity of Mary. As the mother of Jesus, she was the first to learn of his nature and mission, and she was the first to give faith's assent: "Let it be to me according to your word" (Luke 1:38). We picture her nursing him at her breast, teaching him his first words, kissing his bruises when he fell, introducing him to Israel's understanding of the ways of the Lord—the mother who helped him memorize the psalms and say his prayers, even as he grew "in wisdom and in stature, and in favor with God and man" (Luke 2:52).

When, much later, Mary is depicted as praying with the apostles (Acts 1:14), we may imagine that Mary prayed to her son with the words that she had taught him to pray. Contemplating the motherhood of Mary powerfully reinforces—against every form of gnosticism or docetism, whether ancient or modern—our understanding of the full humanity of Jesus the Christ. In the fullness of time he was born of a woman from whom he received all that pertains to his human nature.

We are agreed that it is appropriate, and indeed necessary, to call Mary *Theotokos*—the God-bearer. *Theotokos* means "the one who gave birth to the One who is God," and the title, based on the clear witness of Scripture, was emphasized in the early church to counter the heresy of Nestorius, who divided the human and divine natures of Christ.

Here and elsewhere, what must be said about Mary is inseparably connected with what must be said about Christ. Because Jesus is both true man and true God, and because his human nature and divine nature are inseparable, it is right to call Mary, who is the mother of Jesus, the Mother of God or the God-bearer. Such language is intended first to exalt Jesus Christ and only then to honor Mary. Indeed, in the Magnificat, Mary glorified not herself but God alone.

Mary is always and ever a creature among creatures and no less in need of redemption than any other human being, Jesus only excepted. Mary is always and ever in the role of subordinate and servant. As she said to the angel, "Behold, I am the handmaid of the Lord" (Luke 1:38). Her message, first spoken to the servants at the wedding of Cana, and also to us, is simply this: "Do whatever he tells you" (John 2:5).

We agree with St. Augustine, who wrote: "Indeed the blessed Mary certainly did the Father's will, and so it was for her a greater thing to have been Christ's disciple than to have been his mother, and she was more blessed in her discipleship than in her motherhood. Hers was the happiness of first bearing in her womb him whom she would obey as her master" (Sermon 72A.7).[3]

Mary's act of faith and her giving birth are at the beginning of the incarnate life and mission of the Savior; the New Testament also depicts her gathered with the disciples on the day of Pentecost. She is at the foot of the cross at the close of Christ's earthly ministry. When

---

3. *The Works of Saint Augustine: A Translation for the 21st Century; Sermons,* vol. III/3, trans. Edmund Hill (New York: New City Press, 1991), 287.

other disciples had fled in fear, Mary remained. When from the cross the dying Lord told John to see in Mary his mother and told Mary to see in John her son, we may understand that, symbolically speaking, John represents all the disciples through the ages who will love and honor Mary as the blessed mother of their brother and their Lord.

Mary participates in the suffering of her son, as indeed all Christians are called to do (Phil. 3:10). When the child Jesus was presented in the temple, holy Simeon predicted that a sword would pierce the heart of Mary. Mary stands in solidarity with the church, the pilgrim people of God through time, and is powerfully pertinent to our time in which we witness the increasing persecution of Christians in many parts of the world.

Today there is a new and welcome attentiveness to the role of women in both church and society. In this connection, it is important to underscore that the place of Mary in the plan of salvation is not one of passivity but of courageous faith and love. Catholics and Evangelicals can agree with Pope John Paul II, who wrote in his 1987 encyclical *Redemptoris Mater* (Mother of the Redeemer): "This Marian dimension of Christian life takes on special importance in relation to women and their status. . . . The figure of Mary of Nazareth sheds light on womanhood as such by the very fact that God, in the sublime event of the Incarnation of his Son, entrusted himself to the ministry, the free and active ministry of a woman" (no. 46).

Having addressed matters on which we can speak together, we must also speak to one another about the differences in our understanding of the Blessed Virgin Mary in Christian faith and life. We do so as brothers and sisters in Christ, fully committed to unity in truth.

A Catholic Word to Evangelicals

We believe that Catholic teaching with respect to the Blessed Virgin Mary safeguards the fullness of revelation and deepens our understanding of God's plan of salvation. We here address, all too briefly, four aspects of that doctrine: the perpetual virginity of Mary, her immaculate conception, her bodily assumption into heaven, and her role, along with all the saints, in the communion of the church. We do so in fidelity to "the relation between Sacred Scripture, as the highest authority in matters of faith, and Sacred Tradition as indispensable to the interpretation of the Word of God" (*Ut Unum Sint*, no. 79).

The Bible is the foundation of all Catholic teaching. Catholics also believe, in accordance with Jesus's promise to send the Holy Spirit to teach the church all things (John 14:16), that, under the influence of the Spirit, the gospel of grace is more fully and completely understood. Thus the Catholic Church believes that in its listening to, praying with, and reflecting on the truth of Holy Scripture, the Spirit is active as a divine guide, leading to a rich and comprehensive consideration of God's Word. The Spirit leads the Church to see the full implications of the gospel through the teaching of the early fathers, through ecumenical councils, through prayer and liturgy, through the lives of the saints, and through the study of theologians. All of these help the Church to see more clearly the profound meaning of Christ's message and the extraordinary role of his mother, Mary, in the history of salvation.

The ancient liturgy celebrates Mary as *Aeiparthenos*, the Ever-Virgin. New Testament references to the brothers and sisters of Jesus do not refer to other children of Mary but to children of Joseph by a previous marriage or, more likely, are a biblical manner of referring to close relations (Gen. 13:8; 14:16; 29:15).

Mary was predestined from eternity and uniquely prepared to be the dwelling place of God. Schooled by the New Testament authors in typological reading of the Old Testament, the fathers of the church speak of the womb of Mary as the New Ark of the Covenant, the temple of him who is the New Temple (John 2:21). The Spirit of God hovered over the void at the first creation (Gen. 1:2) and descended as glory over the ark (Exod. 40:34; Num. 9:19–20) and the temple in Jerusalem (1 Kings 8:10–11). And the same Spirit hovered over the womb of Mary, initiating the new creation and new covenant in Christ (Luke 1:35). In the patristic view, Mary's statement that she has no husband and is the handmaid of the Lord is understood as a total and irrevocable vow to dedicate herself to God as a virgin (Luke 1:34, 38). No man may enter the sanctuary thus consecrated to God (Ezek. 44:1–3).

Belief in Mary's perpetual virginity reflects not a denigration of the good of human sexuality but an understanding of the utterly gratuitous nature of God's initiative and the totality of Mary's response of faith. The virginal theme is evident also in the new birth of the faithful, in which participation in the divine life arises "not of blood nor of the will of the flesh nor of the will of man, but of God" (John 1:13). This new life is virginal because it is entirely the gift of the Spirit. The human vocation in relation to God is spousal (2 Cor. 11:2) and is perfectly fulfilled in Mary's virginal motherhood.

All this is by faith. Mary's response is itself God's gift of grace. As with Mary, so also with the church, which "by receiving the word of God in faith becomes herself a mother. By preaching and baptism she brings forth sons, who are conceived by the Holy Spirit and born of God to a new and immortal life. She herself is a virgin who keeps in its entirety and purity the faith she pledged to her spouse" (*Lumen Gentium*, no. 64). Thus, the Catholic Church says with St. Augustine, "Mary remained a virgin in conceiving her Son, a virgin in giving him birth, a virgin in carrying him, a virgin in nursing him at her breast, always a virgin" (*Of Holy Virginity* 3.3).

Under the guidance of the Holy Spirit promised to the church (John 16:12–13), the understanding of the immaculate conception of Mary developed more slowly and not without considerable dispute. In light of the promise of Genesis 3:15, many early Christians saw Mary as the sinless New Eve, the first member of the new creation inaugurated by Christ, the New Adam. Later thinkers, including Thomas Aquinas, acknowledged that there is no creature more holy than the Blessed Virgin but said that she, like all human beings, inherited original sin from Adam and was later purified for her unique mission in the plan of salvation. In the fourteenth century, John Duns Scotus, recognizing that Christ came "in the likeness of sinful flesh" (Rom. 8:3), taught that Christ, out of love for his mother and a desire to reveal his total victory over sin and death, brought his salvation to Mary by preserving her from all sin from the beginning of her existence.

In 1854, Pope Pius IX clarified a long tradition of theological development and piety by formally defining the immaculate conception: "The most Blessed Virgin Mary was, from the first moment of her conception, by a singular grace and privilege of almighty God and by virtue of the merits of Jesus Christ, Savior of the human race, preserved from all stain of original sin" (*Ineffabilis Deus*).

In continuity with scriptural witness and Christian tradition, it is affirmed that Mary is saved by the redemptive work of Jesus Christ alone and is "blessed among women" to be the New Eve who bears the New Adam, the Savior of the world. She is sinless only by virtue of the saving work of Christ. Her assent ("Let it be with me according to your word") is perfect, untainted by sin, and is thus the preeminent model of faith and discipleship, as she is also a sign of hope in Christ's power to undo sin and death in the members of his body, the church. Against every form of Pelagianism, the immaculate conception bears witness to the utter gratuitousness of God's gift of salvation, making clear that it is not dependent upon human merit but is by grace alone (*sola gratia*).

In 1950, also after a long development of the Church's reflection on the role of Mary in the plan of salvation, the assumption of Mary was defined: "Finally, the Immaculate Virgin, preserved free from all stain of original sin, when the course of her earthly life was finished, was taken up body and soul into heavenly glory, and exalted by the Lord as Queen over all things, so that she might be more fully conformed to her Son, the Lord of lords and conqueror of sin and death" (*Munificentissimus Deus*).

"Mary, the all-holy, ever-virgin Mother of God," declares the *Catechism of the Catholic Church* (CCC), "is the masterwork of the mission of the Son and the Spirit in the fullness of time" (721). In her, the Father prepared a dwelling place for the Son and Spirit among men. The annunciation to Mary inaugurates "the fullness of time" (Gal. 4:4 NRSV). In Mary, the mission of the Holy Spirit is conjoined to and ordered to the mission of the Son (John 16:14–15). In Mary, the Holy Spirit fulfills God's loving plan and manifests the Son of the Father, now become the son of the virgin. In her assumption, Mary anticipates the promised destiny of all the faithful, the eschatological icon of the church. "She shines forth on earth until the day of the Lord shall come, a sign of certain hope and comfort to the pilgrim People of God" (*Lumen Gentium*, no. 68).

Mary is the first disciple and mother of the church, which is the communion of saints professed in the Apostles' Creed. The earliest disciples "devoted themselves to the apostles' teaching and fellowship, to the breaking of the bread and the prayers" (Acts 2:42). The communion of saints includes the faithful pilgrims on earth, those who have died and are being prepared for glory (purgatory), and those who already contemplate "in full light, God himself triune and one, exactly as he is" (*Lumen Gentium*, no. 49). All these are in living communion through Christ who has conquered sin and death.

As St. Thomas Aquinas wrote, "Since all the faithful form one body, the good of each is communicated to the other" (*Expositio in Symbolum Apostolorum*, no. 10; Eph. 4:16). Thus, in the communion of saints, the brothers and sisters of Christ, adopted by grace, recognize his mother as their mother. In the words of St. Augustine, "Clearly she is the mother of Christ's members . . . since she has cooperated with love in bringing about the birth of the faithful in the Church. They are the members of the head, but she is physically the mother of the head himself" (*On Holy Virginity* 6.6). When from the cross Jesus commends Mary to John as his mother, John represents the faithful of all time. John welcomes Mary "into his own" (*eis ta idia*), which means not only into his house but into all that is his—his heart and mind and soul (John 19:25–27, 32–37). Thus is Mary rightly recognized as Mother of the Church.

The communion of saints entails a sharing with "the saints in light," they with us and we with them (Col. 1:12). We on earth are permitted to participate in the fulfillment of Christ's mission (Col. 1:24). Mary, with all the saints in heaven, prays for the church on earth. As we ask for the prayers of the church on earth, so also we ask for the prayers of the church in heaven, knowing that "we are surrounded by so great a cloud of witnesses" (Heb. 12:1). The church on earth lives in lively conversation with the church in heaven. Already now, for those who live by faith and not by sight (2 Cor. 5:7), death is vanquished. In drawing closer to Mary, we are drawn closer to Christ, for the entirety of her being is devoted to Christ, and her one will for his disciples is "Do whatever he tells you" (John 2:5). Devotion to Mary, the fully redeemed creature, is directed to the adoration of Christ, true God and true man.

Any mediation attributed to Mary is only part of the mediation of Christ, who is the "one mediator between God and men" (1 Tim. 2:5). "No creature could ever be counted along with the Incarnate Word and Redeemer; but just as the priesthood of Christ is shared in various ways by both his ministers and the faithful, and as the one goodness of God is radiated in different ways among his creatures, so also the unique mediation of the Redeemer does not exclude but rather gives rise to a manifold cooperation which is but a sharing in this one source" (*Lumen Gentium*, no. 62). As John Paul II explains, "Although participated forms of mediation of different kinds and degrees are not excluded, they acquire meaning and value *only* from Christ's own mediation, and they cannot be understood as parallel or complementary to his" (*Redemptoris Missio*, no. 5).

The many titles of Mary—Mother of God, Mother of the Church, Seat of Wisdom, Ark of the Covenant, Queen of Heaven—illuminate the facets of her role in the plan of salvation. They represent centuries of Christian reflection on the greatest of mysteries—that God became man in order that man may share fully in the life of God. "The canticle of Mary, the *Magnificat* (Latin) or *Megalynei* (Byzantine) is the song both of the Mother of God and of the Church; the song of the Daughter of Zion and of the new People of God; the song of thanksgiving for the fullness of graces poured out in the economy of salvation and the song of the poor whose hope is met by the fulfillment of the promises made to our ancestors, 'to Abraham and his children forever'" (*CCC*, 2619).

This, all too briefly stated, is the understanding of Mary and her part in Christian faith and life that we respectfully recommend to our Evangelical brothers and sisters in Christ. We have done so in a manner conscious of the admonition of the Second Vatican Council: "[We] exhort theologians and preachers of the divine word to abstain zealously both from all gross exaggerations as well as from petty narrow-mindedness in considering the singular dignity of the Mother of God. Following the study of Sacred Scripture, the Holy Fathers, the doctors and liturgy of the Church, and under the guidance of the Church's magisterium, let them rightly illustrate the duties and privileges of the Blessed Virgin which always look to Christ, the source of all truth, sanctity, and piety. Let them assiduously keep away from whatever, either by word or deed, could lead separated brethren or any other into error regarding the true doctrine of the Church" (*Lumen Gentium*, no. 67).

We believe that Catholic teaching about Mary safeguards the fullness of revelation and deepens our comprehension of God's plan of salvation. After centuries of misunderstanding between Catholics and Protestants, for which we as Catholics accept our measure of responsibility, our fervent prayer is that this conversation about the Blessed Virgin Mary, the Mother of God, will enhance our unity in Christ.

An Evangelical Word to Catholics

Since its inception in 1994, Evangelicals and Catholics Together has proceeded with two common assumptions: that all who accept Christ as Lord and Savior are brothers and sisters in Christ, and that we recognize spiritual kinship in one another as dialogue partners in this process. These assumptions have been tested over the years in our explorations of many controverted themes including the nature of justification and the relation of Scripture and tradition. This testing is also evident in our current discussions about Mary, the mother of our Lord, her place in the teaching of Holy Scripture, and her role in the history of redemption. We seek here greater mutual understanding of Evangelical and Catholic perspectives on the Blessed Virgin Mary bearing witness to our different understandings of the one apostolic faith. We do so in keeping with the original ECT declaration, which noted that "the differences and disagreements . . . must be addressed more fully and candidly in order to strengthen between us a relationship of trust in obedience to truth." We have always endeavored to speak the truth to one another in love, and we do so here believing that, in the words of the Pilgrims' pastor, John Robinson, the Lord "has yet more truth and light to break forth out of his Holy Word."[4]

In this section of the paper we address three things: the neglect of Marian teaching in Evangelical theology and our hope for its recovery; the issues of Catholic teaching about Mary that still separate us and require prayerful reflection; and a proposal for moving forward.

Evangelicalism is a worldwide renewal movement within the one, holy, catholic, and apostolic church embracing, but not limited to,

---

4. John Robinson, *The Works of John Robinson, Pastor of the Pilgrim Fathers, with a Memoir and Annotations by Robert Ashton* (London: John Snow, 1851), 1:xliv.

puritanism, pietism, and pentecostalism. As such, it claims as its own the trinitarian and christological dogmas of the early church, not because they are ancient or endorsed by any particular denomination but because they are necessarily implied by how the Bible presents God's revelation of himself in the history of Israel and Israel's Messiah, Jesus the Lord. These teachings were also basic to the ecclesial and spiritual renewal in the churches of the West in the sixteenth century generally known as the Reformation. Evangelicals embrace this movement, with its principles of the normative authority of Holy Scripture and justification by faith alone.

With our Catholic brothers and sisters we say without hesitation: Mary is for all Christians. The Reformation has been called a "tragic necessity." The neglect, almost the disappearance, of Mary in Protestant theology belongs to the tragic side. The Reformers rightly rejected an overemphasis on Mary's role in late medieval piety—the sweet mother placating her stern Son—because it obscured the supreme glory of Jesus Christ and salvation through him alone, but they also spoke of Mary with a love and respect that is instructive for us today. As heirs of the Reformation, Evangelicals do well to revisit the Marian thought of the Reformers.

For Luther, Mary is the workshop (*fabrica*) in which God operates to bring about the salvation of the world. Mary is the person and place where God has chosen to enter most deeply into the human story. She is the one who hears the Word of God (*fides ex auditu*), the one who responds in faith and thus is justified by faith alone (*WA* 7:573). The Reformed tradition is more reticent, yet both Zwingli and Bullinger joined in the "Hail Mary, full of grace" not as a prayer to Mary but as an expression of praise in honor of her. Calvin too referred to Mary as "the treasurer of grace" and spoke of how Christ "chose for himself the virgin's womb as a temple in which to dwell" (*Institutes* 2.14.1).

In recent years, Mary has once again become the focus of constructive reflection among Evangelicals, and this is a positive development. There is a place for a biblically precise, theologically robust love and honor of Mary among Evangelicals—not one that claims her as mediatrix or coredemptrix but one that sees her as the figure the Bible presents her to be: the handmaid of the Lord, divinely chosen to give birth to the Messiah, she who stood loyally by Jesus at the cross where he offered "a full, perfect, and sufficient sacrifice for the sins of the whole world" (*Book of Common Prayer*, 1662). Mary's aim was to exalt her Son and to point others to him. We do not detract from Christ by showing proper reverence to his mother.

An important aspect of this reverence is to acknowledge our common confession of Mary's prophetic ministry of proclaiming the message of salvation. Inspired by the Spirit, Mary's Magnificat announces the divine restoration of creation in parallel with Jesus's own proclamation of the year of the Lord's favor (Luke 4:18–19). Mary is not simply a passive instrument of God's plan. She actively participates in the Spirit's charismatic activity, which from generation to generation serves as a model for men and women who seek to proclaim the gospel "in the power of the Spirit." Consequently, there is a pneumatological continuity between Mary's unique vocation and the ongoing vocation of the church that allows Evangelicals, with Ambrose (*Expos. in Luc.* 2.6–7) and Vatican II (*Lumen Gentium*, no. 63), to affirm her role as a type of the church (*ecclesiae typus*).

The common confession of Evangelicals and Catholics includes the virginal conception of Jesus and Mary's role as *Theotokos*, the God-bearer. The latter term has been resisted by some believers because it can be (and has been) confused with pagan notions of fertility cults, goddess worship, and *Magna Mater* (the Great Mother). Yet the debates leading up to the Council of Ephesus (431), which defined Mary as *Theotokos*, were framed by the New Testament witness to the deity of Christ. This title was always christologically driven; it had less to do with the status of Mary than with the unity of divinity and humanity in her son.

To confess Mary as the God-bearer is not to project some notion of a pagan goddess; it is to declare what the Bible says—that Mary was the human mother of the one who is the eternal Son of God. Evangelical theology shines most clearly in its hymnody, and Graham Kendrick's hymn "Meekness and Majesty" (1986) expresses this point well: "Meekness and majesty, / Manhood and Deity, / In perfect harmony, / The Man who is God. / Lord of eternity, / Dwells in humanity, / Kneels in humility / And washes our feet. / O what a mystery, / Meekness and majesty. / Bow down and worship / For this is your God."

Catholics and Evangelicals both confess the historicity of the virginal conception of Jesus. J. Gresham Machen, who published a classic study of the virgin birth of Jesus in 1920, recognized this common ground and declared that the gulf between Rome and the Reformation was negligible compared to the abyss that separated both traditions from others who eviscerated the historic Christian faith. Evangelicals affirm both Mary's virginity and her maternity. Mary was not merely the point of Christ's entrance into the world—as though she were a channel through which he passed as water flows through a pipe. She was truly human and a real mother. Her tender care and life-giving love for Jesus calls for all believers to love and honor her.

Despite all this common ground, however, both Marian dogma and Marian devotion remain contentious issues. Evangelicals understand that the Catholic Church does not equate adoration of God (*latria*) and veneration for Mary (*hyperdoulia*). It seems to many Evangelicals, however, that the devotion of some Catholics to Mary can obscure the preeminence, unique sinlessness, and sole salvific sufficiency of Jesus Christ as well as the common pneumatological ground of worship for all Christians who pray through Christ in the Spirit.

Emphasis on Mary's intercessory role, coupled with prayers to Mary, can create confusion between adoration and veneration—and risks leading people away from, rather than to, the Savior. This is especially true in contexts where devotion to Mary is a deeply in-grained part of cultural identity. We do not think this is the intention of Catholic teaching as expressed in *Lumen Gentium*, and Catholic members of ECT have addressed in helpful ways exaggerations of Marian piety. In an age of syncretism and radical pluralism, the recent statements by Pope Benedict XVI declaring Jesus Christ the one and only Savior are an encouragement to all faithful Christians. We acknowledge that there is little Evangelical reflection on any of these Marian themes, certainly nothing commensurate with the vast Catholic literature in the field. This stems from Protestant neglect of Mary, born of a conviction that the Catholic portrait of Mary exceeds its biblical warrants.

At the same time, disputed questions remain serious points of difference between us. These points represent postbiblical develop-ments in Catholic teaching. Evangelicals also claim continuity with the doctrinal development of biblical teaching in the early church. But the notion of development itself, along with the necessary refutation of error, implies that the church can be, and sometimes has been, mistaken and misled about important matters of faith. Jesus did not guarantee the infallibility of ecclesiastical pronouncements. Jesus did promise instead that the Holy Spirit would lead his disciples into all truth, that true faith would be found on the earth when he returned, and that at the last God would save his people, "in the intervals of sunshine between storm and storm . . . snatching them from the surge of evil, even when the waters rage most furiously" (John Henry Newman).[5]

Article VI of the Thirty-Nine Articles of the Church of England (1563) sets forth the principle of scriptural sufficiency that marks Evangelical thought with reference to these disputed points. "Holy Scripture containeth all things necessary to salvation: so that whatsoever is not read therein, nor may be proved thereby, is not to be required of anyone, that it should be believed as an article of the faith, or be thought requisite or necessary to salvation."

Applying this principle of scriptural sufficiency, we offer brief comments on the following four issues:

1. *Perpetual Virginity.* That a woman named Mary conceived and gave birth to a baby named Jesus without the sexual involvement of a male partner is a truth of biblical revelation (Matt. 1:18–25; Luke 1:26–38). To what extent her physical virginity remained inviolate in the act of her birthgiving (*in partu*) and thereafter (*post partum*) the Bible does not say. Various views were expressed among ancient Christian writers. The *Protoevangelium of James*, for example, describes in graphic detail the exact nature of Mary's virginity (20:1–3). Various themes of later Marian piety are found in this apocryphal work, though Jerome, who himself believed in the perpetual virginity, regarded the work as untrustworthy.

The Bible tells us that Jesus had brothers and sisters and names four of his brothers—James, Joseph, Simon, and Judas (Matt. 13:55–56). Evangelicals commonly maintain that this text refers to the half

5. John Henry Newman, *The Via Media of the Anglican Church* (London: Longmans, Green, and Co., 1901), 1:355.

siblings of Jesus, the subsequent children of Joseph and Mary who lived as husband and wife in the full sense. We do recognize, however, that the Greek word *adelphoi* has a range of meaning and could refer to Jesus's close relatives, either cousins or the children of Joseph by a previous marriage.

In the sixteenth century, Luther, Zwingli, and Calvin all accepted the ever-virgin character of Mary while fully supporting marriage and the inherent goodness of sexuality. Mary's perpetual virginity is an adiaphorous teaching, neither required nor forbidden by Scripture itself. We may regard Mary's virginity as an example of her fidelity to the unique calling she received to become the mother of Jesus, but we may not use it to elevate celibacy above married life, nor to denigrate sexuality as the good creation of God within the sacred bonds of marriage. Some Evangelicals may refer to Mary as ever-virgin, but all acclaim her as blessed because as a virgin she carried the Redeemer in her womb.

2. *Immaculate Conception.* Evangelicals find unnecessary and un-biblical the notion that Mary was preserved from the stain of original sin from the first moment of her conception. Still, we affirm much of what this teaching is intended to convey—that Mary was the object of God's gracious election in Christ; that she was uniquely prepared to become the mother of our Lord; that she is an extraordinary model of the call to discipleship and the life of holiness; that her assent to the purpose of the Lord was itself the result of God's unmerited favor toward her—an example of *sola gratia*; and that she should be honored and called "blessed one" in all places and by all generations.

Much interconfessional discussion has centered on the Greek *kecharitomenē* of Luke 1:28, which the Vulgate renders *gratia plena* and the Douay-Rheims version as "full of grace." In its clearest form, this perfect passive participle expresses divine favor in the passive voice, as in the King James Version: "Hail thou that art highly favoured" (cf. Luther, *holdselige*, and Calvin, *agréable*). Luke 1:28 does not mention Mary's conception, though Scripture does teach that God's redemptive call can take place before birth or even conception (Jer. 1:5; Gal. 1:15).

The concrete manifestation of divine favor occurred through the descent and overshadowing of the Holy Spirit (Luke 1:35), whose sanc-tifying activity enabled Mary's response of faith and thus inaugurated the renewal of all creation in her womb (Luke 1:38). Calvin affirms this point by stating that "to carry Christ in her womb was not Mary's first *blessedness*, but was greatly inferior to the distinction of being born again by the Spirit of God to a new life" (*Commentary on the Harmony of the Gospels*, 42). By divine grace alone Mary was enabled to give birth to the Son of God, and from her alone he received his human nature. It is not to be doubted that this was wrought by the power of God in a way no less miraculous or mysterious than the virginal conception itself.

Immaculate conception is not accepted as a dogma by the churches of the East and was much debated in the West before and after the Reformation. Augustine held to a high view of the personal holiness of Mary but believed that God's abundant grace was conferred on her "for vanquishing sin in every part" (*On Nature and Grace*, 36.42). The idea that Mary was conceived without original sin was rejected by Augustine, Bernard of Clairvaux, and Thomas Aquinas, among other notable teachers of the church. Their thinking about Mary deserves fresh consideration.

Evangelicals confess the sinlessness of Christ but not the sinlessness of Mary. Hebrews 7:26 refers to Jesus as our High Priest. He alone was perfectly "holy, blameless, unstained, separated from sinners." The Bible makes clear that no other human being can claim this (John 8:46; Rom. 3:23; 5:12; 1 Cor. 15:22; 2 Cor. 5:21; Eph. 2:3; Heb. 4:15). Jesus taught his disciples, among whom Mary was the first, to pray "Our Father who art in heaven . . . forgive us our trespasses" (Matt. 6:9, 12). The Bible declares that Christ Jesus came into the world to save sinners, and he was the Savior as well as the son of his blessed mother (1 Tim. 1:15; Luke 1:46–47).

3. *The Bodily Assumption.* The doctrine of the immaculate conception is incongruent with Sacred Scripture because it exempts Mary from original sin and declares that she is thus saved by Jesus in a unique manner. At one level, the doctrine of Mary's bodily assumption applies to Mary what the Bible declares to have happened to the prophets Enoch and Elijah—that she was taken into heaven, body and soul, at the end of her earthly life.

In this way, Mary is believed to have anticipated what many Evangelicals refer to as the rapture of the church at the return of Christ.

Mary's assumption presupposes a number of things that are indeed a part of our common Christian confession: the reality of heaven; the communion of saints; the overcoming of death; the resurrection of the flesh; the certain triumph of Jesus Christ over sin, hell, and the grave; belief in the literal, visible return of Christ in glory; the goodness of creation; and the unity of soul and body for all eternity. None of these biblical truths, however, requires belief in the bodily assumption of Mary, which is without biblical warrant (the vision of Rev. 12:1–6 says nothing about Mary's body being taken into heaven) and has no basis in the early Christian tradition.

The apostolic constitution *Munificentissimus Deus* (1950), in which Pope Pius XII promulgated the dogma of the assumption, does not take a position with respect to Mary's death, yet this is a question of some theological importance. If Mary was taken to heaven without death in the manner of Enoch and Elijah, was this because her body was incorruptible and thus not subject to the fact that "the wages of sin is death" (Rom. 6:23)? On the other hand, if she actually died (without having sinned) and then was raised from the dead to heavenly glory, then her resurrection would seem to be parallel to that of Christ who *alone* died and rose again for our justification (Rom. 4:24–25). Both opinions are present in the apocryphal writings that form the basis of later legends (such as Christ's surrender of the heavenly kingdom to Mary at her coronation in glory), but it seems prudent to follow here the silence of the Scriptures and the reticence of the church fathers of the first three centuries.

4. *Invocation of Mary.* Because Evangelicals take seriously the biblical record of the annunciation and the visitation, we honor and love the Blessed Virgin Mary. We praise God with her and for her, and with the angel Gabriel we hail her as the highly favored mother of the Savior in whom the sanctifying and charismatic presence of the Spirit was at work. We also recognize in her Magnificat a prophetic witness to the redeeming acts of God in salvation history, especially his concern for the poor and downtrodden. We seek to learn to pray like Mary and in her spirit, and we celebrate Jesus's special love for Mary, which extended even to the cross. Because the Spirit unites things separated by space and time, we join our voices in communion with the universal church, with the angels, and with all the saints

in heaven, including Mary, to extol and magnify the Triune God of holiness and love.

Evangelicals do not think that such evocation of Mary leads to her invocation, intercession, or mediation. We do not find in Scripture that Mary has any ongoing redemptive role as the dispenser of grace to sinners. As there is one and only one God, so too there is one and only one mediator between God and human beings, the man Christ Jesus (1 Tim. 2:3–6). We do not deny that, through the Holy Spirit, God uses external means of grace, especially the proclamation of the gospel, to draw lost men and women to the Savior, but he does this in such a way that no creature, in heaven or on earth, shares with Christ the role of redeemer.

Evangelicals affirm that the church is the body of Christ extended throughout time as well as space. The bonds among those who are in Christ are not severed by death, and the struggling church on earth shares one faith and one hope with the noble company of the apostles, martyrs, and all the saints in glory, including Mary. As Jonathan Edwards declared, "The Church in heaven and the Church on earth are more *one* people, *one* city, and *one* family, than is generally imagined" (*Miscellaneous Observations*).

Whether Mary and other departed believers with the Lord in glory can hear and answer words addressed to them from this life, the Bible does not say. Evangelicals believe that through the finished work of Christ on the cross, and by the power of the Spirit who intercedes for us, we may come directly and "boldly to the throne of grace" (Heb. 4:16 NKJV). Although the church triumphant and the church militant join together in common worship by means of the one Spirit (Rev. 5:6–14), there is no mention of prayers to Mary or the saints in the witness of the New Testament and the first two hundred years of the church. Irenaeus observed that the heretical gnostics invoked angels, but he offered no counterpart that the orthodox invoked saints; rather, they invoked the name of Christ alone (*Against Heresies* 1.23; 2.58).

As a safeguard against the temptation to idolatry and because this pattern of piety is not found in the New Testament, most Evangelicals today do not include prayers to Mary and the saints in their worship and personal devotions. At the same time, we acknowledge that the sovereign Lord may choose to reveal himself in extraordinary ways whenever and however he wills.

This Evangelical discussion of Mary raises the question of where we go from here. Our unity as brothers and sisters in Jesus Christ and our desire to move toward a common mission both require that we do so. We affirm with Max Thurian, Brother of Taizé, "Instead of being a cause of division amongst us, Christian reflections on the role of the Virgin Mary should be a cause of rejoicing and a source of prayer."[6] To that end, we Evangelicals offer a few suggestions.

- As theologians committed to unity in truth and unity in love, we will seek together the mind of Christ about Mary. We Evangelicals have sensed the loving pastoral concern of our Catholic partners, and we extend the same to them. We both want to avoid Marian excess on the one hand and Marian narrow-mindedness on the other, but we continue to differ on what is excessive and what is too restrictive. In our approach to one another, we desire the humility so evident in the mother of our Lord.

- Our different perspectives on Mary stem, in part, from our differing understandings of the church and its teaching authority. Both require further elaboration. More attention must also be given to the development of doctrine in the history of the church. Evangelicals need to explain how we can accept the doctrine of the Trinity and the person of Christ developed in the early church while not embracing some later developments. We ask further explanation from Catholics on how doctrinal deviation is checked and on how genuine reformation of dogma can take place.

- Mary's announcement of the kingdom's arrival signals the fulfillment of the biblical prophecy that both "sons and daughters" (Joel 2:28) will serve as instruments of God's grace as they declare his Word to each generation. The sanctity of life is a core conviction of Evangelicals and Catholics Together, and we should give more attention to Mary as a model and an encouragement in our efforts to advance the culture of life.

6. Max Thurian, *Mary, Mother of All Christians* (New York: Herder & Herder, 1964), 7.

- Evangelicals need to consider whether more reflection on Mary would strengthen their relationship with Jesus Christ. We cannot take the incarnation seriously without taking Mary as seriously as the Bible does. The theme of Mary in art, music, and literature is a treasury of the human imagination, but the messages are mixed, reflecting fluctuations in piety and teaching. In Matthias Grünewald's *Isenheim Altarpiece*, Mary and John the Baptist stand on either side of Jesus on the cross and both point to him. Marian devotion at its best ever reflects this posture, and from this kind of spirituality Evangelicals have much to learn.

- If Evangelicals are to recover a proper sense of Mary in the life of faith, it will be through the rediscovery of the Mary of the Bible. Together, Catholics and Evangelicals should study the Bible's witness to Mary—the prophecies of Genesis 3:15 and Isaiah 7:14; her annunciation, visitation, and purification; her witness to the miracles and ministry of Jesus; and her presence at Christmas, Calvary, and Pentecost. Evangelicals do not believe that we come to Jesus through Mary, but we confess that through Jesus we are one with Mary and with all those who, like her, trust in him alone as Savior and Lord. In this sense, Evangelicals and Catholics can sit together in the school of Mary. And thus we will see more clearly the face of God in the face of Christ, proclaiming salvation through his name and by his grace alone to all the world. *Soli Deo gloria!*

A Common Prayer

As Evangelicals and Catholics Together, we recognize that we have not addressed every point of our agreement and difference over Mary, her role in salvation history, and her continuing role in the life of the church. Nonetheless, we have attempted to indicate steps toward a deeper mutual understanding.

As brothers and sisters in Christ who are in lively communion with the saints on earth and the saints in heaven, we together pray—in words Richard John Neuhaus composed for us before he died (on January 8, 2009):

Almighty and gracious God, Father of our Lord and Savior Jesus Christ who was in the fullness of time born of the Blessed Virgin Mary, from whom he received our human nature by which, through his suffering, death, and glorious resurrection, he won our salvation, accept, we beseech you, our giving thanks for the witness of Mary's faith and the courage of her obedience.

Grant to us, we pray, the faithfulness to stand with her by the cross of your Son in his redemptive suffering and the suffering of your pilgrim church on earth. By the gift of your Spirit, increase within us a lively sense of our communion in your Son with the saints on earth and the saints in heaven. May she who is the first disciple be for us a model of faith's response to your will in all things; may her "Let it be with me according to your word" be our constant prayer; may her "Do whatever he tells you" elicit from us a more perfect surrender of obedience to her Lord and ours.

Continue to lead us, we pray, into a more manifest unity of faith and life so that the world may believe and those whom you have chosen may, with the Blessed Virgin Mary and all the saints, rejoice forever in your glory. This we ask in the name of Jesus Christ, who lives and reigns with you and the Holy Spirit, one God forever and forever.

Amen.

8

Freedom

Introduction

· GEORGE WEIGEL

Many of the scholars, pastors, and activists who later collaborated in Evangelicals and Catholics Together had long experience working for religious freedom abroad. Throughout the last decades of European communism, American and Canadian Evangelical Protestants and Catholics were active in organizations like Aid to the Church in Need, Christian Solidarity International, and the Institute on Religion and Democracy, all of which were deeply engaged in the struggle for freedom of worship, catechesis, and ministry behind the Iron Curtain and in Cuba, China, Vietnam, and other countries where Marxism's promise of freedom and equality was known to be a terrible lie. This experience of solidarity in defense of persecuted Christian brethren abroad was, in retrospect, one of the seedbeds from which the Evangelicals and Catholics Together project grew.

Background

That concern for religious freedom continued after the communist crack-up and was reflected in ECT's inaugural statement, which focused on problems created by the US Supreme Court's attempt to "balance" the "free exercise" and "no establishment" provisions of the First Amendment, often to the detriment of the free exercise of religious conviction, individually and corporately. ECT believed that this misconstrual of the Constitution inexorably led to the phenomenon that Richard John Neuhaus had dubbed the "naked public square," which both Evangelicals and Catholics understood as a profound distortion of democratic public life: if citizens were legally proscribed (or culturally discouraged) from bringing into public life the sources of their deepest moral convictions—which in America were, in the main, religious sources—then something was seriously awry in the American democratic experiment.[1]

Over the twenty years of Evangelicals and Catholics Together, that concern has not abated but intensified. It is one of the great ironies, and great tragedies, of the post–Cold War world that in democracies old and new, including the United States and Canada, religious conviction has been increasingly marginalized as a source of moral argument in public life. But that, ECT members might say, we saw coming. What few, if any, ECT participants could have imagined in 1994 was the dumbing down of the very concept of religious freedom that took place in the second decade of the third Christian millennium.

In the United States, for example, the Obama administration rarely if ever used the term "religious freedom" in describing its international human rights policy. Rather, it substituted "freedom of worship" for religious freedom and then linked that diminished notion of the first freedom to what Secretary of State Hillary Rodham Clinton described as the right to "love the way we choose"—code language for what had come to be known as the LGBT agenda. Domestically, in its implementation of the Affordable Care Act (Obamacare), the administration issued regulations that put severe pressure on religious

---

1. Richard John Neuhaus, *The Naked Public Square: Religion and Democracy in America* (Grand Rapids: Eerdmans, 1984).

institutions and religious employers to conform their health insurance policies to the "reproductive health" standards decreed by the US Department of Health and Human Services, which included the mandatory provision of contraceptives and abortion-inducing "contraceptive" drugs. Evangelical Protestant and Catholic institutions and employers joined forces with the Becket Fund for Religious Liberty and other public interest legal organizations to contest this gross abridgment of religious freedom. At the same time, the members of Evangelicals and Catholics Together believed it was necessary that a statement be made in support of religious freedom *in full*; the result was *In Defense of Religious Freedom*.

The Statement

In the conversations that preceded this statement, ECT emphasized time and again that religious freedom in full included both the right of individuals to believe, worship, witness, and conduct their professional and business lives as conviction and conscience required and the right of religious institutions to conduct their affairs according to their own creeds and moral codes. Religious conviction, ECT members insisted, is not a matter of personal lifestyle choice involving weekend leisure activities such as worship. Religious conviction is by its very nature community forming, and those communities ought to be able to conduct their affairs—ministry, religious education, social service, the provision of health care—in a manner consonant with their convictions. Here, ECT members were reiterating the legal position established in the United States by the 1993 Religious Freedom Restoration Act (RFRA) (which, in fact, some ECT members had helped conceive and shepherd through a congressional process marked by virtually unanimous bipartisan support). But such a reaffirmation of what seemed obvious in 1993 was, unfortunately, essential in 2012, after years of attempts by the Obama administration's Justice Department to hollow out RFRA.

These subtle, and sometimes not-so-subtle, forms of religious discrimination were apparent throughout the Western world. When a Canadian pastor is convicted by an ironically named "human rights tribunal" of engaging in "hate speech" for preaching biblical truth in his church, or when a British couple is forbidden to adopt children because of their Christian convictions about what a "family" means, the withering away of religious freedom in full is under way, just as much as it is when employers and Christian institutions face severe monetary penalties for refusing to bend their convictions to the conventions of "reproductive choice." That withering away of religious freedom was one warning signal that what Pope Benedict XVI called the "dictatorship of relativism"—the use of coercive state power to impose moral relativism on all of society—was not a fantasy but a disturbing aspect of contemporary public life, one that threatened the very foundations of Western democracy. In defending religious freedom, ECT believed we were defending the bedrock democratic idea that the state exists to serve civil society and cannot do so if it so encroaches on the social space occupied by civil society that that space effectively disappears. To defend religious freedom for all, ECT members believed, was to defend the limited, constitutional state against the tendency of all modern states to extend their power into every crevice of society.

ECT's membership was not only concerned about the cause of religious freedom in the West. Over the twenty years of the ECT project, persecution of Christians throughout the world had intensified, largely but not exclusively at the hands of Islamists and jihadists. There was nothing subtle about this phenomenon: Christians were being harassed, tortured, and murdered for their faith in the Lord Jesus Christ, and too often Western governments were content to let these atrocities pass in silence. It seemed to the members of Evangelicals and Catholics Together that a solemn obligation of solidarity required effective witness and action on behalf of persecuted brethren throughout the world; as such, ECT pledged to summon all the members of our communities to the fulfillment of that obligation.

ECT is profoundly aware that, in the twentieth and twenty-first centuries, we are living in the greatest period of persecution in Christian history. The witness of the martyrs calls to us from within the communion of saints, challenging us to be bold and unflagging in the defense of religious freedom in full and for all. At the same time, our obligations as citizens of two of the world's oldest democracies require us to be witnesses with our everyday neighbors, in the United States and Canada, to the threats to religious freedom that have been seeping into our societies, often unnoticed but never without consequences.

In Defense of Religious Freedom was intended to answer that call from those who have shed their blood for Christ in our times and to fulfill at least a part of that civic obligation.

In Defense of Religious Freedom

(2012)

Eighteen years ago, this fellowship of Evangelical and Catholic pastors, theologians, and educators was formed to deepen the dialogue among our communities on issues of common concern, to explore theological common ground, and to offer in public life a common witness born of Christian faith. Since our founding in 1994, we have addressed, together, such important public policy questions as the defense of life, even as we have proposed to our communities patterns of theological understanding on such long-disputed questions as the gift of salvation, the authority of Scripture, and the call to holiness in the communion of saints. We hope that this collaboration has been a service to both church and society; it has certainly drawn us closer together as brothers and sisters in Christ, and for that we are grateful to the Lord of all mercies.

At the beginning of our common work on behalf of the gospel, it did not seem likely that religious freedom would be one of our primary concerns. The communist project in Europe had collapsed; the commitment of Christian believers to defeat totalitarianism through the weapons of truth had triumphed; and throughout the world, a new era of religious freedom seemed at hand.

We are now concerned—indeed, deeply concerned—that religious freedom is under renewed assault around the world. While the threats to freedom of faith, religious practice, and religious participation in public affairs in Islamist and communist states are widely recognized, grave threats to religious freedom have also emerged in the developed democracies. In the West, certain religious beliefs are now regarded as bigoted. Pastors are under threat, both cultural and legal, for preaching biblical truth. Christian social-service and charitable agencies are forced to cease cooperation with the state because they

136

will not bend their work to what Pope Benedict XVI has called the "dictatorship of relativism."

Proponents of human rights, including governments, have begun to define religious freedom down, reducing it to a bare "freedom of worship." This reduction denies the inherently public character of biblical religion and privatizes the very idea of religious freedom, a view of freedom such as one finds in those repressive states where Christians can pray only so long as they do so behind closed doors. It is no exaggeration to see in these developments a movement to drive religious belief, and especially orthodox Christian religious and moral convictions, out of public life.

Given these circumstances, we offer this statement, *In Defense of Religious Freedom*, as a service due to God and to the common good. The God who gave us life gave us liberty. The God who has called us to faith asks that we defend the possibility that others may make similarly free acts of faith. By reaffirming the fundamental character of religious freedom, we contribute to the defense of freedom and to human flourishing, in our countries and throughout the world.

In making this statement, we confess, and we call all Christians to confess, that Christians have often failed to live the truths about freedom that we have preached: by persecuting one another, by persecuting those of other faiths, and by using coercive methods of proselytism. At times Christians have also employed the state as an instrument of religious coercion. Even some of the greatest leaders in the history of Christianity failed to live up to their own best ideals. As the Second Vatican Council's declaration on religious freedom, *Dignitatis Humanae*, puts it, "In the life of the People of God, as it has made its pilgrim way through the vicissitudes of human history, there has at times appeared a way of acting that was hardly in accord with the spirit of the Gospel or even opposed to it" (no. 12). It is this memory of Christian sinfulness that gives us all the more reason to defend the religious freedom of all men and women today.

What Religious Freedom Is

As believers in the God of Abraham, Isaac, and Jacob, who reveals himself fully in the Lord Jesus, we find the deepest source of religious freedom in the form or nature of the human person created by God. Human beings have been created with the capacity to know God, the will to seek God, and a spiritual thirst for God. In Genesis 1:26, the Bible teaches us that only human beings are made "in the image of God." No one bears this image (*imago Dei*) more than others; no one has the right to assert that by reason of race, tribe, ethnicity, class, or sex his imaging of God is superior to another.

In a world of manifest and innumerable inequalities, this radical equality of all men and women before God is the bond that allows us to speak meaningfully of a human family, a human race, in which we share mutual obligations—including the obligation to recognize and honor that sanctuary of conscience in which each person can meet the divine source of life. Any power, be it cultural or political, that puts unwarranted impediments in the path of the human quest for truth, which culminates in the human quest for God, is violating the order of creation.

These truths have already been stated in several Christian documents:

- In the 1986 *Instruction on Christian Freedom and Liberation* issued by the Congregation for the Doctrine of the Faith, we read that "God wishes to be adored by people who are free" (no. 44).
- In the National Association of Evangelicals' 2006 *Statement on Religious Freedom*, this fundamental freedom is described as "the distinctive characteristic of the American project—what Roger Williams called 'the livelie experiment.' . . . It is an inalienable right that precedes the state itself."
- In the 2010 *Cape Town Commitment*, Evangelical Christians of the Lausanne Movement declared, "Let us strive for the goal of religious freedom for all people. This requires advocacy before governments on behalf of Christians and people of other faiths who are persecuted."

Human freedom, and especially religious freedom, reflects God's design for creation and his pattern of redemption. Religious freedom is thus grounded in the character of God as revealed in the Bible *and* in the moral structure of the world that we can know through reason. It is precisely as Evangelical and Catholic Christians that we affirm, on the authority of the Bible, religious freedom for all, even as we are prepared to defend religious freedom in public life through arguments drawn from reason.

Religious freedom is a fundamental right. As the American founders put it, it is "unalienable." Religious freedom is thus a right that exists before the state. The just state recognizes this right of persons and protects it in law. In doing so, the state recognizes the limits of its own capacity: it cannot coerce consciences; it cannot compel belief. For the state that recognizes and protects religious freedom is not an omnicompetent state, but rather a state that acknowledges the rights of conscience and the prerogatives of the institutions that men and women freely sustain to express and pass on their religious convictions. It recognizes its duty to serve, and not to impede, those communities of civil society. Thus the recognition of religious freedom in full is a crucial barrier to the totalitarian temptation that seems to exist in all forms of political modernity.

In sum, religious freedom has both personal and public dimensions. It is grounded in the dignity of the human person as possessed of a thirst for the truth and a capacity to know it. The state that recognizes religious freedom as inherent and inalienable, a civil right protected by law, thereby acknowledges its incompetence over the sanctuary of human conscience. Religious freedom is fundamental both to the freedom of the individual human person and to the sustaining of just and limited governments.

The Genealogy of Religious Freedom

It is because Evangelicals and Catholics Together confess Jesus Christ as head of the church and of our consciences that we insist that there can be no compulsion whatsoever in the act of faith. Here, the Lord himself is our witness.

The New Testament, whose basic confession of faith was distilled by the first generation of Christians to the simple affirmation that "Jesus is Lord," never depicts Jesus the Lord as coercing faith. Quite the contrary: Jesus reasoned with his listeners, instructed them in parables, called them to repent, and invited them to believe the good news of God's kingdom. When his disciples asked him to call down fire from heaven to destroy those who refused to receive him, Jesus rebuked them (Luke 9:52–55). Shortly thereafter, Jesus sent his disciples on a mission with the explicit instruction to respect others' freedom (Luke 10:1–12). Even the Risen One, whom the church confesses as the Lord of the cosmos and of history, speaks of himself as one who invites: "Behold, I stand at the door and knock; if anyone hears my voice and opens the door, I will come in and eat with him, and him with me" (Rev. 3:20). The first chapters in the history of the church, the Acts of the Apostles, show the first Christians preaching conversion and demonstrating by the quality of their lives and their witness that God's kingdom is "established" by the ministry of the Word and the works of the Holy Spirit (Acts 12:24). They acknowledged the authority and value of the state (Rom. 13) even as they recognized the limits of its reach (Acts 5:29).

Recognizing the failures of Christians to live in accord with these convictions in the past, we also ask that the history of religious freedom be understood in its full amplitude. The genealogy of religious freedom is a rich and complex one; its story does not begin in modern times. It begins in the Jewish and Christian understanding of human dignity and freedom.

In the fourth century, Lactantius (whom the Renaissance humanists called the "Christian Cicero") wrote, "Religion cannot be a matter of coercion." A century later, the greatest of the Latin fathers of the church, St. Augustine, wrote in his *Commentary on the Gospel of St. John*, "When force is applied, the will cannot be aroused. You can be compelled to enter a church against your will; to approach the altar against your will; to receive the sacrament against your will. But you cannot believe against your will. No one can believe except willingly."[2] The greatest of the medieval theologians, St. Thomas Aquinas, insisted that no one should be compelled to the faith "because to believe depends on the will" (*Summa theologiae*, II-II, q. 10, a.8).

In his 1523 treatise *Temporal Authority: To What Extent It Should Be Obeyed*, Martin Luther declared that the state has no authority

---

2. *The Works of Saint Augustine: A Translation for the 21st Century; Homilies on the Gospel of John*, trans. Edmund Hill (New York: New City Press, 2009), 451.

over the soul, and he demarcated the limits of government in the spiritual realm: "It has laws which extend no further than to life and property and external affairs on earth, for God cannot and will not permit anyone but himself to rule over the soul. Therefore, where the temporal authority presumes to prescribe laws for the soul, it encroaches upon God's government and only misleads souls and destroys them." Luther's contemporary John Calvin believed that in the face of "overbearing tyranny," a Christian must "venture boldly to groan for freedom" (Letter 136). He protested the intrusions on the church's freedoms of assembly and speech.

In early American history, the Puritan dissenter Roger Williams founded the colony of Rhode Island in the conviction that the bloody persecution of men for their religious convictions was "contrary to Scripture." In the sixth point of his *Plea for Religious Liberty* (1644), Williams wrote that it is "the will and command of God" that permission be granted to Jews, Muslims, and other non-Christians alike in their worship and in the exercise of their consciences, so that the only sword used in matters of the soul should be "the sword of God's Spirit, the Word of God." Just before the American Revolution, the Baptist pastor Isaac Backus grounded his *Appeal to the Public for Religious Liberty* (1773) in the teaching and example of Jesus, stating that "our Lord has most plainly forbidden us, either to assume or to submit to any such [compulsion] in religion."

In our own time, the 2010 Lausanne *Cape Town Commitment* called Christians to "being committed to advocate and speak up for those who are voiceless under the violation of their human rights," and declared, "Let us strive for the goal of religious freedom for all people. This requires advocacy before governments on behalf of Christians *and* people of other faiths who are persecuted."

Finally, the Second Vatican Council, after careful consultation with Protestant observers, summarized and restated many of these themes in *Dignitatis Humanae*. We, as Evangelicals and Catholics Together, fully affirm the teaching of this declaration that

> the human person has a right to religious freedom. This freedom means that all men are to be immune from coercion on the part of individuals or of social groups or of any human power, in such wise

that no one is to be forced to act in a manner contrary to his own beliefs, whether privately or publicly, whether alone or in association with others, within due limits. . . . This right of the human person to religious freedom is to be recognized in the constitutional law whereby society is governed and thus it is to become a civil right. (no. 2)

Religious Freedom in the Architecture of Democracy

As we have argued, just government recognizes and protects those rights that are built into human nature by God and that can be known by both reason and revelation. The most basic of these fundamental rights is religious freedom, which is most basic because it touches what is deepest in the human spirit: our thirst for the truth, which Christians believe is in fact a thirst for God. Religious freedom, then, grounds the freedom of speech, of assembly, of the press, and all other freedoms. Absent religious freedom, there is no freedom in the deepest meaning of the word. Absent religious freedom, democracy crumbles.

The fundamental human right of religious freedom precludes the establishment of a religion to which all citizens must conform. That is why the First Amendment to the United States Constitution wisely links the free exercise of religion to its prohibition of "laws respecting an establishment of religion." The prohibition of an establishment of religion is one crucial means to advance the end of the free exercise of religion. Thus "no establishment" and "free exercise" are not in tension, as much modern jurisprudence understands them to be. Nor does "no establishment" demand a naked public square, shorn of religiously informed moral conviction. The "separation of church and state" is intended to protect freedom *for* religious conviction; it is not intended to promote religion's exile from public life.

It is essential for the full expression of religious freedom that believers be welcome, in law and in social custom, to bring their religiously based moral convictions into the ongoing public debate over how we ought to order our common life. Religiously informed moral argument does not establish religion or impose sectarian values on a pluralistic society. Such charges are undemocratic, for they deny to fellow citizens and religious communities the right to bring the sources of their deepest convictions into public life. For their part, believers often have the resources to make their arguments in the public square in ways that every citizen, irrespective of religious belief or the lack thereof, can engage. Thus we seek neither a naked nor a sacred public square, but a civil public square open to the full range of convictions.

Religious Freedom in Peril

As the Pew Forum on Religion and Public Life has noted, Christians face harassment in more countries than any other religious group. In the words of the World Evangelical Alliance, Christians are "the largest single group in the world . . . being denied human rights on the basis of their faith."

Overt persecution of Christians is widespread in many Islamic societies. Christians are murdered by radical Islamists in churches in Egypt and Iraq. Bibles are not permitted in Saudi Arabia, and the Saudi national curriculum continues to teach students to "kill" Jews and apostates, view Christians as enemies, and spread the Islamic faith through "jihad"—a teaching it promotes by funding the distribution of extremist textbooks throughout the world. In some Islamic states, conversion to another religion is a capital offense. In Iran, a Christian pastor who refused to recant his faith has been brought to trial for apostasy. In Pakistan, blasphemy laws forbid any criticism, however mild, of Islam. Muslim persecution of Christians is not confined to one area of the world, for these practices can be found in Indonesia and northern Nigeria as well as the Middle East, North Africa, the Persian Gulf, and the Indian subcontinent. Nor is it likely that the "Arab Spring" will lead to a springtime of religious freedom in the Islamic heartland and beyond. Indeed, if radical Islamists come to power, the situation of Christians and other religious minorities will become even more perilous.

Islamic societies are not alone in their persecution of Christians. The remaining communist states in Asia—North Korea, the People's Republic of China, and Vietnam—and "postcommunist" states such as Belarus, Turkmenistan, and Uzbekistan restrict religious freedom in their determination to control all aspects of social life. In India,

Christians are persecuted by Hindu radicals who burn orphanages and schools for no reason other than their Christian sponsorship; here, too, conversion to Christ can be life-threatening.

Religious freedom is under assault even in countries where the language of human rights is part of the public moral vocabulary. In Canada, for example, Evangelical pastors have been fined by "human rights commissions" for preaching biblical morality in matters of human sexuality. In Great Britain, couples have been denied foster children because of their commitment to teach the young the moral truths inscribed in the Bible. In Poland, a Catholic magazine editor was fined by a court for speaking the truth about abortion. In these and other instances, coercive state power is being deployed to impose a secularist agenda on society while driving religious faith and practice out of public life.

By these and other means, "religious freedom" is reduced to a private lifestyle choice. In Europe and Canada, what amounts to state-established secularism erodes the exercise of full religious freedom by impeding the public witness of Christian communities. It also substantially threatens the free exercise of religious belief in preaching and catechesis.

In the United States, religious freedom is being encroached upon and reduced through the courts, in administrative policy, and in our culture. For example, the Equal Employment Opportunity Commission (EEOC), through the office of the solicitor general, recently challenged the long-standing interpretation of the "ministerial exception" to antidiscrimination and other employment laws in *Hosanna-Tabor v. EEOC*. The legal arguments presented by officials from the executive branch of government would have dramatically reduced the constitutional protections that allow Christian communities to choose their ministers according to their own criteria. Fortunately, in a unanimous decision, the Supreme Court of the United States affirmed the ministerial exception.

While the Supreme Court has protected the right to determine religious leaders, the capacity of religious believers to form and sustain distinctive institutions is threatened today. The United States Department of Health and Human Services has proposed "preventive services" regulations that require provision of FDA-approved contraceptives, including abortifacients like Ella, and sterilization. These regulations threaten the religious freedom of insurers, employers, schools, and other religious enterprises that conscientiously oppose contraception and abortion. Limiting conscience protections to those in religious institutions that serve only their own members, as some have proposed, criminalizes the public witness of religious organizations such as Catholic universities and other religious social welfare institutions.

Administrative and regulatory policies pose further threats to religious freedom. Christian doctors, nurses, pharmacists, and other health-care providers are being put at professional risk by policies that compel all health-care workers to undertake procedures and provide prescription drugs that many of them regard as immoral.

We also note that the attempt to redefine marriage through coercive state power has already brought pressure to bear on Christian ministers, despite exceptions provided in legislation. Further, in no state where the redefinition of marriage has passed the legislature has the religious institution exception provided all the religious freedom protections needed for individuals and groups that oppose the legalization of same-sex unions in those states.

The Renewal of Religious Freedom

We live in the greatest period of persecution in the history of Christianity. In the twentieth century, noble martyrs like Dietrich Bonhoeffer and Blessed Jerzy Popieluszko gave their lives for Christ amid a cloud of witnesses greater in number than those martyred for the Name in the previous nineteen centuries of Christian history. That witness continues today in the self-sacrifice of men like Shahbaz Bhatti, a Christian cabinet officer murdered because of his defense of the religious freedom of all of his fellow Pakistanis.

As Evangelicals and Catholics who seek to honor the witness of these and other martyrs, we pledge to work together for the renewal of religious freedom in our countries and around the world. We will resist the legal pressure brought on Christians in the medical profession, the armed forces, and elsewhere to participate in actions that they deem immoral on the grounds of both faith and reason.

We acknowledge that the state enjoys its own sphere of competence. But we remind the modern democratic state that it is a limited state. We applaud the United States Supreme Court's decision to sustain the long-held ministerial exception. In the same spirit of concern for religious liberty, we ask that legislators formulate explicit conscience protections for health-care workers. And we counsel legislators to intervene and reverse the coercive efforts at the Department of Health and Human Services and other agencies to mandate health coverage and adoption procedures that will force religious institutions to betray their foundational principles. In these and other areas, we must vigilantly defend religious freedom.

We also join together in asking our federal governments to defend religious freedom in conducting the foreign policy of the United States and Canada. We recognize the complexities into which such a commitment inevitably leads; we also see the evidence of history, which teaches that religiously free societies are better for their people, and safer for the world, than societies in which persecution is culturally and legally affirmed. Thus we call on our public officials to undertake prudent measures to advance the cause of religious freedom in full.

In all of this, we believe we are acting as Christians have been commanded to act and speaking as citizens of mature democracies ought to speak. Our faith in Jesus Christ as Lord and Savior, and our baptism in the name of the Most Holy Trinity, compels us to defend the religious freedom of all who are created in the image of God. Our gratitude for the religious freedom that has been a hallmark of North America for over two centuries compels us to work to defend religious freedom in the United States and Canada and to work for the religious freedom of others in all lands. For the sake of the common good, we, Evangelicals and Catholics Together, urge our fellow citizens and our public officials to join us in the renewal of religious freedom: to defend religious freedom for all persons and to guard against its erosion in our societies.

9

Marriage

Introduction

TIMOTHY GEORGE AND THOMAS G. GUARINO

ECT has harbored long-standing concerns about the state of marriage in North America and in the Western world in general. Marriage, which is both a Christian and a natural reality, is the very foundation of society and civilization. It has been significantly weakened in the late twentieth and early twenty-first centuries by several factors: divorce has become widespread; there exists an easygoing acceptance of premarital sex and cohabitation; out-of-wedlock births have notably increased; a contraceptive mentality has taken hold of many couples; and, in general, there has been a commodification of human sexuality.

Background

These factors alone would have impelled Evangelicals and Catholics Together to address the institution of marriage from a biblical and theological perspective. But the advent of same-sex "marriage" has

147

added a powerful urgency to our deliberations. How has the institution of marriage been lived across various times and cultures? Most crucially, what does biblical revelation and human reason teach us about the nature of marriage?

For two years, these questions were ardently discussed by ECT. During that time, we reached virtual unanimity on the biblical teaching about marriage. While a few matters still separate us, such as the permissibility of divorce and contraception (and even here we are much closer than is usually thought), we are completely united on the fundamental truth that is under challenge by contemporary culture: that marriage is a lifelong covenantal union based on the complementarity of men and women. The most recent ECT statement is evidence of our common witness concerning the biblical truth about marriage and family life.

Contemporary society now leans—and leans strongly—toward the position that we inhabit a world of competing and multiple interpretations without a clearly defined center. As a consequence, it is more and more held that civil society must tolerate—and, indeed, must endorse—any nonviolent point of view. Only by sanctioning a wide-ranging tolerance, it is argued, will justice and equality be achieved. In this view, we must learn to live with a vast panorama of interpretations concerning the nature and meaning of life, including the nature and meaning of marriage. Marriage is no longer "given" to us as a preexistent reality inscribed in the very form of the world, a reality that serves as a criterion and norm for human action. Rather, we are told, men and women must be allowed to *create* truth and meaning through their personal and autonomous interpretations of human existence, including their interpretation of the institution of marriage. But this position—that human beings create their own understanding of life and of reality itself—is at antipodes with the natural and Christian understanding of marriage. And this difference is at the root of the ongoing conflict over how justice properly reigns in contemporary society.

The Statement

In answer to this increasingly accepted point of view—that one creates the truth and meaning about marriage through one's subjective interpretation—ECT juxtaposes the understanding that is sanctioned by Holy Scripture: marriage is a privileged sign of Christ's union with his church, and it only serves as that sign when a man and a woman are joined together in a stable union.

Of course, the statement adds that the complementarity of male and female in marriage has been the rule and norm across diverse cultures for millennia. There is a discernible "form"—and so a discernible truth—mediated by the world which is not simply the result of the individual's self-definition. Marriage is not subject, then, to a supposed "plasticity" or malleability whereby the institution can be re-imaged in variable and self-determined forms. Virtually all societies have recognized this natural meaning of marriage.

But the present document concentrates on the Christian and biblical understanding of marriage. Among the statement's principal affirmations are these: marriage is not a socially constructed reality but is rooted in the nature of humanity itself; human beings have a nature which is given by God and which must be respected. Only in this way is true freedom fulfilled. Important Christian teachers—Augustine, Luther, Calvin, and the bishops gathered at Vatican II—have with one voice defended marriage as a stable and permanent union between a man and a woman. They and the entire Christian tradition teach, with St. Paul's Letter to the Ephesians, that the marriage bond represents the union existing between Christ and his church. Indeed, if Christians cannot affirm the uniqueness of marriage between a man and a woman, they can no longer affirm that marriage is a "profound mystery," a supernatural sign of Christ's relationship with his bride, the church.

Christians have every right to affirm this understanding in the public square. As Evangelicals and Catholics Together stated in its original 1994 statement and has repeated frequently in subsequent years, the "separation of church and state" can never mean the separation of public life and public policy from the moral convictions of the nation's citizenry. Trying to separate religious and moral beliefs from public life represents the discredited attempt to impose upon society a naked public square—as if there exists a "value-free" point of view that is not itself riddled with prior theoretical commitments.

As this ECT statement makes clear, Christians are already experiencing censure for upholding the truth about marriage. This will likely continue and, indeed, grow more intense in the future. Speech about marriage is already being assiduously policed and the new orthodoxy zealously imposed. Those who refuse to conform are increasingly regarded as outside the boundaries of reasonable and humane discourse. But intensified intolerance toward the biblical and Christian understanding of marriage will cause us neither to yield in our convictions nor to tire of their firm defense.

Future Prospects

From its foundation in 1994, Evangelicals and Catholics Together has dedicated itself to specifically theological issues and to cultural issues harboring significant theological dimensions. In this statement on marriage, these two elements are conjoined inasmuch as the institution of marriage is both a universal reality and one about which the Bible teaches at great length, in both the Old and New Testaments.

The present statement deals primarily with marriage and only tangentially with human sexuality. While the issue of same-sex "marriage" was a significant trigger for our discussions, this document is not about human sexuality and Christian life per se. ECT could profitably examine the issue of sexuality and faithful Christian discipleship in the future. Men and women are embodied, sexual beings. How are we to understand human sexuality in the clear light of divine truth? How, for example, are single men and women—both those with heterosexual and those with homosexual inclinations—to be brought more fully and effectively into the following of Christ and the life of the church? How can Christians best respond to the degradation of sexuality that has taken place in many societies, particularly through pornography and the exaltation of fornication and adultery frequently found in the media? Our common, biblical faith on the vast majority of issues related to human sexuality is strong and undivided. How can ECT place that biblical understanding at the fruitful service of the church and of society at large?

The Two Shall Become One Flesh: Reclaiming Marriage

(2015)

In the Gospel of St. Mark, the Lord Jesus teaches that "from the beginning of creation God made them male and female." He then declares a great and beautiful truth inscribed in creation: "For this reason a man shall leave his father and mother and be joined to his wife, and the two shall become one flesh. So they are no longer two but one flesh" (Mark 10:6–8).

For centuries, Christians have proclaimed these words at weddings, for they express the gift of marriage long recognized by all humanity and acknowledged by men and women of faith: marriage is the union of a man and a woman. This truth is being obscured, even denied, today. Because of that, the institution of marriage, which is essential to the well-being of society, is being undermined.

As Christians, it is our responsibility to bear witness to the truth about marriage as taught by both revelation and reason—by the Holy Scriptures and by the truths inscribed on the human heart. These age-old truths explain why Christians celebrate marriage—the coming together of a man and woman in a binding union of mutual support—as one of the glories of the human race. Marriage is the primordial human institution, a reality that existed long before the establishment of what we now know as the state.

As the most venerable and reliable basis for domestic happiness, marriage is the foundation of a just and stable society. Yet in our times this institution has been gravely weakened by the sexual revolution and the damage it has done to marriage and the family: widespread divorce; the dramatic increase in out-of-wedlock births; the casual acceptance of premarital sex and cohabitation; and a contraceptive mentality which insists that sex has an arbitrary relation to procreation. In this environment, families fragment, the poor suffer, and children are especially vulnerable and at risk. The decline of marriage culture is evident throughout the world, and where it is evident, the common good is imperiled.

Christians have too often been silent about biblical teaching on sex, marriage, and family life. Too many have accommodated themselves to the spirit of our age. As Evangelicals and Catholics who speak to and from our various communities of faith, we are committed to setting forth the Christian teaching on marriage. In a few matters, we do not speak with one voice: we hold somewhat different views about the morality of contraception, the legitimacy of divorce, and clerical celibacy. But on the crucial and fundamental truth that marriage is a stable union based on the complementarity of male and female, we are fully united.

In this statement we speak as Christians to Christians, using the language of the faith. Our hope is to clarify and reclaim the truth about marriage. If we are to remain faithful to the Scriptures and to the unanimous testimony of Christian tradition, there can be no compromise on marriage. We cannot allow our witness to be obscured by the confusions into which our culture and society have fallen. Drawing our confidence from the Lord's own Word, we take to heart the apostle's injunction: "Preach the word, be urgent in season and out of season, convince, rebuke, and exhort, be unfailing in patience and in teaching" (2 Tim. 4:2).

Marriage, Christianly Considered

> God created man in his own image, in the image of God he created him; male and female he created them. And God blessed them and God said to them, "Be fruitful and multiply." (Gen. 1:27–28)

Maleness, femaleness, and their complementarity are among the central organizing principles of creation. When, in the biblical flood account, Noah brings the entire animal kingdom onto the ark, he does so in pairs: male and female. Maleness and femaleness are essential components of our unique dignity as human beings created in the image of God, for through these realities we participate in the divine creativity and its fruitfulness. Thus, from a Christian point of view, sexual union must be approached with reverence and in recognition of its intrinsic potential for new life.

Our sexual acts have spiritual and moral dimensions; they are not merely physical or biological. The Old Testament often uses sexual imagery to describe how well or how poorly we are living our relationship to God (marital fidelity, nuptial joy, fertility, harlotry, sexual defilement, and childlessness). For good or ill, our sexual acts affect the image of God we bear. What we do sexually either honors or dishonors the imprint of the divine that is uniquely borne by human beings. As Jesus teaches, this is even true of sexual desire: "Every one who looks at a woman lustfully has already committed adultery with her in his heart" (Matt. 5:28). Thus Christians, instructed by the Lord, have, from the earliest days of the church, taught an ethic of sexual self-discipline, recognizing that sex involves our souls as well as our bodies.

> Therefore a man leaves his father and his mother and cleaves to his wife, and they become one flesh. (Gen. 2:24)

Marriage creates "one body," a new reality, ennobling the sexual union of a man and a woman by ordering it toward a common life that promotes the good of the couple, the family, and the community as a whole. Marriage creates a unique social union not based on blood relations or common descent ("a man *leaves* his father and his mother and cleaves to his wife"); thus marriage is also the primordial institution of human society. Martin Luther called it the "first estate," which precedes both church and civil government. As such, the institution of marriage is a foundation of a just political order and the nursery of civic virtue, as spouses exercise mutual responsibility for raising their children.

> What therefore God has joined together, let not man put asunder. (Mark 10:9)

When challenged about the lawfulness of divorce, Jesus cited Genesis, stating clearly that the human act of joining together in marriage is at the same time God's work. We leave our parents and cleave to our spouses—a human act encouraged by our sexual instincts and shaped by the historical institution of marriage—*and* God joins us together. Because God's grace is at work in marriage, Jesus teaches us that our marital unions are capable of lifelong fidelity, signified by the prophet's use of marriage as an image of God's enduring covenant with Israel: "I have loved you with an everlasting love" (Jer. 31:3). In the union created by marriage, the Lord affirms, we participate in the power of God's everlasting love. Though the dissolution of marriages is treated differently in various Christian churches, we together confess that marriage was originally ordained by God to be indissoluble.

> For this reason a man shall leave his father and mother and be joined to his wife, and the two shall become one flesh. This mystery is a profound one, and I am saying that it refers to Christ and the church. (Eph. 5:31–32)

Like Jesus, Paul the apostle quotes the teaching of Genesis that, when a man leaves his parents and cleaves to his wife, he is united with her in one flesh. But Paul also teaches that the bond between man and woman in marriage is a great sign of the union between Christ and the church. It is, the apostle writes, a "profound mystery" that signifies the intimate relation between Christ and his bride, the church (Rev. 21:2), and proclaims Christ's unifying power, which in his death and resurrection "has broken down the dividing wall of hostility" between Jew and gentile (Eph. 2:14), making the Lord himself "our peace." In this bond of peace, the church comes together as one body, sharing "one Lord, one faith, one baptism, one God and Father of us all" (Eph. 4:5–6). Marriage, similarly, is a bond of peace, in which male and female find their intended unity. In Christ Jesus, marriage serves as a redemptive sign that the great chasm separating creature from Creator has been bridged and that the original unity intended by God has been restored, both among us and between humanity and its Creator.

As Evangelicals and Catholics we do not agree on the status of marriage as a sacrament of the church. But we affirm strongly and without qualification, following the clear testimony of Holy Scripture, that *marriage is a unique and privileged sign of the union of Christ with his people and of God with his Creation—and it can only serve as that sign when a man and a woman are solemnly joined together in a permanent union.*

Christian Teachers

For two millennia, great Christian teachers have proclaimed the biblical understanding of marriage. In the early church, Augustine defined the three goods of marriage. The first good is *children*: marriage provides the fitting and proper context for us to fulfill our natural desire for sexual union, to respect the intrinsic possibility of fertility in that union, and to accept responsibility for the children that union produces. The second good is *fidelity*: as a social institution supported by cultural and legal sanctions, marriage encourages an exclusive commitment that expresses what is noblest in the human aspiration to solidarity and that calls us beyond the selfishness and self-centeredness that can erode and ultimately destroy social life. Augustine also identifies a third good, *permanence*: marriage is a natural *sign* pointing toward a supernatural reality. He refers here to the mysterious way in which marriage creates an indissoluble bond that points us toward God's covenantal fidelity. As the prophet Hosea said: "I will betroth you to me forever; I will betroth you to me in righteousness and in justice, in steadfast love, and in mercy" (Hos. 2:19).

Martin Luther, too, saw marriage as a sign that points beyond itself to even greater truths, as he taught in his sermon "On the Estate of Marriage":

> The Church's great teachers say that marriage is a sacrament. A sacrament is a sacred sign of something spiritual, holy, heavenly, and eternal. . . . It is an outward and spiritual sign of the greatest, holiest, worthiest, and noblest thing that has ever existed or ever will exist: the union of the divine and the human natures in Christ. The holy apostle Paul says that as man and wife united in the estate of matrimony are two in one flesh, so God and man are united in the one person Christ, and so Christ and Christendom are one body. It is indeed a wonderful

sacrament, as Paul says (Eph. 5:32), that the estate of marriage truly signifies such a great reality. Is it not a wonderful thing that God is man and that he gives himself to man and will be his, just as the husband gives himself to his wife and is hers? But if God is ours, then everything is ours. Consider this matter with the respect it deserves. Because the union of man and woman signifies such a great mystery, the estate of marriage has to have this special significance.[1]

Luther also addressed the question of who can marry, stressing the complementarity of male and female:

Therefore, each one of us must have the kind of body God has created for us. I cannot make myself a woman, nor can you make yourself a man; we do not have that power. But we are exactly as he created us: I a man and you a woman. . . . Each should honor the other's image and body as a divine and good creation that is well-pleasing.[2]

John Calvin understood marriage as a covenant based on God's covenant with us. Like Luther, Calvin held that God is the author of marriage:

When a marriage takes place between a man and a woman, God presides and requires a mutual pledge from both. Hence Solomon in Proverbs 2:17 calls marriage the covenant of God, for it is superior to all human contracts. So also Malachi (2:14) declares that God as it were makes the marriage and by his authority joins the man to the woman, and sanctions the alliance. . . .[3] Marriage is not ordained by men. We know that God is its author and that it is solemnized in his name. The Scripture says that it is a holy covenant, and therefore calls it divine.[4]

The fathers of the Second Vatican Council sounded similar themes in their teaching on marriage in the *Pastoral Constitution on the Church in the Modern World*:

1. *Luther's Works* (Philadelphia: Fortress, 1966), 44:10.
2. Ibid., 45:17–18.
3. John Calvin, *Commentaries on the Twelve Minor Prophets*, vol. 5, *Zechariah and Malachi*, trans. John Owen (Edinburgh: Calvin Translation Society, 1849), 552–53.
4. John Calvin, *Sermons on the Epistle to the Ephesians* (Edinburgh: The Banner of Truth Trust, 1973), 565.

God himself is the author of marriage and has endowed it with various benefits and with various ends in view: all of these have a very important bearing on the continuation of the human race, on the personal development and eternal destiny of every member of the family, on the dignity, stability, peace, and prosperity of the family and of the whole human race. By their very nature the institution of marriage and married love are ordered to the procreation and education of offspring and find in them their crowning glory. Thus the man and the woman, who are "no longer two but one" (Matt. 19:6), help and serve each other by their marriage partnership; they become conscious of their unity and experience it more deeply from day to day. . . . Christ the Lord has abundantly blessed this love, which is rich in its various features, coming as it does from the spring of divine love and modeled on Christ's own union with the Church. . . . Authentic married love is caught up into divine love and enriched by the redemptive power of Christ . . . with the result that the spouses are effectively led to God . . . and together they render glory to God. (no. 48)

Our Situation Today

Marriage is in crisis throughout the Western world. The data from the United States alone tell an unmistakable—and unmistakably sad—story. Fifty years ago, some 70 percent of American adults were married; today the figure is just over 50 percent. Then, more than 90 percent of children lived with their natural parents; today fewer than two-thirds do. The birth rate has declined, and the abortion rate has climbed from less than 1 percent of live births to over 20 percent.

Everyone suffers from the current crisis in marriage, but some suffer more than others. A growing class divide is becoming alarmingly clear. College-educated men and women marry and are unlikely to get divorced. The less educated are less likely to marry, and those who do so are three times more likely to get divorced. Rates of illegitimacy are even more striking. A very small percentage of college-educated women have children out of wedlock (6 percent). Nearly half of women without a college education now have children out of wedlock.

In considering the demise of marriage culture and the decline of the institution of marriage, we are profoundly aware of the challenge posed by the Lord, that "as you did it to one of the least of these my brethren, you did it to me" (Matt. 25:40). The effects of the decline of marriage on children are dramatic, unequal, and deeply disturbing. Among the well-educated and economically well-off, the traditional family remains the norm. This is no longer true for children born to less educated and less affluent women. By age fourteen, nearly half these children no longer live with both parents, posing dire consequences for their futures. Young men raised in broken families are more likely to go to prison. Young women in these circumstances are more likely to become pregnant as unwed teenagers. The dramatic decline of marriage is a major factor in the misery of many in our society.

The erosion of marriage degrades our common culture as well. A contraceptive mentality encourages the notion of sex as purely recreational, a matter of private pleasure. Widespread divorce and serial cohabitation undermine our sense of stability and commitment in human relations.

Christians are implicated in this decline. Evangelicals and Catholics are more likely to divorce than they were fifty years ago. Moreover, Christians have adopted to no small extent the contraceptive mindset that in society at large has separated sex from reproduction and so weakened the centrality and attraction of marriage.

Too often, Christians lack the courage to which both the cross and resurrection summon us. Like the disciples taken aback at Jesus's strong words about divorce, we shrink from the full truth and deny the nobility of Christian teaching on sexuality, making excuses for our own failures and for those in our communities. We fail to hold one another and our communities accountable. We forget that the covenant of marriage carries obligations of fidelity and mutual love and is morally binding on the spouses. We forget that the Bible again and again reminds us we must die to sin and live solely for Christ.

The words of the Ten Commandments, "Thou shalt not commit adultery" (Exod. 20:14), are reaffirmed in the New Testament (Rom. 13:9). Drawing on the Scriptures, Christian teaching about human sexuality seeks to respect the sanctity of marriage and to guard its potential for a deep and lasting union. We cannot reclaim marriage unless we reclaim the clear Christian witness that our sexual desires must be ordered to their proper end: male-female union in the context of marriage.

A Parody of Marriage

The crisis of marriage culture in our times now poses a direct and fundamental challenge to the very nature of marriage. By redefining marriage to allow a union between two persons of the same sex— Spouse 1 and Spouse 2—a kind of alchemy is performed, not merely on the institution, but on human nature itself. In such a world, the distinction between men and women is denied social recognition, and marriage is no longer a unique bond uniting male and female. It becomes an instrument created by the state to give official status to the relationship between two generic human beings.

In these circumstances, what the state defines as marriage no longer embodies God's purposes in creation. An easy acceptance of divorce damages marriage; widespread cohabitation devalues marriage. But so-called same-sex marriage is a graver threat, because what is now given the name of marriage in law is a parody of marriage.

We are today urged to embrace an abstract conception of human nature that ignores the reality of our bodies: human beings are no longer to be understood as either male or female. Our culture encourages us to exalt our personal desires and choices over the created order. Instead of freely accepting God's gift, we seek to dominate (and even alter) nature, constructing our own moral truths. The result is a deceptive pseudo-freedom that degrades our humanity. Genuine freedom is found in obedience to God's order: in freely choosing, as a matter of grace and moral habit, what is good and what makes for true beatitude.

No one should doubt or deny what is at stake here. To sustain the fiction of same-sex marriage, the natural family must be deconstructed. Birth certificates will no longer list "father's name" and "mother's name" but Parent 1/Parent 2, a change already made on certificates issued in some jurisdictions that recognize same-sex marriage. In this brave new world, the family—the institution on which our social order rests—is being redefined as a socially constructed unit, constituted by our sovereign will, not by nature itself. And if a "family" is anything I want or choose it to be, the corrosive individualism that already leaves too many people lonely and disconnected in twenty-first-century Western society is intensified.

For centuries, parents of adopted children have been acknowledged as legal parents. And we warmly commend the generous practice of adoption. But this was understood as a humane exception to the more fundamental rule of natural descent.

Today, however, the most basic principles of family life are being reconstructed around exceptions. Because the male-female difference must be erased to make way for same-sex marriage, the procreative potential of the male-female union must be set aside as well. A child's parents are whomever legal documents designate as Parent 1 or Parent 2—or, as California documents now allow, Parent 3 or Parent 4. Thus, children are exposed to the risk of coming into the world as strangers, in which the biological ties that form the natural family are arbitrarily broken. The law no longer recognizes the primordial, complementary natural roles of mother and father. The natural family as the fundamental context defining where we have come from and who we are is set aside. The family becomes a creation of the state, and where the family is a creation of the state, children become, in important legal respects, the property of the state.

The revolution in our marriage and family law, already well advanced, marches under the banners of freedom and equality. But these noble ideals are here gravely misapplied. When society systematically denies the difference between male and female in law and custom, our fundamental dignity is diminished, the image of God within us is obscured, unreality becomes legally established, and those who refuse to conform are regarded as irrational bigots. Further, as same-sex couples are granted the right to marry, they will inevitably assert a "right to children" as well. But children are a gift, not a right. Forgetting this adds powerful pressure for the expansion of radical forms of reproductive technology—such as sperm and egg donation along with surrogacy, which involves contracting with a woman for the carrying of a pregnancy for intended parents.

Freedom itself is severely compromised when our speech about the difference and complementarity of male and female must be policed and any dissent from the new orthodoxies assiduously suppressed. It is increasingly difficult to affirm that marriage is the union of a man and a woman without being ruled outside the boundaries of reasonable public conversation. And once opposition to same-sex marriage is judged to be discriminatory, no institution that declines to substitute unreality for reality will remain unaffected. Some individuals are already being censured and others have lost their jobs because of their public commitment to marriage as the union of a man and a woman.

As Christians, we must state, unambiguously, that same-sex marriage contradicts the gospel. As we have noted, Holy Scripture teaches that marriage, as ordered by God, is a mysterious sign of the union of Christ and the church. This sign is dependent on the profound complementarity of male and female. A conception of marriage that allows for same-sex unions denies this element of difference, rendering it unable to signify the mystical union of Christ and his church.

As Evangelicals and Catholics committed to the gospel's invitation to discipleship, we are acutely aware of many ways in which our broken lives need the healing and reconciling power of God's grace. Moreover, we share the widespread and proper desire of Christians today to repent of injustices against those who experience same-sex attraction and to discern more effective ways for all single people to participate in the life of the church. However, faithful Christian witness cannot accommodate itself to same-sex marriage. It disregards the created order, threatens the common good, and distorts the gospel.

A Clear Witness

We, Evangelicals and Catholics together, affirm the truth and the reality of marriage as a covenant between a man and a woman, established by free and mutual consent and by God's action. This marital union is intended to be permanent and is fully consummated in consensual sexual intercourse open to procreation.

In affirming this we do not dispute the evident fact of hormonal and chromosomal irregularities, nor of different sexual attractions and desires. As Christians, however, we must insist that our sexual desires, orientations, and proclivities do not provide a basis for re-defining marriage. As is the case in all aspects of human life, our inclinations, desires, and actions must be judged by the Word of God (Rom. 1:21–24).

We must also reject the contemporary presumption—which is widespread and even influences our churches in many ways—that human fulfillment requires the satisfaction of sexual desire. While the Bible calls all Christians to chastity, it also holds up the celibate life as one honorable vocation in light of the example of our Lord himself and his teaching that there are some who are eunuchs "for the sake of the kingdom of heaven" (Matt. 19:12). Thus, with two thousand years of Christian tradition, we affirm that the integral development of the human person is possible without sexual intimacy. In the early centuries of the church's history, the presence of men and women committed to a celibate life had already become a distinctive mark of the Christian community. Freely choosing celibacy or living the single life in faithfulness to Christ offers a unique kind of service to the church and the world.

Finally, in our witness to the truth about marriage, we reject the canard that the Christian view is based solely on "sectarian" religious truths. Throughout history and across all cultures, marriage has been understood to be the union of male and female and is organized around the procreative potential of that union. Rituals and forms of marriage are extraordinarily diverse, and conditions for dissolution vary widely. But across all cultures marriage seeks to establish a per-manent bond that promotes marital fidelity, not least for the raising of children. All this evidence testifies to the truth that marriage as the union of male and female is part of the created order, "from the beginning," as Jesus himself teaches (Mark 10:6).

The truth about marriage, accessible to all and ennobled by reve-lation, is being systematically dismantled and dismissed as hoary prejudice. Within the span of a decade, same-sex marriage has not only been legally recognized, but its acceptance has been declared an index of one's status as a citizen committed to liberty and justice for all. How and why such a cultural and legal revolution has taken place so quickly is for historians and sociologists to explain. Our task is different. We must say, as clearly as possible, that same-sex unions, even when sanctioned by the state, are not *marriages*. Christians who wish to remain faithful to the Scriptures and Christian tradition cannot embrace this falsification of reality, irrespective of its status in law.

Light and Salt

A society that seeks to erase the difference between male and female in marriage is asking us to believe something we know *is not* true and *cannot* be true. If the truth about marriage can be displaced by social and political pressure operating through the law, other truths can be set aside as well. And that displacement can lead, in due course, to the coercion and persecution of those who refuse to acknowledge the state's redefinition of marriage, which is beyond the state's competence.

The same exaltation of false freedom used to justify abortion—the liberty to redefine the very nature of the human person—is now at work in the revolution of same-sex marriage. When the autonomous will of man dictates morality—and even reality—life will be defined for the benefit of the powerful and at the expense of the weak, the order of creation will be violated, and the gospel itself will eventually be declared an enemy of society. And if Christians discard the most fundamental, visible, and universal fact of our bodies—that we are created male and female—we can no longer confess the words of the Creed: "I believe in one God, maker of heaven and earth, and of all things visible and invisible."

We thus face a difficult and dangerous situation. A society that identifies the two parties in marriage as Spouse 1 and Spouse 2 has lost sight of a deep truth of human nature. We must do everything in our power to distinguish this falsification of marriage from its true form as the lifelong union of a man and a woman. In some contexts, consistent testimony to the truth about marriage may require clergy to refuse to serve as officers of the state by signing marriage licenses. Whatever courses of action are deemed necessary, the coming years will require careful discernment. All Christians and men and women of goodwill must work to rebuild the culture of marriage and live lives that attest to the joy and beauty of marriage. On this basis alone can we succeed.

This will not be easy. The proponents of these so-called marriages are powerful, and they do not hesitate to use the tools of calumny to defeat their opponents. Keeping in mind the obligation to speak the truth in love, we must find ways to distinguish true marriage from its distortion, and we must do so without abandoning the public square. We owe our fellow citizens a socially engaged witness to the truth about marriage, which, with the family, is the unalterable foundation of a healthy, humane society.

The time is approaching—indeed, in some instances it has already arrived—when Christians in this country will suffer abuse for upholding the truth about marriage. We encourage our fellow Christians to stand firm in obedience to Christ, for that obedience is the most compassionate service we can offer society. In doing so, we must strive to heal the wounds of a confused and broken culture, to foster human flourishing, and to honor the God who created human beings in his own image, male and female. For Christ said, "I came that they may have life, and have it abundantly" (John 10:10).

Soli Deo gloria.

Epilogue

The Continuing Importance
of Evangelical-Catholic Dialogue

R. R. RENO AND KEVIN J. VANHOOZER

We are called to confess "one Lord, one faith, one baptism" (Eph. 4:5). Sadly, one of the most powerful arguments against the truth of the gospel is our failure to do so. Jesus teaches that we should be one so that the world may believe that the Father has sent him—that he is truly the Son of God (John 17:21). The sad truth is that we're not one. While we confess that same Lord, share in many ways a common faith, and together baptize in the name of the Father, Son, and Holy Spirit, we are divided. This lack of unity in Christ is one of the most significant impediments to the truth of the gospel.

The Present Dialogue: Where We Are

It should therefore come as good news to Christians everywhere that two communities in North America, who throughout our history have regarded one another with mistrust—sometimes even competing for the hearts and minds of converts—have sought to repair the wound of disunity. We are not an official dialogue. Nothing we do has an imprimatur, or any endorsements from our churches for that matter. But for the past twenty years, Evangelicals and Catholics Together has succeeded in communicating with one another, often reaching consensus on vital issues of mutual concern. As much as possible, we seek to be one in Christ.

There is good precedent for fellowship, however informal and ad hoc, focused on discerning our common life in the Lord. Christians have been discussing the significance of Jesus Christ since he rose from the dead. "That very day"—the day of Jesus's resurrection—two of his disciples were on a seven-mile trek from Jerusalem to Emmaus. While they were walking, they were "talking with each other about all these things that had happened" (Luke 24:14). "These things" refer to what happened to Jesus of Nazareth (Luke 24:19) and to reports of the empty tomb and Jesus's resurrection (Luke 24:22–24). Two thousand years later, ECT has picked up the discussion about Jesus and his significance for today. The conversation on the road to Emmaus continues, now between two communions rather than two individuals. Begun in 1994, our long discussions have been measured in years rather than miles. But the reality is the same. Meaningful dialogue takes time—to speak, listen, and hear. It is our hope that our time spent together conversing about our Lord and Savior will contribute in some small way to the unity to which Christ calls us. Good dialogue does not paper over differences. Our goal has been to clarify the core commitments of our traditions. This allows us to remove misunderstandings that have created unnecessary division. It also provides a basis for restating our difference, but with a more generous mutual understanding, as well as a firm basis for cooperation and common witness where possible. We acknowledge one another as disciples. This affirmation of a shared Christian identity is the all-important presupposition that underlies each of our published agreements. There has been joy in the mutual recognition that both communities are indeed seeking to follow the way of Jesus Christ. Both serve the same Lord who "has broken down in his flesh the dividing wall of hostility" (Eph. 2:14 ESV).

Past Dialogues: Precedent at Regensburg

ECT is no novelty. We are not the first to walk the road to Emmaus. There have been previous attempts by Evangelicals and Catholics to come together to discuss "the things about Jesus of Nazareth" (Luke 24:19 NRSV). Largely forgotten in the annals of religious conflict is one fleeting bright spot: a two-year period in mid-sixteenth-century Germany when Catholics and Protestants engaged in serious dialogue under the watchful eye of Emperor Charles V. Evangelicals may be surprised to learn that the Protestant Reformers made a sincere yet ultimately unsuccessful effort to preserve communion with the Roman Catholic Church through a series of dialogues from 1536 to 1557. Evangelicals may be even more surprised to learn that Calvin was one of the Protestant participants in a number of these meetings, including the Regensburg Colloquy (1541), where he represented the city of Strasbourg.[1] Catholics may be surprised to learn that, prior to the Council of Trent (1545–63), a number of Catholic theologians were sympathetic to Protestant understandings of original sin and other doctrines. Protestant and Catholic theologians reached agreement on the doctrine of justification at the Regensburg Colloquy, some 450 years before ECT did it again in 1997 with *The Gift of Salvation*. Both sides at Regensburg consented to article 5 on "The Justification of Man."[2] Calvin did not have high hopes for the colloquy in general, but he was positive about article 5, which he believed preserved "the substance of the true doctrine."[3] Peter Matheson's verdict is therefore unnecessarily harsh: "The dialogue between Protestantism and Catholicism at the Diet of Regensburg in 1541 did not fail. It never took place."[4] In the end, it was not the doctrine of justification by faith—the doctrine on which Luther said the church stands

1. Calvin was a delegate, though not always a happy camper. See Maarten Stolk, "Calvin and Rome," in *The Calvin Handbook*, ed. Herman J. Sekderhuis (Grand Rapids: Eerdmans, 2009), 104–12 (esp. 108–9).

2. An English translation of the article is available as appendix 1 in A. N. S. Lane, *Justification by Faith in Catholic-Evangelical Dialogue: An Evangelical Assessment* (New York: T&T Clark, 2002), 233–37.

3. Letter to Farel, May 11, 1541, cited in Lane, *Justification by Faith*, 56.

4. Peter Matheson, *Cardinal Contarini at Regensburg* (Oxford: Oxford University Press, 1972), 181.

or falls—that derailed the Regensburg Colloquy. Rather, it was the nature of the authority of the church that proved a hurdle too high to jump. So it remains today, perhaps, in which case we should not tire of theological discussion but rather do as did those at Regensburg. ECT, far from being a novelty, is another lap in the good race that seeks the prize of Christian unity. We should not disguise or distort the differences that divide us, but we are duty bound to preach in deeds of dialogue the unity Christ promises.

The Future: Are We There Yet?

Evangelical-Catholic dialogue is urgent. For example, as Evangelicals, we often have superficial views of what Catholics believe when they affirm the doctrines of the Virgin Mary's immaculate conception and bodily assumption into heaven. And as Catholics, we have equally superficial views of Evangelical affirmations of the gracious sufficiency of Jesus's atoning sacrifice on the cross. The spiritual discipline of ecumenical dialogue involves patient listening, sympathetic understanding, and a willingness to probe the deeper concerns that often lead our traditions to read Scripture with different emphases and interpret the Great Tradition along different lines. This discipline allows us to come to a deeper understanding of one another's traditions—and our own. It is possible to be convinced of the truth of one's position and to be open to the possibility that one may not fully possess the truth. In this way, dialogue in the service of Christ is, at its best, conducive of both humility and truth. It keeps us honest to God and to one another. We all see through our traditions as through a mirror, dimly. Furthermore, there are things we may find easier to retrieve by continuing rather than halting our dialogue. As Catholics, we need continually to retrieve the gospel (the *evangel*). Christ is the Alpha and the Omega. He can never be too much at the center of our preaching. As Evangelicals, we need continually to retrieve catholicity. The Holy Spirit is living and active, taking no holidays from history. Evangelicals are not the first or the only people that have received the gospel.

At its best, ECT encourages the development of "Evangelical Catholics." Such people do not adopt Evangelical modes of worship or the doctrinal particularities of Protestant confessions, but they admire Evangelicals' passion for the Bible and for "always reforming" the life of the church by centering it on the gospel of Jesus Christ.[5] Our dialogue also encourages "Catholic Evangelicals." Such people do not adopt Catholic devotional practices or recent dogmas, but they recognize the importance of doing theology in the Great Tradition. They see that their work and ministry is supported by a great cloud of witnesses.[6] ECT faces important challenges. The first is to clarify the issue of "dogmatic rank," that is, the relative importance of the doctrines that continue to divide us. Catholics have the concept of the "hierarchy of truths." This reminds Evangelicals (and Catholics as well) that not all doctrines are created equal. Some are closer to the mystery of salvation in Jesus Christ than others. Evangelicals have an important affirmation: "In essentials, unity." But they do not always agree about what counts as an "essential"! Some Evangelicals have begun to develop criteria for distinguishing between matters of first, second, and third dogmatic rank.[7] The greater challenge will be to find criteria on which Evangelicals and Catholics can agree.

The second concerns the nature of theological agreement. Evangelicals have a long tradition of unity among different strands of the Protestant theological and confessional tradition. This reminds Catholics that the specific formulations of their magisterial traditions, while definitive for them, are not exhaustive. (It also reminds Evangelicals that specific traditions of biblical interpretation are not exhaustive.) There are other ways of expressing the same theological truth. Work needs to be done to outline the possibilities for diverse

5. See, for example, George Weigel, *Evangelical Catholicism: Deep Reform in the 21st-Century Church* (New York: Basic Books, 2013).

6. See, for example, Michael Allen and Scott R. Swain, *Reformed Catholicity: The Promise of Retrieval for Theology and Biblical Interpretation* (Grand Rapids: Baker Academic, 2015), and W. David Buschart and Kent Eilers, *Theology as Retrieval: Receiving the Past, Renewing the Church* (Downers Grove, IL: InterVarsity, 2015).

7. See Al Mohler, "Confessional Evangelicalism," in *Four Views on the Spectrum of Evangelicalism*, ed. Andrew Naselli and Collin Hansen (Grand Rapids: Zondervan, 2011), 77–80; and Kevin Vanhoozer, "Improvising Theology according to the Scriptures: An Evangelical Account of the Development of Doctrine," in *Building on the Foundations of Evangelical Theology*, ed. Gregg Allison and Steve Wellum (Wheaton: Crossway, 2015).

formulations of essential theological truths, as well as the limits of diversity.

Finally, Evangelicals and Catholics are "together" in ways that could not have been imagined even a few decades ago. Who would have imagined a common statement on the Virgin Mary? Yet we still do not celebrate a common *communion*. The togetherness of Evangelicals and Catholics Together remains incomplete. We continue to fall short of the Lord's prayer for his church "that they may be one" (John 17:22). Strictly speaking, because we cannot share the Lord's Supper, we are "together" only on the road, not at table. We have not yet reached Emmaus. Let us pray that we soon reach the common table there.

Acknowledgments

T he editors would like to thank the many people who have helped
with this volume over the course of the past two years. The contributors to this book have worked hard to ensure that Evangelicals
and Catholics Together remains an ongoing encounter of theological
understanding and mutual respect. We thank all the members of ECT,
past and present, who have contributed to the spiritual fraternity and
theological commitment that this ecumenical initiative represents.

We would also like to thank the Institute on Religion and Public
Life for kindly hosting our meetings in New York City over the past
twenty years. We express our appreciation to R. R. Reno, editor of
the Institute's journal, *First Things*, for allowing staff members to
attend to the task of proofreading our statements. We thank Lauren
Wilson, who coordinated this assignment, and Sandra Laguerta, B. D.
McClay, and Gregory Pine, O.P., for their invaluable assistance.

We would also like to convey our appreciation to the Chuck Colson Center and Prison Fellowship Ministries for the generous support they have provided for the continuing work of Evangelicals and
Catholics Together.

Timothy George extends his appreciation to Le-Ann Little, his
administrative assistant, and to Dr. B. Coyne and Jason Odom, his
research associates.

Thomas G. Guarino would like to thank his dean, the Rev. Dr. Joseph Reilly, and Cathy Xavier for her kind assistance with a variety of book-related tasks. He also thanks the dean of Seton Hall University Libraries, Dr. John Buschman, for kindly providing space for research and writing. Finally, he expresses his gratitude to Dr. William Storrar, the director of the Center of Theological Inquiry, for always extending a warm welcome when he was working in the Princeton area.

Finally, we offer an inadequate word of thanks to Davida Goldman of *First Things*. From the beginning, she has worked quietly, but with deft efficiency, to ensure that our meetings have been productive.

Timothy George
Thomas G. Guarino

Appendix

Signers of the Documents

N ote: "Participants" took part in the discussions that produced the documents. "Endorsers" signed on afterward. Institutional affiliations are given to identify the signers and do not signify institutional support of the documents. Signatory lists are printed here as they originally appeared at the time of publication.

1. *Evangelicals and Catholics Together: The Christian Mission in the Third Millennium* (1994)

PARTICIPANTS: Mr. Charles Colson (Prison Fellowship), Fr. Juan Diaz-Vilar, S.J. (Catholic Hispanic Ministries), Fr. Avery Dulles, S.J. (Fordham University), Bishop Francis George, O.M.I. (Diocese of Yakima [Washington]), Dr. Kent Hill (Eastern Nazarene College), Dr. Richard Land (Christian Life Commission of the Southern Baptist Convention), Dr. Larry Lewis (Home Mission Board of the Southern Baptist Convention), Dr. Jesse Miranda (Assemblies of God), Msgr. William Murphy (Chancellor of the Archdiocese of Boston), Fr. Richard John Neuhaus (Institute on Religion and Public Life), Mr. Brian O'Connell (World Evangelical Fellowship), Mr. Herbert Schlossberg

(Fieldstead Foundation), Archbishop Francis Stafford (Archdiocese of Denver), Mr. George Weigel (Ethics and Public Policy Center), Dr. John White (Geneva College and the National Association of Evangelicals)

ENDORSERS: Dr. William Abraham (Perkins School of Theology), Dr. Elizabeth Achtemeier (Union Theological Seminary [Virginia]), Mr. William Bentley Ball (Harrisburg, Pennsylvania), Dr. Bill Bright (Campus Crusade for Christ), Professor Robert Destro (Catholic University of America), Fr. Augustine Di Noia, O.P. (Dominican House of Studies), Fr. Joseph P. Fitzpatrick, S.J. (Fordham University), Mr. Keith Fournier (American Center for Law and Justice), Bishop William Frey (Trinity Episcopal School for Ministry), Professor Mary Ann Glendon (Harvard Law School), Dr. Os Guinness (Trinity Forum), Dr. Nathan Hatch (University of Notre Dame), Dr. James Hitchcock (St. Louis University), Professor Peter Kreeft (Boston College), Fr. Matthew Lamb (Boston College), Mr. Ralph Martin (Renewal Ministries), Dr. Richard Mouw (Fuller Theological Seminary), Dr. Mark Noll (Wheaton College), Mr. Michael Novak (American Enterprise Institute), John Cardinal O'Connor (Archdiocese of New York), Dr. Thomas Oden (Drew University), Dr. J. I. Packer (Regent College [British Columbia]), Rev. Pat Robertson (Regent University), Dr. John Rodgers (Trinity Episcopal School for Ministry), Bishop Carlos A. Sevilla, S.J. (Archdiocese of San Francisco)

2. *The Gift of Salvation* (1997)

EVANGELICAL PROTESTANT PARTICIPANTS: Dr. Gerald L. Bray (Beeson Divinity School), Dr. Bill Bright (Campus Crusade for Christ), Dr. Harold O. J. Brown (Trinity Evangelical Divinity School), Mr. Charles Colson (Prison Fellowship), Bishop William C. Frey (Episcopal Church), Dr. Timothy George (Beeson Divinity School), Dr. Os Guinness (Trinity Forum), Dr. Kent R. Hill (Eastern Nazarene College), Rev. Max Lucado (Oak Hills Church of Christ [San Antonio, Texas]), Dr. T. M. Moore (Chesapeake Theological Seminary), Dr. Richard Mouw (Fuller Theological Seminary), Dr. Mark A. Noll

(Wheaton College), Mr. Brian F. O'Connell (Interdev), Dr. Thomas Oden (Drew University), Dr. J. I. Packer (Regent College [British Columbia]), Dr. Timothy R. Phillips (Wheaton College), Dr. John Rodgers (Trinity Episcopal School for Ministry), Dr. Robert A. Seiple (World Vision US), Dr. John Woodbridge (Trinity Evangelical Divinity School)

ROMAN CATHOLIC PARTICIPANTS: Dr. James J. Buckley (Loyola College of Maryland), Father J. A. Di Noia, O.P. (Dominican House of Studies), Father Avery Dulles, S.J. (Fordham University), Mr. Keith Fournier (Catholic Alliance), Father Thomas Guarino (Seton Hall University), Dr. Peter Kreeft (Boston College), Father Matthew L. Lamb (Boston College), Father Eugene LaVerdiere, S.S.S. (Emmanuel), Father Francis Martin (John Paul II Institute for Studies on Marriage and Family), Mr. Ralph Martin (Renewal Ministries), Father Richard John Neuhaus (Religion and Public Life), Mr. Michael Novak (American Enterprise Institute), Father Edward Oakes, S.J. (Regis University), Father Thomas P. Rausch, S.J. (Loyola Marymount University), Mr. George Weigel (Ethics and Public Policy Center), Dr. Robert Louis Wilken (University of Virginia)

3. *Your Word Is Truth* (2002)

EVANGELICAL PROTESTANT PARTICIPANTS: Dr. Harold O. J. Brown (Reformed Theological Seminary), Mr. Charles Colson (Prison Fellowship), Dr. Timothy George (Beeson Divinity School), Dr. Kent R. Hill (Eastern Nazarene College), Dr. Frank A. James (Reformed Theological Seminary), Dr. Cheryl Bridges Johns (Church of God School of Theology), Dr. T. M. Moore (Cedar Springs Presbyterian Church), Dr. Thomas Oden (Drew University), Dr. J. I. Packer (Regent College [British Columbia]), Dr. Timothy R. Phillips (Wheaton Graduate School of Theology), Dr. John Woodbridge (Trinity Evangelical Divinity School)

ROMAN CATHOLIC PARTICIPANTS: Dr. James J. Buckley (Loyola College of Maryland), Avery Cardinal Dulles, S.J. (Fordham University), Father Thomas Guarino (Seton Hall University), Father

Joseph T. Lienhard, S.J. (Fordham University), Father Francis Martin (John Paul II Institute for Studies on Marriage and Family), Father Richard John Neuhaus (Institute on Religion and Public Life), Father Edward T. Oakes, S.J. (Regis University), Dr. Robert Louis Wilken (University of Virginia)

4. *The Communion of Saints* (2003)

EVANGELICAL PROTESTANT PARTICIPANTS: Dr. Harold O. J. Brown (Reformed Theological Seminary), Mr. Charles Colson (Prison Fellowship), Dr. Timothy George (Beeson Divinity School), Dr. Kent R. Hill (Eastern Nazarene College), Dr. Cheryl Bridges Johns (Church of God School of Theology), Dr. T. M. Moore (Cedar Springs Presbyterian Church), Dr. Thomas Oden (Drew University), Dr. J. I. Packer (Regent College [British Columbia])

ROMAN CATHOLIC PARTICIPANTS: Dr. James J. Buckley (Loyola College of Maryland), Dr. Peter Casarella (Catholic University of America), Avery Cardinal Dulles, S.J. (Fordham University), Father Thomas Guarino (Seton Hall University), Father Francis Martin (John Paul II Institute for Studies on Marriage and Family), Father Richard John Neuhaus (Institute on Religion and Public Life), Edward T. Oakes, S.J. (Mundelein Seminary), Mr. George Weigel (Ethics and Public Policy Center), Dr. Robert Louis Wilken (University of Virginia)

5. *The Call to Holiness* (2005)

EVANGELICAL PROTESTANT PARTICIPANTS: Dr. Harold O. J. Brown (Reformed Theological Seminary), Mr. Charles Colson (Prison Fellowship), Dr. Timothy George (Beeson Divinity School), Dr. Kent Hill (Church of the Nazarene), Dr. Cheryl Bridges Johns (Church of God School of Theology), Rev. T. M. Moore (Cedar Springs Presbyterian Church), Dr. Thomas Oden (Drew University Emeritus), Dr. J. I. Packer (Regent College [British Columbia]), Dr. Sarah Sumner (Azusa Pacific University), Dr. Kevin J. Vanhoozer (Trinity Evangelical Divinity School), Dr. John Woodbridge (Trinity Evangelical Divinity School)

ROMAN CATHOLIC PARTICIPANTS: Dr. James J. Buckley (Loyola College of Maryland), Dr. Peter Casarella (Catholic University of America), Dr. Gary Culpepper (Providence College), Avery Cardinal Dulles, S.J. (Fordham University), Fr. Thomas Guarino (Seton Hall University), Dr. Matthew Levering (Ave Maria College), Fr. Francis Martin (Mother of God Community), Fr. Richard John Neuhaus (*First Things*), Fr. Edward T. Oakes, S.J. (Mundelein Seminary), Mr. George Weigel (Ethics and Public Policy Center), Dr. Robert Louis Wilken (University of Virginia)

6. *That They May Have Life* (2006)

EVANGELICAL PROTESTANT PARTICIPANTS: Dr. Harold O. J. Brown (Reformed Theological Seminary), Mr. Charles Colson (Prison Fellowship), Dr. Timothy George (Beeson Divinity School), Dr. Kent Hill (Church of the Nazarene), Dr. Frank James (Reformed Theological Seminary), Dr. Cheryl Bridges Johns (Church of God School of Theology), Rev. T. M. Moore (The Wilberforce Forum, Prison Fellowship), Dr. Thomas Oden (Drew University Emeritus), Dr. J. I. Packer (Regent College [British Columbia]), Dr. Sarah Sumner (Azusa Pacific University), Dr. Kevin J. Vanhoozer (Trinity Evangelical Divinity School), Dr. John Woodbridge (Trinity Evangelical Divinity School)

ROMAN CATHOLIC PARTICIPANTS: Dr. James J. Buckley (Loyola College of Maryland), Dr. Peter Casarella (Catholic University of America), Dr. Gary Culpepper (Providence College), Avery Cardinal Dulles, S.J. (Fordham University), Fr. Thomas Guarino (Seton Hall University), Fr. Arthur Kennedy (University of St. Thomas), Dr. Matthew Levering (Ave Maria University), Fr. Francis Martin (Mother of God Community), Fr. Richard John Neuhaus (Institute on Religion and Public Life), Fr. Edward T. Oakes, S.J. (Mundelein Seminary), Mr. George Weigel (Ethics and Public Policy Center), Dr. Robert Louis Wilken (University of Virginia)

ENDORSERS: Alan K. Andrews (CEO, The Navigators), Mrs. Jill Briscoe (author and speaker), Dr. Bryan Chapell (president, Covenant Theological Seminary), Dr. David S. Dockery (president, Union

University), Dr. Os Guinness (senior fellow, The Trinity Forum), Dr. David P. Gushee (Graves Professor of Moral Philosophy, Union University), Ted A. Haggard (president, National Association of Evangelicals), Bill Hybels (pastor, Willow Creek Community Church), Dr. Duane Litfin (president, Wheaton College), Dr. Richard Mouw (president, Fuller Theological Seminary), David Neff (editor and vice president, *Christianity Today*), Tony Perkins (president, Family Research Council), Dr. Cornelius Plantinga (president, Calvin Theological Seminary), Dr. Ron Sider (president and founder, Evangelicals for Social Action), Joni Eareckson Tada (founder, Joni and Friends International Disability Center), Rick Warren (pastor, Saddleback Church), Dr. James White (president, Gordon-Conwell Theological Seminary)

7. *Do Whatever He Tells You: The Blessed Virgin Mary in Christian Faith and Life* (2009)

EVANGELICAL PROTESTANT PARTICIPANTS: Mr. Charles Colson (Colson Center for Christian Worldview), Dr. Dale Coulter (Regent University), Dr. Joel Elowsky (Eastern University), Dr. Timothy George (Beeson Divinity School), Dr. Frank James (Gordon-Conwell Theological Seminary), Dr. Cheryl Bridges Johns (Pentecostal Theological Seminary), Dr. T. M. Moore (Prison Fellowship), Dr. Thomas Oden (Drew University), Dr. J. I. Packer (Regent College [British Columbia]), Dr. Cornelius Plantinga (Calvin Theological Seminary), Dr. Sarah Sumner (A. W. Tozer Theological Seminary), Dr. Kevin J. Vanhoozer (Wheaton College), Dr. John Woodbridge (Trinity Evangelical Divinity School)

ROMAN CATHOLIC PARTICIPANTS: Dr. Joseph Bottum (*First Things*), James J. Buckley (Loyola College of Maryland), Dr. Peter Casarella (DePaul University), Dr. Gary Culpepper (Providence College), Avery Cardinal Dulles (1918–2008) (Fordham University), Fr. Thomas Guarino (Seton Hall University), Fr. Arthur Kennedy (St. John's Seminary of Boston), Dr. Matthew Levering (University of Dayton), Fr. Richard John Neuhaus (1936–2009) (*First Things*),

Fr. Francis Martin (Sacred Heart Major Seminary of Detroit), Fr. James Massa (National Conference of Catholic Bishops), Fr. Edward T. Oakes, S.J. (Mundelein Seminary of Chicago), Mr. George Weigel (Ethics and Public Policy Center), Dr. Robert Louis Wilken (University of Virginia)

8. *In Defense of Religious Freedom* (2012)

EVANGELICAL PROTESTANT PARTICIPANTS: Charles Colson (Prison Fellowship), Dale Coulter (Regent University School of Divinity), Joel Elowsky (Concordia University Wisconsin), Timothy George (Beeson Divinity School), Cheryl Bridges Johns (Pentecostal Theological Seminary), Thomas Oden (Eastern University), J. I. Packer (Regent College [British Columbia]), Cornelius Plantinga (Calvin Theological Seminary), Sarah Sumner (A. W. Tozer Theological Seminary), Kevin J. Vanhoozer (Wheaton College), John Woodbridge (Trinity Evangelical Divinity School)

ROMAN CATHOLIC PARTICIPANTS: Peter Casarella (DePaul University), Gary Culpepper (Providence College), Thomas Guarino (Seton Hall University), Matthew Levering (University of Dayton), David Mills (*First Things*), Edward T. Oakes, S.J. (Mundelein Seminary of Chicago), R. R. Reno (*First Things*), George Weigel (Ethics and Public Policy Center), Robert Louis Wilken (Providence College)

ENDORSERS: Daniel Akin (Southeastern Baptist Theological Seminary), Gary Anderson (University of Notre Dame), Leith Anderson (National Association of Evangelicals), Hadley Arkes (Amherst College), John C. Cavadini (University of Notre Dame), William T. Cavanaugh (DePaul University), Francesco C. Cesareo (Assumption College), Charles J. Chaput, O.F.M. Cap. (Archdiocese of Philadelphia), Michael Cromartie (Ethics and Public Policy Center), Lawrence S. Cunningham (University of Notre Dame), Daniel Delgado (Third Day Missions Church), David S. Dockery (Union University), Timothy Cardinal Dolan (Archdiocese of New York), Robert Duncan (Anglican Church in North America), Philip W. Eaton (Seattle Pacific University), Thomas F. Farr (Georgetown University), Douglas Farrow

(McGill University), Jim Garlow (Skyline Church), Francis Cardinal George, O.M.I. (Archdiocese of Chicago), Mary Ann Glendon (Harvard Law School), Paul J. Griffiths (Duke Divinity School), Ken Hagerty (Renewing American Leadership), Alec Hill (InterVarsity Christian Fellowship), Kent R. Hill (World Vision), Russell Hittinger (University of Tulsa), Reinhard Hütter (Duke Divinity School), Stanton L. Jones (Wheaton College), Peter A. Lillback (Westminster Theological Seminary), James Liske (Prison Fellowship), Paul R. McHugh (Johns Hopkins University School of Medicine), Wilfred M. McClay (University of Tennessee at Chattanooga), Michael W. McConnell (Stanford Law School), George D. McKinney (St. Stephen's Cathedral Church of God in Christ), Gilbert Meilaender (Valparaiso University), Eric Metaxas (Socrates in the City), Stephen D. Minnis (Benedictine College), Jennifer Roback Morse (Ruth Institute), David Neff (*Christianity Today*), Stephen Noll (Uganda Christian University), Thomas J. Olmsted (Diocese of Phoenix), Daniel Philpott (University of Notre Dame), Tony Perkins (Family Research Council), Timothy Samuel Shah (Berkley Center for Religion, Peace, and World Affairs), Ronald J. Sider (Palmer Theological Seminary at Eastern University), Robert B. Sloan, Jr. (Houston Baptist University), Thomas Joseph White, O.P. (Dominican House of Studies in Washington, DC), G. Bryant Wright, Jr. (Right from the Heart Ministries)

9. *The Two Shall Become One Flesh: Reclaiming Marriage* (2015)

EVANGELICAL PROTESTANT PARTICIPANTS: Dale Coulter (Regent University), Joel Elowsky (Concordia Seminary), Robert Gagnon (Pittsburgh Theological Seminary), Timothy George (Beeson Divinity School), Jennifer Lahl, Peter Leithart (Theopolis Institute), Kevin J. Vanhoozer (Trinity Evangelical Divinity School), John Woodbridge (Trinity Evangelical Divinity School)

ROMAN CATHOLIC PARTICIPANTS: Juan-Diego Brunetta, O.P. (Dominican Province of St. Joseph), Eduardo Echeverria (Sacred Heart Major Seminary), Douglas Farrow (McGill University), Thomas G.

Guarino (Seton Hall University), Matthew Levering (Mundelein Seminary), Francesca Murphy (University of Notre Dame), Russell Reno (*First Things*), George Weigel (Ethics and Public Policy Center), Robert Wilken (Institute on Religion and Public Life)

ENDORSERS: Daniel L. Akin (Southeastern Baptist Theological Seminary), Paul Allen (Concordia University, Montreal), Ryan Anderson (The Heritage Foundation), Foley Beach (Archbishop, Anglican Church in North America), Francis J. Beckwith (Baylor University), Matthew W. Bennett (Christian Union), Ernest Caparros (University of Ottawa [Emeritus]), Bruce J. Clemenger (Evangelical Fellowship of Canada), Christian Elia (Catholic Civil Rights League), Thomas F. Farr (Georgetown University), Maggie Gallagher (American Principles Project), Mark Galli (*Christianity Today*), Robert P. George (Princeton University), Sherif Girgis (Princeton University), Reinhard Hütter (Duke University), Jim Liske (Prison Fellowship Ministries), Dale A. Meyer (Concordia Seminary, St. Louis), Balázs M. Mezei (Pazmany Peter Catholic University), J. Michael Miller (Archbishop of Vancouver), John J. Myers (Archbishop of Newark), Aidan Nichols, O.P. (Blackfriars, Cambridge), J. I. Packer (Regent College), Terrence Prendergast (Archbishop of Ottawa), Robert Reynolds (Christian Legal Fellowship, Canada), Eugene F. Rivers III (Seymour Institute for Black Church and Policy Studies), Jacqueline C. Rivers (Seymour Institute for Black Church and Policy Studies), Brian C. Stiller (World Evangelical Alliance), Mark Tooley (Institute on Religion and Democracy), Olivier-Thomas Venard, O.P. (École Biblique et Archéologique Française in Jerusalem), Rick Warren (Saddleback Church), Thomas Joseph White, O.P. (Washington, DC), Paul Winter (elder, Bruderhof Communities), John Witte, Jr. (Emory University)

List of Contributors

Dale M. Coulter is associate professor of historical theology at Regent University, Virginia Beach, Virginia.

Timothy Dolan is archbishop of New York.

Timothy George is the founding dean of Beeson Divinity School of Samford University (Birmingham, Alabama) and chair of the Doctrine and Christian Unity Commission of the Baptist World Alliance.

Thomas G. Guarino is professor of systematic theology at Seton Hall University, South Orange, New Jersey.

Cheryl Bridges Johns is the Robert E. Fisher professor of spiritual renewal and Christian formation at Pentecostal Theological Seminary, Cleveland, Tennessee.

Thomas C. Oden, professor of theology emeritus at Drew University (Madison, New Jersey), is director of the Center for Early African Christianity at Eastern University in Philadelphia.

J. I. Packer is the Board of Governors' professor of theology at Regent College in Vancouver, British Columbia.

R. R. Reno is editor of *First Things*.

Kevin J. Vanhoozer is research professor of systematic theology at Trinity Evangelical Divinity School, Deerfield, Illinois.

George Weigel is distinguished senior fellow of the Ethics and Public Policy Center (Washington, DC), where he holds the William E. Simon Chair in Catholic Studies.

Robert Louis Wilken is chairman of the board of directors of the Institute on Religion and Public Life.

Index of Scripture References